I0834429

JOHN G. WHITTIER'S WRITINGS.

OLD PORTRAITS AND MOD. SKETCHES. Price 75 cents.

MARGARET SMITH'S JOURNAL. Price 75 cents.

SONGS OF LABOR, AND OTHER POEMS. Boards. 50 cts.

THE CHAPEL OF THE HERMITS.

OLIVER WENDELL HOLMES'S WRITINGS.

POETICAL WORKS. With fine Portrait. Boards. $1.00.

ASTRÆA. Fancy paper. Price 25 cents.

ALFRED TENNYSON'S WRITINGS.

POETICAL WORKS. With Portrait. 2 vols. Boards. $1.50.

THE PRINCESS. Boards. Price 50 cents.

IN MEMORIAM. Cloth. Price 75 cents.

THOMAS DE QUINCEY'S WRITINGS.

CONFESSIONS OF AN ENGLISH OPIUM-EATER, AND SUSPIRIA DE PROFUNDIS. With Portrait. Price 75 cents.

BIOGRAPHICAL ESSAYS. Price 75 cents.

MISCELLANEOUS ESSAYS. Price 75 cents.

THE CÆSARS. Price 75 cents.

LIFE AND MANNERS. Price 75 cents.

LITERARY REMINISCENCES. 2 Vols. Price $1.50.

NARRATIVE AND MISCELLANEOUS PAPERS. 2 Vols. Price $1 50.

GRACE GREENWOOD'S WRITINGS.

GREENWOOD LEAVES. 1st & 2d Series. $1.25 each.

POETICAL WORKS. With fine Portrait. Price 75 cents.

HISTORY OF MY PETS. With six fine Engravings. Scarlet cloth. Price 50 cents.

RECOLLECTIONS OF MY CHILDHOOD. With six fine Engravings. Scarlet cloth. Price 50 cents.

EDWIN P. WHIPPLE'S WRITINGS.

ESSAYS AND REVIEWS. 2 Vols. Price $2.00.

LECTURES ON SUBJECTS CONNECTED WITH LITERATURE AND LIFE. Price 63 cents.

WASHINGTON AND THE REVOLUTION. Price 20 cts.

HENRY GILES'S WRITINGS.

LECTURES, ESSAYS, AND MISCELLANEOUS WRITINGS. 2 Vols. Price $1.50.

CHRISTIAN THOUGHT ON LIFE. Price 75 cents.

WILLIAM MOTHERWELL'S WRITINGS.

POEMS, NARRATIVE AND LYRICAL. New edition.

POSTHUMOUS POEMS. Boards. Price 50 cents.

MINSTRELSY, ANC. AND MOD. 2 Vols. Boards. $1.50.

JAMES RUSSELL LOWELL'S WRITINGS.

COMPLETE POETICAL WORKS. Revised, with Additions. In two volumes, 16mo. Boards. Price $1.50.

SIR LAUNFAL. New Edition. Price 25 cents.

MISCELLANEOUS.

LYDIA: A WOMAN'S BOOK. By Mrs. NEWTON CROSLAND. 16mo. Paper, 50 cents. Cloth, 75 cents.

ENGLISH TALES AND SKETCHES. By Mrs. CROSLAND. 1 vol. Cloth. Price $1.00.

JOSEPH T. BUCKINGHAM'S PERSONAL MEMOIRS AND RECOLLECTIONS OF EDITORIAL LIFE. With Portrait. 2 vols. 16mo. Price $1.50.

VILLAGE LIFE IN EGYPT. By the Author of 'Adventures in the Lybian Desert.' 2 vols. 16mo. Price $1.25.

PALISSY THE POTTER. By the Author of 'How to make Home Unhealthy.' 2 vols. 16mo. Price $.150.

WILLIAM MOUNTFORD. THORPE: A QUIET ENGLISH TOWN, AND HUMAN LIFE THEREIN. 16mo. Price $1.00.

JAMES FREEMAN CLARKE. ELEVEN WEEKS IN EUROPE, AND WHAT MAY BE SEEN IN THAT TIME. 16mo. Price $1.00.

CAPT. MAYNE REID. THE DESERT HOME, OR THE ADVENTURES OF A LOST FAMILY IN THE WILDERNESS. 12 Engravings. 16mo. Price $1.00.

WILLIAM WORDSWORTH'S BIOGRAPHY. By Dr. C. WORDSWORTH. 2 Vols. Price $2.50.

ROBERT BROWNING. POETICAL WORKS. 2 Vols. $2.00.

BARRY CORNWALL. ENGLISH SONGS AND OTHER SMALL POEMS. Enlarged Edition. Price $1.00.

BARRY CORNWALL. ESSAYS AND TALES IN PROSE. 2 Vols. Price $1.50.

RICHARD MONCKTON MILNES. POEMS OF MANY YEARS. Boards. Price 75 cents.

CHARLES MACKAY'S POEMS. 1 Vol. Cloth. Price $1.00.

PHILIP JAMES BAILEY. THE ANGEL WORLD AND OTHER POEMS. Price 50 cents.

GOETHE'S WILHELM MEISTER. Translated by CARLYLE. 2 Vols. Price $2 50.

GOETHE'S FAUST. Price 75 cents.

CHARLES SPRAGUE. POETICAL AND PROSE WRITINGS. With fine Portrait. Boards. Price 75 cents.

CHARLES SUMNER. ORATIONS AND SPEECHES. 2 Vols. Price $2.50.

GEORGE S. HILLARD. THE DANGERS AND DUTIES OF THE MERCANTILE PROFESSION. Price 25 cents.

HORACE MANN. A FEW THOUGHTS FOR A YOUNG MAN. Price 25 cents.

F. W. P. GREENWOOD. SERMONS OF CONSOLATION. $1.00.

HENRY ALFORD'S POEMS. Just out.

HENRY T. TUCKERMAN. POEMS. Cloth. Price 75 cents.

BAYARD TAYLOR. POEMS. Cloth. Price 63 cents.

R. H. STODDARD. POEMS. Cloth. Price 63 cents.

JOHN G. SAXE. POEMS. With Portrait. Boards, 63 cents. Cloth, 75 cents.

REJECTED ADDRESSES. By HORACE and JAMES SMITH. Boards, Price 50 cents. Cloth, 63 cents.

WARRENIANA. By the Authors of Rejected Addresses. Price 63 cents.

MEMORY AND HOPE. A BOOK OF POEMS, REFERRING TO CHILDHOOD. Cloth. Price $2.00.

ALDERBROOK. By FANNY FORESTER. 2 Vols. Price $1.75.

HEROINES OF THE MISSIONARY ENTERPRISE. 75 cts.

MEMOIR OF THE BUCKMINSTERS, FATHER AND SON. By Mrs. LEE. Price $1.25.

THE SOLITARY OF JUAN FERNANDEZ. By the Author of Picciola. Price 50 cents.

THE BOSTON BOOK. Price $1.25.

ANGEL-VOICES. Price 38 cents.

FLORENCE, AND OTHER TALES. By Mrs. LEE. 50 cts

SIR ROGER DE COVERLEY. Price 75 cents.

EACH OF THE ABOVE POEMS AND PROSE WRITINGS, MAY BE HAD IN VARIOUS STYLES OF HANDSOME BINDING.

ESSAYS ON THE POETS,

AND

OTHER ENGLISH WRITERS.

BY

THOMAS DE QUINCEY,

AUTHOR OF

"*CONFESSIONS OF AN ENGLISH OPIUM-EATER*," *ETC. ETC.*

BOSTON:
TICKNOR, REED, AND FIELDS.
MDCCCLIII.

THURSTON, TORRY, AND EMERSON, PRINTERS.

CONTENTS.

ON WORDSWORTH'S POETRY.

HERETOFORE, upon one impulse or another, I have retraced fugitive memorials of several persons celebrated in our own times; but I have never undertaken an examination of any man's writings. The one labor is, comparatively, without an effort; the other is both difficult, and, with regard to contemporaries, is invidious. In genial moments the characteristic remembrances of men expand as fluently as buds travel into blossoms; but criticism, if it is to be conscientious and profound, and if it is applied to an object so unlimited as poetry, must be almost as unattainable by any hasty effort as fine poetry itself. 'Thou hast convinced me,' says Rasselas to Imlac, 'that it is impossible to be a poet;' so vast had appeared to be the array of qualifications. But, with the same ease, Imlac might have convinced the prince that it was impossible to be a critic. And hence it is, that, in the sense of absolute and philosophic criticism, we have little or none; for, before *that* can exist, we must have a good psychology; whereas, at present, we have none at all.

If, however, it is more difficult to write critical sketches than sketches of personal recollections, often it is much less connected with painful scruples. Of books, resting only on grounds which, in sincerity, you believe to be true, and speaking without anger or scorn, you can hardly say the thing which *ought* to be taken amiss. But of men and women you dare not, and must not, tell all that chance may have revealed to you. Sometimes you are summoned to silence by pity for that general human infirmity, which you also, the writer, share. Sometimes you are checked by the consideration, that perhaps your knowledge of the case was originally gained under opportunities allowed by confidence or by unsuspecting carelessness. Sometimes the disclosure would cause quarrels between parties now at peace. Sometimes it would carry pain, such as you could not feel justified in carrying, into the mind of him who was its object. Sometimes, again, if right to be told, it might be difficult to prove. Thus, for one cause or another, some things are sacred, and some things are perilous, amongst any personal revelations that else you might have it in your power to make. And seldom, indeed, is your own silent retrospect of such connections altogether happy. 'Put not your trust in princes, nor in the sons of princes,' — this has been the warning, — this has been the farewell moral, winding up and pointing the experience of dying statesmen. Not less truly it might be said — 'Put not your trust in the intellectual princes of your age:' form no connections too close with any who live only in the atmosphere of admiration and praise. The love or the friendship of such people rarely contracts itself into the narrow circle of individuals. You, if you are brilliant like themselves, they will hate;

you, if you are dull, they will despise. Gaze, therefore, on the splendor of such idols as a passing stranger. Look for a moment as one sharing in the idolatry; but pass on before the splendor has been sullied by human frailty, or before your own generous homage has been confounded with offerings of weeds.

Safer, then, it is to scrutinize the works of eminent poets, than long to connect yourself with themselves, or to revive your remembrances of them in any personal record. Now, amongst all works that have illustrated our own age, none can more deserve an earnest notice than those of the Laureate; and on some grounds, peculiar to themselves, none so much. Their merit in fact is not only supreme but unique; not only supreme in their general class, but unique as in a class of their own. And there is a challenge of a separate nature to the curiosity of the readers, in the remarkable contrast between the first stage of Wordsworth's acceptation with the public and that which he enjoys at present. One original obstacle to the favorable impression of the Wordsworthian poetry, and an obstacle purely self-created, was his theory of poetic diction. The diction itself, without the theory, was of less consequence; for the mass of readers would have been too blind or too careless to notice it. But the preface to the second edition of his Poems, (2 vols. 1799-1800,) compelled them to notice it. Nothing more injudicious was ever done by man. An unpopular truth would, at any rate, have been a bad inauguration, for what, on *other* accounts, the author had announced as 'an experiment.' His poetry was already an experiment as regarded the quality of the subjects selected, and as regarded the mode of treating them. That was surely trial enough for the reader's untrained sensibilities, without the unpopular truth besides, as to the diction. But, in the mean time, this truth, besides being unpopular, was also, in part, false: it was true, and it was *not* true. And it was not true in a double way. Stating broadly, and allowing it to be taken for his meaning, that the diction of ordinary life, in his own words, 'the very language of man,' was the proper diction for poetry, the writer meant no such thing; for only a *part* of this diction, according to his own subsequent restriction, was available for such a use. And, secondly, as his own subsequent practice showed, even this part was available only for peculiar classes of poetry. In his own exquisite 'Laodamia,' in his 'Sonnets,' in his 'Excursion,' few are his obligations to the idiomatic language of life, as distinguished from that of books, or of prescriptive usage. Coleridge remarked, justly, that 'The Excursion' bristles beyond most poems with what are called 'dictionary' words; that is, polysyllabic words of Latin or Greek origin. And so it must ever be, in meditative poetry upon solemn philosophic themes. The gamut of ideas needs a corresponding gamut of expressions; the scale of the thinking, which ranges through *every* key, exacts, for the artist, an unlimited command over the entire scale of the instrument which he employs. Never, in fact, was there a more erroneous direction than that given by a modern rector of the Glasgow University to the students, — viz. that they should cultivate the Saxon part of our language, at the cost of the Latin part.

Nonsense. Both are indispensable ; and, speaking generally, without stopping to distinguish as to subjects, both are *equally* indispensable. Pathos, in situations which are homely, or at all connected with domestic affections, naturally moves by Saxon words. Lyrical emotion of every kind, which, (to merit the name of *lyrical*,) must be in the state of flux and reflux, or, generally, of agitation, also requires the Saxon element of our language. And why? Because the Saxon is the aboriginal element; the basis, and not the superstructure: consequently it comprehends all the ideas which are natural to the heart of man and to the elementary situations of life. And, although the Latin often furnishes us with duplicates of these ideas, yet the Saxon, or monosyllabic part, has the advantage of precedency in our use and knowledge; for it is the language of the nursery, whether for rich or poor, in which great philological academy no toleration is given to words in '*osity*' or '*ation*.' There is, therefore, a great advantage, as regards the consecration to our feelings, settled, by usage and custom, upon the Saxon strands, in the mixed yarn of our native tongue. And, universally, this may be remarked — that, wherever the passion of a poem is of that sort which *uses*, *presumes*, or *postulates* the ideas, without seeking to extend them, Saxon will be the 'cocoon,' (to speak by the language applied to silk-worms,) which the poem spins for itself. But, on the other hand, where the motion of the feeling is *by* and *through* the ideas, where, (as in religious or meditative poetry — Young's, for instance, or Cowper's,) the pathos creeps and kindles underneath the very tissues of the thinking, there the Latin will predominate ; and so much so that, whilst the flesh, the blood and the muscle, will be often almost exclusively Latin, the articulations only, or hinges of connection, will be anglo-Saxon.

But a blunder, more perhaps from thoughtlessness and careless reading, than from malice on the part of the professional critics, ought to have roused Wordsworth into a firmer feeling of the entire question. These critics have fancied that, in Wordsworth's estimate, whatsoever was plebeian was also poetically just in diction ; not as though the impassioned phrase were sometimes the vernacular phrase, but as though the vernacular phrase were universally the impassioned. They naturally went on to suggest, as a corollary, which Wordsworth could not refuse, that Dryden and Pope must be translated into the flash diction of prisons and the slang of streets, before they could be regarded as poetically costumed. Now, so far as these critics were concerned, the answer would have been — simply to say, that much in the poets mentioned, but especially of the racy Dryden, actually *is* in that vernacular diction for which Wordsworth contended ; and, for the other part, which is *not*, frequently it *does* require the very purgation, (if *that* were possible,) which the critics were presuming to be so absurd. In Pope, and sometimes in Dryden, there is much of the unfeeling and the prescriptive slang which Wordsworth denounced. During the eighty years between 1660 and 1740, grew up that scrofulous taint in our diction, which was denounced by Wordsworth as technically 'poetic language ;' and, if Dryden and Pope were less infected than others, this was merely because their understandings were finer. Much there is in both poets, as regards diction, which *does* require correction. And if, *so* far, the critics should resist Wordsworth's principle of reform, not he, but they, would have been found the patrons of deformity. This course would soon have turned the tables upon the critics. For the poets, or the class of poets, whom they unwisely selected as models, susceptible of no correction, happen to be those who chiefly require it. But *their* foolish selection ought not to have intercepted or clouded the question when put in another shape, since in this shape it opens into a very troublesome dilemma. Spenser, Shakspeare, the Bible of 1610, and Milton, — how say you, William Wordsworth, — are these right and true as to diction, or are they not? If you say they *are*, then what is it that you are proposing to change? What room for a revolution? Would you, as Sancho says, have 'better bread than is made of wheat?' But if you say, no, they are *not*; then, indeed, you open a fearful range to your own artillery, but in a war greater than you could, apparently, have contemplated. In the first case, that is, if the leading classics of the English literature are, in quality of diction and style, loyal to the canons of sound taste, then you cut away the *locus standi* for yourself as a reformer: the reformation applies only to secondary and recent abuses. In the second, if they also are faulty, you undertake an *onus* of hostility so vast that you will be found fighting against the stars.

It is clear, therefore, that Wordsworth erred, and

caused unnecessary embarrassment, equally to the attack and to the defence, by not assigning the names of the parties offending, whom he had specially contemplated. The bodies of the criminals should have been had into court. But much more he erred in another point, where his neglect cannot be thought of without astonishment. The whole appeal turned upon a comparison between two modes of phraseology; each of these, the bad and the good, should have been extensively illustrated; and, until that is done, the whole dispute is an aërial subtilty, equally beyond the grasp of the best critic and the worst. How *could* a man so much in earnest, and so deeply interested in the question, commit so capital an oversight? *Tantamne rem tam negligenter?* The truth is, that, at this day, after a lapse of forty-seven years, and some discussion, the whole question moved by Wordsworth is still a *res integra.* And for this reason, that no sufficient specimen has ever been given of the particular phraseology which each party contemplates as good or as bad: no man, in this dispute, steadily understands even himself; and, if he did, no other person understands him for want of distinct illustrations. Not only the answer, therefore, is still entirely in arrear, but even the question has not yet practically explained itself so as that an answer to it could be possible.

Passing from the diction of Wordsworth's poetry to its matter, the least plausible objection ever brought against it, was that of Mr. Hazlitt: 'One would suppose,' he said, 'from the tenor of his subjects, that on this earth there was neither marrying nor giving in marriage.' But as well might it be said of Aristophanes: 'One would suppose, that in Athens no such thing had been known as sorrow and weeping.' Or Wordsworth himself might say reproachfully to some of Mr. Hazlitt's more favored poets: 'Judging by *your* themes, a man must believe that there is no such thing on our planet as fighting and kicking.' Wordsworth has written many memorable poems, (for instance, 'On the Tyrolean and the Spanish Insurrections;' 'On the Retreat from Moscow;' 'On the Feast of Brougham Castle,') all sympathizing powerfully with the martial spirit. Other poets, favorites of Mr. Hazlitt, have never struck a solitary note from this Tyrtæan lyre; and who blames them? Surely, if every man finds his powers limited, every man would do well to respect this silent admonition of nature, by not travelling out of his appointed walk, through any coxcombry of sporting a spurious versatility. And in this view, what Mr. Hazlitt made the reproach of the poet, is amongst the first of his praises. But there is another reason why Wordsworth could not meddle with festal raptures like the glory of a wedding-day. These raptures are not only too brief, but (which is worse) they tend downwards: even for as long as they last, they do not move upon an ascending scale. And even *that* is not their worst fault: they do not diffuse or communicate themselves: the wretches chiefly interested in a marriage are so selfish, that they keep all the rapture to themselves. Mere joy, that does not linger and reproduce itself in reverberations or mirrors, is not fitted for poetry. What would the sun be itself, if it were a mere blank orb of fire that did not multiply its splendors through millions of rays refracted and reflected; or if its glory were not endlessly caught, splintered, and thrown back by atmospheric repercussions?

There is, besides, a still subtler reason, (and one that ought not to have escaped the acuteness of Mr. Hazlitt,) why the muse of Wordsworth could not glorify a wedding festival. Poems no longer than a sonnet he *might* derive from such an impulse: and one such poem of his there really is. But whosoever looks searchingly into the characteristic genius of Wordsworth, will see that he does not willingly deal with a passion in its direct aspect, or presenting an unmodified contour, but in forms more complex and oblique, and when passing under the shadow of some secondary passion. Joy, for instance, that wells up from constitutional sources, joy that is ebullient from youth to age, and cannot cease to sparkle, he yet exhibits in the person of Matthew,[1] the village schoolmaster, as touched and overgloomed by memories of sorrow. In the poem of 'We are Seven,' which brings into day for the first time a profound fact in the abysses of human nature, namely, that the mind of an infant cannot admit the idea of death, any more than the fountain of light can comprehend the aboriginal darkness, [a truth on which Mr. Ferrier has since commented beautifully in his 'Philosophy of Consciousness;'] the little mountaineer, who furnishes the text for this lovely strain, she whose fulness of

---

[1] See the exquisite poems, so little understood by the commonplace reader, of *The Two April Mornings,* and *The Fountain.*

life could not brook the gloomy faith in a grave, is yet (for the effect upon the reader) brought into connection with the reflex shadows of the grave : and if she herself has *not*, the reader *has*, the gloom of that contemplation obliquely irradiated, as raised in relief upon his imagination, even by *her*. Death and its sunny antipole are forced into connection. I remember again to have heard a man complain, that in a little poem having for its very subject the universal diffusion and the gratuitous diffusion of joy —

> 'Pleasure is spread through the earth,
> In stray gifts to be claim'd by whoever shall find,'

a picture occurs which overpowered him with melancholy : it was this —

> 'In sight of the spires
> All alive with the fires
> Of the sun going down to his rest,
> In the broad open eye of the solitary sky,
> They dance, — there are three, as jocund as free, —
> While they dance on the calm river's breast.'[1]

Undeniably there is [and without ground for complaint there is] even here, where the spirit of gaiety is pro-

[1] Coleridge had a grievous infirmity of mind as regarded pain. He could not contemplate the shadows of fear, of sorrow, of suffering, with any steadiness of gaze. He was, in relation to that subject, what in Lancashire they call *nesh*, *i. e.* soft, or effeminate. This frailty claimed indulgence, had he not erected it at times into a ground of superiority. Accordingly, I remember that he also complained of this passage in Wordsworth, and on the same ground, as being too overpoweringly depressing in the fourth line, when modified by the other five.

fessedly invoked, an oblique though evanescent image flashed upon us of a sadness that lies deep behind the laughing figures, and of a solitude that is the real possessor in fee of all things, but is waiting an hour or so for the dispossession of the false dancing tenants.

An inverse case, as regards the three just cited, is found in the poem of 'Hart-leap-well,' over which the mysterious spirit of the noon-day, Pan, seems to brood. Out of suffering is there evoked the image of peace. Out of the cruel leap, and the agonizing race through thirteen hours; out of the anguish in the perishing brute, and the headlong courage of his final despair,

'Not unobserved by sympathy divine,'—

out of the ruined lodge and the forgotten mansion, bowers that are trodden under foot, and pleasure-houses that are dust, the poet calls up a vision of *palingenesis;* he interposes his solemn images of suffering, of decay, and ruin, only as a visionary haze through which gleams transpire of a trembling dawn far off, but surely on the road.

'The pleasure-house is dust: behind, before,
This is no common waste, no common gloom;
But Nature in due course of time once more
Shall here put on her beauty and her bloom.

She leaves these objects to a slow decay,
That what we are, and have been, may be known;
But, at the coming of the milder day,
These monuments shall all be overgrown.'

This influx of the joyous into the sad, and of the sad into the joyous, this reciprocal entanglement of darkness in light, and of light in darkness, offers a subject too occult for popular criticism; but merely to have suggested it, may be sufficient to account for Wordsworth not having chosen a theme of pure garish sunshine, such as the hurry of a wedding-day, so long as others, more picturesque or more plastic, were to be had. A wedding-day is, in many a life, the sunniest of its days. But unless it is overcast with some event more tragic than could be wished, its uniformity of blaze, without shade or relief, makes it insipid to the mere bystander. Accordingly, all *epithalamia* seem to have been written under the inspiration of a bank-note.

Far beyond these causes of repulsiveness to ordinary readers was the class of subjects selected, and the mode of treating them. The earliest line of readers, the van in point of time, always includes a majority of the young, the commonplace, and the unimpassioned. Subsequently, these are sifted and winnowed, as the rear ranks come forward in succession. But at first it was sure to ruin any poems, that the situations treated are not those which reproduce to the fancy of readers their own hopes and prospects. The meditative are interested by all that has an interest for human nature. But what cares a young lady, dreaming of lovers kneeling at her feet, for the agitations of a mother forced into resigning her child? or of a shepherd at eighty parting for ever amongst mountain solitudes with an only son of seventeen, innocent and hopeful, whom soon afterwards the guilty town seduces into ruin irreparable? Romances and novels in verse constitute the poetry which is *immediately* successful;

and that is a poetry, it may be added, which, after one generation, is unsuccessful for ever.

But this theme is too extensive. Let us pass to the separate works of Wordsworth; and, in deference to the opinion of the world, let us begin with 'The Excursion.' This poem, as regards its opening, seems to require a recast. The inaugurating story of Margaret is in a wrong key, and rests upon a false basis. It is a case of sorrow from desertion. So at least it is represented. Margaret loses, in losing her husband, the one sole friend of her heart. And the wanderer, who is the presiding philosopher of the poem, in retracing her story, sees nothing in the case but a wasting away through sorrow, at once natural in its kind, and preternatural in its degree.

There is a story somewhere told of a man who complained, and his friends complained, that his face looked almost always dirty. The man explained this strange affection out of a mysterious idiosyncrasy in the face itself, upon which the atmosphere so acted as to force out stains or masses of gloomy suffusion, just as it does upon some qualities of stone in vapory weather. But, said his friend, had you no advice for this strange affection? Oh yes: surgeons had prescribed: chemistry had exhausted its secrets upon the case: magnetism had done its best: electricity had done its worst. His friend mused for some time, and then asked: 'Pray, amongst these painful experiments, did it ever happen to you to try one that I have read of, viz. a basin of soap and water?' And perhaps, on the same principle, it might be allowable to ask the philosophic wanderer, who washes the case of Margaret with so many coats of metaphysical varnish, but ends with finding all unavailing, 'Pray, amongst your other experiments, did you ever try the effect of a guinea?' Supposing this, however, to be a remedy beyond his fortitude, at least he might have offered a little rational advice, which costs no more than civility. Let us look steadily at the case. The particular calamity under which Margaret groaned was, the loss of her husband, who had enlisted. There is something, even on the husband's part, in this enlistment, to which the reader can hardly extend his compassion. The man had not gone off, it is true, as a heartless deserter of his family, or in profligate quest of pleasure: cheerfully he would have stayed and worked, had trade been good: but, as it was *not*, he found it impossible to support the spectacle of domestic suffering: he takes the bounty of a recruiting sergeant, and off he marches with his regiment. Nobody reaches the summit of heartlessness at once: and, accordingly, in this early stage of his desertion, we are not surprised to find that part (but what part?) of the bounty had been silently conveyed to his wife. So far we are barely not indignant: but as time wears on we become highly so; for no letter does he ever send to his poor forsaken partner, either of tender excuse, or of encouraging prospects. Yet, if *he had* done this, still we must condemn him. Millions have supported (and supported without praise or knowledge of man) that trial from which he so weakly fled. Even in this, and going no further, he was a voluptuary. Millions have heard and acknowledged, as a secret call from Heaven, the summons, not only to take their own share of household suffering, as a mere sacrifice to the spirit of manliness, but also to stand the far sterner trial of witnessing the same privations in a wife and little childen. To evade this, to slip his neck out of the yoke, when God summons a poor man to such a trial, is the worst form of cowardice. And Margaret's husband, by adding to this cowardice subsequently an entire neglect of his family, not so much as intimating the destination of the regiment, forfeits his last hold upon our lingering sympathy. But with *him*, it will be said, the poet has not connected the leading thread of the interest. Certainly not: though in some degree by a reaction from *his* character depends the respectability of Margaret's grief. And it is impossible to turn away from his case entirely, because from the act of the enlistment is derived the whole movement of the story. Here it is that we must tax the wandering philosopher with treason. He found so luxurious a pleasure in contemplating a pathetic *phthisis* of heart in the abandoned wife, that the one obvious counsel in her particular distress which dotage could not have overlooked he suppresses. And yet this in the revolution of a week would have brought her effectual relief. Surely the regiment, into which her husband had enlisted, bore some number: it was the king's 'dirty half-hundred' — or the rifle brigade — or some corps known to men and the Horse Guards. Instead, therefore, of suffering poor Margaret to loiter at a gate, looking for answers to her questions from vagrant horsemen, a process which reminds one of a sight, sometimes extorting at once smiles and deep pity, in the crowded thoroughfares of

London, namely, a little child innocently asking with tearful eyes from strangers for the mother whom it has lost in that vast wilderness — the wanderer should at once have inquired for the station of that detachment which had enlisted him. This *must* have been in the neighborhood. Here he would have obtained all the particulars. That same night he would have written to the War-Office; and in a very few days, an official answer, bearing the indorsement, *On H. M.'s Service*, would have placed Margaret in communication with the truant. To have overlooked a point of policy so broadly apparent as this, vitiates and nullifies the very basis of the story. Even for a romance it will not do; far less for a philosophic poem dealing with intense realities. No such case of distress could have lived for one fortnight, nor have survived a single interview with the rector, the curate, the parish-clerk, with the schoolmaster, the doctor, the attorney, the innkeeper, or the exciseman.

But, apart from the vicious mechanism of the incidents, the story is even more objectionable by the doubtful quality of the leading character from which it derives its pathos. Had any one of us readers held the office of coroner in her neighborhood, he would have found it his duty to hold an inquest upon the body of her infant. This child, as every reader could depose, (*now* when the details have been published by the poet,) died of neglect; not through direct cruelty, but through criminal self-indulgence. Self-indulgence in what? Not in liquor, yet not altogether in fretting. Sloth, and the habit of gadding abroad, were most in fault. The wanderer himself might have been called as a witness for the crown, to prove that the infant was left to sleep in solitude for hours: the key even was taken away, as if to intercept the possibility (except through burglary) of those tender attentions from some casual stranger, which the unfeeling mother had withdrawn. The child absolutely awoke whilst the philosopher was listening at the door. It cried; but finally hushed itself to sleep. That looks like a case of Dalby's carminative. But this crisis could not have been relied on: tragical catastrophes arise from neglected crying; ruptures in the first place, a very common result in infants; rolling out of bed, followed by dislocation of the neck; fits, and other short cuts to death. It is hardly any praise to Margaret that she carried the child to that consummation by a more lingering road.

This first tale, therefore, must and will, if Mr. Wordsworth retains energy for such recasts of a laborious work, be cut away from its connection with 'The Excursion.' This is the more to be expected from a poet aware of his own importance and anxious for the perfection of his works, because nothing in the following books depends upon this narrative. No timbers or main beams need to be sawed away; it is but a bolt that is to be slipped, a rivet to be unscrewed. And yet, on the other hand, if the connection is slight, the injury is great: for we all complain heavily of entering a temple dedicated to new combinations of truth through a vestibule of falsehood. And the falsehood is double; falsehood in the adjustment of the details, (however separately possible,) falsehood in the character which, wearing the mask of profound sentiment, does apparently repose upon dyspepsy and sloth.

Far different in value and in principle of composition is the next tale in 'The Excursion.' This occupies the fourth book, and is the impassioned record from the infidel solitary of those heart-shaking chapters in his own life which had made him what the reader finds him. Once he had not been a solitary; once he had not been an infidel: now he is both. He lives in a little urn-like valley (a closet-recess from Little Langdale by the description) amongst the homely household of a yeoman: he is become a bitter cynic; and not against man alone, or society alone, but against the laws of hope or fear upon which both repose. If he endures the society with which he is now connected, it is because, being dull, that society is of few words; it is because, being tied to hard labor, that society goes early to bed, and packs up its dulness at eight, P. M. in blankets; it is because, under the acute inflictions of Sunday, or the chronic inflictions of the Christmas holidays, that dull society is easily laid into a magnetic sleep by three passes of metaphysical philosophy. The narrative of this misanthrope is grand and impassioned; not creeping by details and minute touches, but rolling through capital events, and uttering its pathos through great representative abstractions. Nothing can be finer than when, upon the desolation of his household, upon the utter emptying of his domestic chambers by the successive deaths of children and youthful wife, just at that moment the mighty phantom of the French Revolution rises solemnly above the horizon; even then new earth and new heavens are promised to human nature; and suddenly the solitary man, translated by the frenzy of human grief into the frenzy of supernatural hopes, adopts these radiant visions for the darlings whom he has lost —

> 'Society becomes his glittering bride,
> And airy hopes his children.'

Yet it is a misfortune in the fate of this fine tragic movement, rather than its structure, that it tends to collapse: the latter strains, colored deeply by disappointment, do not correspond with the grandeur of the first. And the hero of the record becomes even more painfully a contrast to himself than the tenor of the incidents to their earlier tenor. Sneering and querulous comments upon so broad a field as human folly, make poor compensation for the magnificence of youthful enthusiasm. But may not this defect be redressed in a future section of the poem? It is probable, from a hint dropped by the author, that one collateral object of the philosophical discussions is — the reconversion of the splenetic infidel to his ancient creed in some higher form, and to his ancient temper of benignant hope: in which case, what *now* we feel to be a cheerless depression, will sweep round into a noble reascent — quite on a level with the aspirations of youth, and differing, not in degree, but only in quality of enthusiasm. Yet, if this is the poet's plan, it seems to rest upon a misconception. For how should the sneering sceptic, who has actually found solace in Voltaire's 'Candide,' be restored to the benignities of faith and hope by argument? It was not in this way that he lost his station amongst Christian believers. No false philosophy it had been which wrecked his Christian spirit of hope; but, on the contrary, his bankruptcy in hope which wrecked his Christian philosophy. Here, therefore, the poet will certainly find himself in an 'almighty fix:' because any possible treatment, which could restore the solitary's former self, such as a course of sea-bathing, could not interest the reader; and reversely, any successful treatment through argument that could interest the philosophic reader, would not, under the circumstances, seem a plausible restoration for the case.

What is it that has made the recluse a sceptic? Is it the reading of bad books? In that case he may be reclaimed by the arguments of those who have read better. But not at all. He has become the unbelieving cynic that he is, 1st, through his own domestic calamities predisposing him to *gloomy* views of human nature; and, 2dly, through the overclouding of his high-toned expectations from the French Revolution, which has disposed him, in a spirit of revenge for his own disappointment, to *contemptuous* views of human nature. Now, surely the dejection which supports his gloom, and the despondency which supports his contempt, are not of a nature to give way before philosophic reasonings. Make him happy by restoring what he has lost, and his genial philosophy will return of itself. Make him triumphant by realizing what had seemed to him the golden promises of the French Revolution, and his political creed will moult her sickly feathers. Do this, and he is still young enough for hope; but less than this restoration of his morning visions will not call back again his morning happiness;

and breaking spears with him in logical tournaments will mend neither his hopes nor his temper.

Indirectly, besides, it ought not to be overlooked, that, as respects the French Revolution, the whole college of philosophy in 'The Excursion,' who are gathered together upon the case of the recluse, make the same mistake that *he* makes. Why is the recluse disgusted with the French Revolution? Because it had not fulfilled many of his expectations; and, of those which it *had* fulfilled, some had soon been darkened by reverses. But really this was childish impatience. If a man depends for the exuberance of his harvest upon the splendor of the coming summer, you do not excuse him for taking prussic acid because it rains cats and dogs through the first ten days of April. All in good time, we say; take it easy; make acquaintance with May and June before you do anything rash. The French Revolution has not, even yet, [1845] come into full action. It was the explosion of a prodigious volcano, which scattered its lava over every kingdom of every continent, everywhere silently manuring them for social struggles; this lava is gradually fertilizing all; the revolutionary movement is moving onwards at this hour as inexorably as ever. Listen, if you have ears for such spiritual sounds, to the mighty tide even now slowly coming up from the sea to Milan, to Rome, to Naples, to Vienna. Hearken to the gentle undulations already breaking against the steps of that golden throne which stretches from St. Petersburgh to Astrachan; — tremble at the hurricanes which have long been mustering about the pavilions of the Ottoman Padishah. All these are long swells setting in from the French Revolution. Even as regards France herself, that which gave the mortal offence to the sympathies of the solitary was the Reign of Terror. But how thoughtless to measure the cycles of vast national revolutions by metres that would not stretch round an ordinary human passion. Even to a frail sweetheart, you would grant more indulgence than to be off in a pet because some transitory cloud arose between you. The Reign of Terror was a mere fleeting phasis. The Napoleon dynasty was nothing more. Even that scourge, which was supposed by many to have *mastered* the Revolution, has itself passed away upon the wind,—leaving no wreck, relic, or record behind, except precisely those changes which it worked, *not as an enemy to the Revolution*, [which also it was,] *but as its servant and its tool.* See, even whilst we speak, the folly of that cynical sceptic who would not allow time for great natural processes of purification to travel onwards to their birth, or wait for the evolution of natural results;—the storm that shocked him has wheeled away;—the frost and the hail that offended him have done their office;—the rain is over and gone;—happier days have descended upon France;—the voice of the turtle is heard in all her forests;—man walks with his head erect;—bastiles are no more;—every cottage is searched by the golden light of law; and the privileges of conscience are consecrated for ever.

Here, then, the poet himself, the philosophic wanderer, the learned vicar, are all equally in fault with the solitary sceptic; for they all agree in treating his disappointment as sound and reasonable in itself; but blameable only in relation to those exalted hopes which he never ought to have encouraged. Right, (they say,) to consider the French Revolution, now, as a failure : but *not* right originally, to have expected that it should succeed. Whereas, in fact, it *has* succeeded ; it is propagating its life ; it is travelling on to new births — conquering, and yet to conquer.

It is not easy to see, therefore, how the Laureate can avoid making some change in the constitution of his poem, were it only to rescue his philosophers, and, therefore, his own philosophy, from the imputation of precipitancy in judgment. They charge the sceptic with rash judgment *à parte ante ;* and, meantime, they themselves are more liable to that charge *à parte post.* If he, at the first, hoped too much, (which is not clear, but only that he hoped too impatiently,) they afterwards recant too blindly. And this error they will not, themselves, fail to acknowledge, as soon as they awaken to the truth, that the Revolution did not close on the 18th Brumaire, 1799, at which time it was only arrested or suspended, in one direction, by military shackles, but is still mining under ground, like the ghost in Hamlet, through every quarter of the globe.[1]

[1] The reader must not understand the writer as unconditionally approving of the French Revolution. It is his belief that the resistance to the Revolution was, in many high quarters, a sacred duty ; and that this resistance it was which forced out, from the Revolution itself, the benefits which it has since diffused. To speak by the language of mechanics, the case was one which illustrated the composition of forces. Neither the Revolution singly, nor the resistance to the Revolution

In paying so much attention to 'The Excursion,' (of which, in a more extended notice, the two books entitled, 'The Churchyard amongst the Mountains,' would have claimed the profoundest attention,) we yield less to our own opinion than to that of the public. Or, perhaps, it is not so much the public as the vulgar opinion, governed entirely by the consideration that 'The Excursion' is very much the longest poem of its author; and, secondly, that it bears currently the title of a *philosophic* poem; on which account it is presumed to have a higher dignity. The big name and the big size are allowed to settle its rank. But in this there is much delusion. In the very scheme and movement of 'The Excursion' there are two defects which interfere greatly with its power to act upon the mind as a whole, or with any effect of unity; so that, infallibly, it will be read, by future generations, in parts and fragments; and, being thus virtually dismembered into many small poems, it will scarcely justify men in allowing it the rank of a long one. One of these defects is the *undulatory* character of the course pursued by the poem, which does not ascend uniformly, or even keep one steady level, but trespasses, as if by forgetfulness, or chance, into topics furnishing little inspiration, and not always closely connected with the presiding theme. In part this

singly, was calculated to regenerate social man. But the two forces in union, where the one modified, mitigated, or even neutralized the other, at times; and where, at times, each entered into a happy combination with the other, yielded for the world those benefits which, by its separate tendency, either of the two was fitted to stifle.

arises from the accident that a slight tissue of narrative connects the different sections; and to this the movement of the narrative, the fluctuations of the speculative themes, are in part obedient: the succession of the incidents becomes a law for the succession of the thoughts, as oftentimes it happens that these incidents are the proximate occasions of the thoughts. Yet, as the narrative is not of a nature to be moulded by any determinate principle of coercing passion, but bends easily to the caprices of chance and the moment, unavoidably it stamps, by reaction, a desultory or even incoherent character upon the train of the philosophic discussions. You know not what is coming next; and, when it *does* come, you do not always know *why* it comes. This has the effect of crumbling the poem into separate segments, and causes the whole (when looked at *as* a whole), to appear a rope of sand. A second defect lies in the colloquial form which the poem sometimes assumes. It is dangerous to conduct a philosophic discussion by *talking*. If the nature of the argument could be supposed to roll through logical quillets, or metaphysical conundrums, so that, on putting forward a problem, the interlocutor could bring matters to a crisis, by saying, 'Do you give it up?'—in that case there might be a smart reciprocation of dialogue, of swearing and denying, giving and taking, butting, rebutting, and 'surrebutting;'[1] and this would

[1] 'Surrebutting:' this is not, directly, a term from Aristotle's mint, but indirectly it is; for it belongs to the old science of 'special pleading,' which, in part, is an offset from the Aristotelian logic.

confer an interlocutory or *amœbæan* character upon the process of altercation. But the topics, and the quality of the arguments being *moral*, in which always the reconciliation of the feelings is to be secured by gradual persuasion, rather than the understanding to be floored by a solitary blow, inevitably it becomes impossible that anything of this brilliant conversational sword-play, cut-and-thrust, 'carte' and 'tierce,' can make for itself an opening. Mere decorum requires that the speakers should be prosy. And you yourself, though sometimes disposed to say, 'Do now, dear old soul, cut it short,' are sensible that he *cannot* cut it short. Disquisitions, in a certain key, can no more turn round upon a sixpence than a coach-and-six. They must have sea-room to 'wear' ship, and to tack. This in itself is often tedious; but it leads to a worse tediousness: a practised eye sees from afar the whole evolution of the coming argument; and then, besides the pain of hearing the parties preach, you hear them preach from a text which already in germ had warned you of all the buds and blossoms which it was laboriously to produce. And this *second* blemish, unavoidable if the method of dialogue is adopted, becomes more painfully apparent through a *third*, almost inalienable from the natural constitution of the subjects concerned. It is, that in cases where a large interest of human nature is treated, such as the position of man in this world, his duties, his difficulties, many parts become necessary as transitional or connecting links, which, *per se*, are not attractive, nor can by any art be made so. Treating the whole theme *in extenso*, the poet is driven, by natural corollary, or by objection too obvious to be evaded, into discussions not chosen by his own taste, but dictated by the logic or the tendencies of the question, and by the impossibility of dismissing with partiality any one branch of a subject which is essential to the integrity of the speculation, simply because it is at war with the brilliancy of its development.

Not, therefore, in 'The Excursion' must we look for that reversionary influence which awaits Wordsworth with posterity. It is the vulgar superstition in behalf of big books and sounding titles; it is the weakness of supposing no book entitled to be considered a power in the literature of the land, unless physically it is weighty, that must have prevailed upon Coleridge and others to undervalue, by comparison with the direct philosophic poetry of Wordsworth, those earlier poems which are all short, but generally scintillating with gems of far profounder truth. Let the reader understand, however, that by 'truth,' I understand, not merely that truth which takes the shape of a formal proposition, reducible to 'mood' and 'figure;' but truth which suddenly strengthens into solemnity an impression very feebly acknowledged previously, or truth which suddenly unveils a connection between objects always before regarded as irrelate and independent. In astronomy, to gain the rank of discoverer, it is not required that you should reveal a star absolutely new: find out with respect to an old star some new affection — as, for instance, that it has an ascertainable parallax — and immediately you bring it within the verge of a human interest; or of some old familiar planet, that its satellites suffer periodical eclipses, and immediately you bring it within the verge of terrestrial uses. Gleams of steadier vision, that brighten into certainty appearances else doubtful, or that unfold relations else unsuspected, are not less discoveries of truth than the revelations of the telescope, or the conquests of the diving bell. It is astonishing how large a harvest of new truths would be reaped, simply through the accident of a man's feeling, or being made to feel, more *deeply* than other men. He sees the same objects, neither more nor fewer, but he sees them engraved in lines far stronger and more determinate : and the difference in the strength makes the whole difference between consciousness and sub-consciousness. And in questions of the mere understanding, we see the same fact illustrated : the author who rivets notice the most, is not he that perplexes men by truths drawn from fountains of absolute novelty, — truths unsunned as yet, and obscure from that cause ; but he that awakens into illuminated consciousness old lineaments of truth long slumbering in the mind, although too faint to have extorted attention. Wordsworth has brought many a truth into life both for the eye and for the understanding, which previously had slumbered indistinctly, for all men.

For instance, as respects the eye, who does not acknowledge instantaneously the strength of reality in that saying upon a cataract seen from a station two miles off, that it was 'frozen by distance ?' In all nature, there is not an object so essentially at war with the stiffening of frost, as the headlong and desperate life of a cataract ; and yet notoriously the effect of distance is to lock up this frenzy of motion into the most petrific column of stillness. This effect is perceived at once when pointed out; but how few are the eyes that ever *would* have perceived it for themselves! Twilight, again, — who before Wordsworth ever distinctly noticed its *abstracting* power? — that power of removing, softening, harmonizing, by which a mode of obscurity executes for the eye the same mysterious office which the mind so often within its own shadowy realms executes for itself. In the dim interspace between day and night, all disappears from our earthly scenery, as if touched by an enchanter's rod, which is either mean or inharmonious, or unquiet, or expressive of temporary things. Leaning against a column of rock, looking down upon a lake or river, and at intervals carrying your eyes forward through a vista of mountains, you become aware that your sight rests upon the very same spectacle, unaltered in a single feature, which once at the same hour was beheld by the legionary Roman from his embattled camp, or by the roving Briton in his 'wolf-skin vest,' lying down to sleep, and looking

> ——'through some leafy bower,
> Before his eyes were closed.'

How magnificent is the summary or abstraction of the elementary features in such a scene, as executed by the poet himself, in illustration of this abstraction daily executed by nature, through her handmaid Twilight! Listen, reader, to the closing strain, solemn as twilight is solemn, and grand as the spectacle which it describes: —

'By him [*i. e.* the roving Briton] was seen,
The self-same vision which *we* now behold,
At thy meek bidding, shadowy Power, brought forth,
These mighty barriers, and the gulf between;
The floods, the stars, — a spectacle as old
As the beginning of the heavens and earth.'

Another great field there is amongst the pomps of nature, which, if Wordsworth did not first notice, he certainly has noticed most circumstantially. I speak of cloud-scenery, or those pageants of sky-built architecture, which sometimes in summer, at noon-day, and in all seasons about sunset, arrest or appal the meditative; 'perplexing monarchs' with the spectacle of armies manœuvring, or deepening the solemnity of evening by towering edifices that mimic — but which also in mimicking mock — the transitory grandeurs of man. It is singular that these gorgeous phenomena, not less than those of the *Aurora Borealis*, have been so little noticed by poets. The *Aurora* was naturally neglected by the southern poets of Greece and Rome, as not much seen in their latitudes.[1] But the cloud-

[1] But then, says the reader, why was it not proportionably the more noticed by poets of the north? Certainly, that question is fair. And the answer, it is scarcely possible to doubt, is this: — That until the rise of Natural Philosophy, in Charles the Second's reign, *there was no name* for the appearance; on which account, some writers have been absurd enough to believe that the Aurora did not exist, noticeably, until about 1690. Shakspeare, in his journey down to Stratford, (always performed on horseback,) must often have been belated: he must sometimes have seen, he could not but have admired, the fiery skirmishing of the Aurora. And yet, for want of a word to fix and identify the object, how could he introduce it as an image or allusion in his writings?

architecture of the daylight belongs alike to north and south. Accordingly, I remember one notice of it in Hesiod, a case were the clouds exhibited

'The beauteous semblance of a flock at rest.'

Another there is, a thousand years later, in Lucan: amongst the portents which prefigured the dreadful convulsions destined to shake the earth at Pharsalia, is noticed by him some fiery coruscation of arms in the heavens; but, so far as I recollect, the appearances might have belonged equally to the workmanship of the clouds or the Aurora. Up and down the next eight hundred years, are scattered evanescent allusions to these vapory appearances; in Hamlet and elsewhere, occur gleams of such allusions; but I remember no distinct picture of one before that in the 'Antony and Cleopatra' of Shakspeare, beginning,

'Sometimes we see a cloud that's dragonish.'

Subsequently to Shakspeare, these notices, as of all phenomena whatsoever that demanded a familiarity with nature in the spirit of love, became rarer and rarer. At length, as the eighteenth century was winding up its accounts, forth stepped William Wordsworth, of whom, as a reader of all pages in nature, it may be said that, if we except Dampier, the admirable buccaneer, and some few professional naturalists, he first and he last looked at natural objects with the eye that neither will be dazzled from without nor cheated by preconceptions from within. Most men look at nature in the hurry of a confusion that distinguishes nothing; *their* error is from without. Pope, again, and many who live in towns,[1] make such blunders as that of supposing the moon to tip with silver the hills *behind* which she is rising, not by erroneous use of their eyes, (for they use them not at all,) but by inveterate preconceptions. Scarcely has there been a poet with what could be called a learned eye, or an eye *extensively* learned, before Wordsworth. Much affectation there has been of that sort since *his* rise, and at all times much counterfeit enthusiasm: but the sum of the matter is this, that Wordsworth had his passion for nature fixed in his blood; — it was a necessity, like that of the mulberry-leaf to the silk-worm; and through his commerce with nature did he live and breathe. Hence it was, viz., from the *truth* of his love, that his knowledge grew; whilst most others, being merely hypocrites in their love, have turned out merely *charlatans* in their knowledge. This chapter, therefore, of *sky* scenery, may be said to have been revivified amongst the resources of poetry by Wordsworth — rekindled, if not absolutely kindled. The sublime scene indorsed upon the draperies of the storm in 'The Excursion,' — that wit-

[1] It was not, however, that all poets then lived in towns; neither had Pope himself generally lived in towns. But it is perfectly useless to be familiar with nature unless there is a public trained to love and value nature. It is not what the individual sees that will fix itself as beautiful in his recollections, but what he sees under a consciousness that others will sympathize with his feelings. Under any other circumstances familiarity does but realize the adage, and 'breeds contempt.' The great despisers of rural scenery are rustics.

nessed upon the passage of the Hamilton Hills in Yorkshire, — the solemn 'sky prospect' from the fields of France, are unrivalled in that order of composition; and in one of these records Wordsworth has given first of all the true key-note of the sentiment belonging to these grand pageants. They are, says the poet, speaking in a case where the appearance had occurred towards night,

> 'Meek nature's evening comment on the shows
> And all the fuming vanities of earth.'

Yes, that is the secret moral whispered to the mind. These mimicries express the laughter which is in heaven at earthly pomps. Frail and vapory are the glories of man, even as the parodies of those glories are frail which nature weaves in clouds.

As another of those natural appearances which must have haunted men's eyes since the Flood, but yet had never forced itself into *conscious* notice until arrested by Wordsworth, I may notice an effect of *iteration* daily exhibited in the habits of cattle: —

> 'The cattle are grazing,
> Their heads never raising;
> There are forty feeding like one.'

Now, merely as a *fact*, and if it were nothing more, this characteristic appearance in the habits of cows, when all repeat the action of each, ought not to have been overlooked by those who profess themselves engaged in holding up a mirror to nature. But the fact has also a profound meaning as a hieroglyphic. In all animals which live under the protection of man a life of peace and quietness, but do not share in his labors or in his pleasures, what we regard is the species, and not the individual. Nobody but a grazier ever looks at one cow amongst a field of cows, or at one sheep in a flock. But as to those animals which are more closely connected with man, not passively connected, but actively, being partners in his toils and perils and recreations, such as horses, dogs, falcons, they are regarded as individuals, and are allowed the benefit of an individual interest. It is not that cows have not a differential character, each for herself; and sheep, it is well known, have all a separate physiognomy for the shepherd who has cultivated their acquaintance. But men generally have no opportunity or motive for studying the individualities of creatures, however otherwise respectable, that are too much regarded by all of us in the reversionary light of milk, and beef, and mutton. Far otherwise it is with horses, who share in man's martial risks, who sympathize with man's frenzy in hunting, who divide with man the burdens of noonday. Far otherwise it is with dogs, that share the hearths of man, and adore the footsteps of his children. These man loves: of these he makes dear, though humble friends. These often fight for *him;* and for them he will sometimes fight. Of necessity, therefore, every horse and every dog is an individual — has a sort of personality that makes him *separately* interesting — has a beauty and a character of his own. Go to Melton, therefore, and what will you see? Every man, every horse, every dog, glorying in the plentitude of life, is in a different attitude, motion, gesture, action. It is not there the sublime unity which you must seek, where forty are like one ; but the sublime infinity, like that of ocean, like that of Flora, like that of nature, where no repetitions are endured, no leaf the copy of another leaf, no absolute identity, and no painful tautologies. This subject might be pursued into profounder recesses; but in a popular discussion it is necessary to forbear.

A volume might be filled with such glimpses of novelty as Wordsworth has first laid bare, even to the apprehension of the *senses.* For the *understanding*, when moving in the same track of human sensibilities, he has done only not so much. How often (to give an instance or two) must the human heart have felt that there are sorrows which descend far below the region in which tears gather; and yet who has ever given utterance to this feeling until Wordsworth came with his immortal line —

'Thoughts that do often lie too deep for tears ?'

This sentiment, and others that might be adduced, (such as 'The child is father of the man,') have even passed into the popular mind, and are often quoted by those who know not *whom* they are quoting. Magnificent, again, is the sentiment, and yet an echo to one which lurks amongst all hearts, in relation to the frailty of merely human schemes for working good, which so often droop and collapse through the unsteadiness of human energies, —

——— 'foundations must be laid
In Heaven.

How ? Foundations laid in realms that are *above* ? But *that* is at war with physics ; — foundations must be laid *below.* Yes ; and even so the poet throws the mind yet more forcibly on the hyperphysical character — on the grandeur transcending all physics — of those shadowy foundations which alone are enduring.

But the great distinction of Wordsworth, and the pledge of his increasing popularity, is the extent of his sympathy with what is *really* permanent in human feelings, and also the depth of this sympathy. Young and Cowper, the two earlier leaders in the province of meditative poetry, are too circumscribed in the range of their sympathies, too exclusive, and oftentimes not sufficiently profound. Both these poets manifested the quality of their strength by the quality of their public reception. Popular in some degree from the first, they entered upon the inheritance of their fame almost at once. Far different was the fate of Wordsworth; for, in poetry of this class, which appeals to what lies deepest in man, in proportion to the native power of the poet, and his fitness for permanent life, is the strength of resistance in the public taste. Whatever is too original will be hated at the first. It must slowly mould a public for itself; and the resistance of the early thoughtless judgments must be overcome by a counter resistance to itself, in a better audience slowly mustering against the first. Forty and seven years it is since William Wordsworth first appeared as an author. Twenty of those years he was the scoff of the world, and his poetry a byword of scorn. Since then, and more than once, senates have rung with acclamations to the echo of his name. Now at this moment, whilst we are talking about him, he has entered upon his seventy-sixth year.

For himself, according to the course of nature, he cannot be far from his setting; but his poetry is but now clearing the clouds that gathered about its rising. Meditative poetry is perhaps that which will finally maintain most power upon generations more thoughtful; and in this department, at least, there is little competition to be apprehended by Wordsworth from anything that has appeared since the death of Shakspeare.

PERCY BYSSHE SHELLEY.

THERE is no writer named amongst men, of whom, so much as of Percy Bysshe Shelley, it is difficult for a conscientious critic to speak with the truth and the respect due to his exalted powers, and yet without offence to feelings the most sacred, which too memorably he outraged. The indignation which this powerful young writer provoked, had its root in no personal feelings — those might have been conciliated; in no worldly feelings — those might have proved transitory; but in feelings the holiest which brood over human life, and which guard the sanctuary of religious truth. Consequently, which is a melancholy thought for any friend of Shelley's, the indignation is likely to be co-extensive and co-enduring with the writings that provoked it. That bitterness of scorn and defiance which still burns against his name in the most extensively meditative section of English society, viz. the religious section, is not of a nature to be propitiated: selfish interests, being wounded, might be compensated; merely human interests might be soothed; but interests that transcend all human valuation, being *so* insulted, must upon principle reject all human ransom or conditions of human compromise. Less than penitential recantation could not be accepted: and *that* is now impossible. 'Will ye *transact* with God?' is the indignant language of Milton in a case of that nature. And in this case the language of many pious men said aloud,—'It is for God to forgive: but we, his servants, are bound to recollect, that this young man offered to Christ and to Christianity the deepest insult which ear has heard, or which it has entered into the heart of man to conceive.' Others, as in Germany, had charged Christ with committing suicide, on the principle that he who tempts or solicits death by doctrines fitted to provoke that result, is virtually the causer of his own destruction.... But in this sense every man commits suicide, who will not betray an interest confided to his keeping under menaces of death; the martyr, who perishes for truth, when by deserting it he might live; the patriot, who perishes for his country, when by betraying it he might win riches and honor. And, were this even otherwise, the objection would be nothing to Christians — who, recognising the Deity in Christ, recognise his unlimited right over life. Some, again, had pointed their insults at a part more vital in Christianity, if it had happened to be as vulnerable as they fancied. The new doctrine introduced by Christ, of forgiveness to those who injure or who hate us,—on what footing was it placed? Once, at least in appearance, on the idea, that by assisting or forgiving an enemy, we should be eventually 'heaping coals of fire upon his head.' Mr. Howdon, in a very clever book [*Rational Investigation of the Principles of Natural Philosophy: London*, 1840,] calls this 'a fiendish idea,' (p. 290): and I acknowledge that to myself, in one part of my boyhood, it *did* seem a refinement of malice. My subtilizing habits, however, even in those days, soon suggested to me that this aggravation of guilt in the object of our forgiveness was not held out as the motive to the forgiveness, but as the result of it; secondly, that perhaps no aggravation of his guilt was the point contemplated, but the salutary stinging into life of his remorse, hitherto sleeping; thirdly, that every doubtful or perplexing expression must be overruled and determined by the prevailing spirit of the system in which it stands. If Mr. Howdon's sense were the true one, then this passage would be in pointed hostility to every other part of the Christian ethics.[2]]

These were affronts to the Founder of Christianity, offered too much in the temper of malignity. But Shelley's was worse; more bitter, and with less of countenance, even in show or shadow, from any fact, or insinuation of a fact, that Scripture suggests. In his 'Queen Mab,' he gives a dreadful portrait of God; and that no question may arise, of *what* God? he names him; it is Jehovah. He asserts his existence; he affirms him to be 'an almighty God, and vengeful as almighty.' He goes on to describe him as the 'omnipotent fiend,' who found 'none but slaves' [Israel in Egypt, no doubt] to be 'his tools,' and none but 'a murderer' [Moses, I presume] 'to be his accomplice in crime.' He introduces this dreadful Almighty as speaking, and as speaking thus, —

> 'From an eternity of idleness
> I, God, awoke; in seven days' toil made earth
> From nothing; rested; and created man.'

But man he hates; and he goes on to curse him; till at the intercession of 'the murderer,' who is electrified into pity for the human race by the very horror of the divine curses, God promises to send his son — only, however, for the benefit of a few. This son appears; the poet tells us that —

—— 'the Incarnate came; humbly he came,
Veiling his horrible Godhead in the shape
Of man, scorn'd by the world, his name unheard
Save by the rabble of his native town.'

The poet pursues this incarnate God as a teacher of men; teaching, 'in semblance,' justice, truth, and peace; but underneath all this, kindling 'quenchless flames,' which eventually were destined

—— 'to satiate, with the blood
Of truth and freedom, his malignant soul.'

He follows him to his crucifixion; and describes him, whilst hanging on the cross, as shedding malice upon a reviler, — *malice on the cross!*

'A smile of godlike malice reillumined
His fading lineaments:'

and his parting breath is uttered in a memorable curse.

This atrocious picture of the Deity, in his dealings with man, both pre-Christian and post-Christian, is certainly placed in the mouth of the wandering Jew. But the internal evidence, as well as collateral evidence from without, make it clear that the Jew, (whose version of scriptural records nobody in the poem disputes,) here represents the person of the poet. Shelley had opened his career as an atheist; and as a proselytizing atheist. But he was then a boy. At the date of 'Queen Mab' he was a young man. And we now find him advanced from the station of an atheist to the more intellectual one of a believer in God and in the mission of Christ; but of one who fancied himself called upon to defy and to hate both, in so far as they had revealed their relations to man.

Mr. Gilfillan* thinks that 'Shelley was far too harshly treated in his speculative boyhood;' and it strikes him 'that, had pity and kind-hearted expostulation been tried, instead of reproach and abrupt expulsion, they might have weaned him from the dry dugs of Atheism to the milky breast of the faith and "worship of sorrow;" and the touching spectatacle had been renewed, of the demoniac sitting, "clothed, and in his right mind," at the feet of Jesus.' I am not of that opinion: and it is an opinion which seems to question the *sincerity* of Shelley, — that quality which in him was deepest, so as to form the basis of his nature, if we allow ourselves to think that, by personal irritation, he had been piqued into infidelity, or that by flattering conciliation he could have been bribed back into a profession of Christianity. Like a wild horse of the Pampas, he would have thrown up his heels, and *whinnied* his disdain of any man coming to catch *him* with a bribe of oats. He had a constant vision of a manger and a halter in the rear of all such caressing tempters, once having scented the gales of what he thought perfect freedom,

* 'Gallery of Literary Portraits.'

from the lawless desert. His feud with Christianity was a craze derived from some early wrench of his understanding, and made obstinate to the degree in which we find it, from having rooted itself in certain combinations of ideas that, once coalescing, could not be shaken loose; such as, that Christianity underpropped the corruptions of the earth, in the shape of wicked governments that might else have been overthrown, or of wicked priesthoods that, but for the shelter of shadowy and spiritual terrors, must have trembled before those whom they overawed. Kings that were clothed in bloody robes; dark hierarchies that scowled upon the poor children of the soil; these objects took up a permanent station in the background of Shelley's imagination, not to be dispossessed more than the phantom of Banquo from the festival of Macbeth, and composed a towering Babylon of mystery that, to *his* belief, could not have flourished, under any umbrage less vast than that of Christianity. Such was the inextricable association of images that domineered over Shelley's mind: such was the hatred which he built upon that association, — an association casual and capricious, yet fixed and petrified as if by frost. Can we imagine the case of an angel touched by lunacy? Have we ever seen the spectacle of a human intellect, exquisite by its functions of creation, yet in one chamber of its shadowy house already ruined before the light of manhood had cleansed its darkness? Such an angel, such a man, — if ever such there were, — such a lunatic angel, such a ruined man, was Shelley, whilst yet standing on the earliest threshold of life.

Mr. Gilfillan, whose eye is quick to seize the lurking and the stealthy aspect of things, does not overlook the absolute midsummer madness which possessed Shelley upon the subject of Christianity. Shelley's total nature was altered and darkened when that theme arose: transfiguration fell upon him. He that was so gentle, became savage; he that breathed by the very lungs of Christianity — that was so merciful, so full of tenderness and pity, of humility, of love and forgiveness, then raved and screamed like an idiot whom once I personally knew, when offended by a strain of heavenly music at the full of the moon. In both cases, it was the sense of perfect beauty revealed under the sense of morbid estrangement. This it is, as I presume, which Mr. Gilfillan alludes to in the following passage, (p. 104): 'On all *other* subjects the wisest of the wise, the gentlest of the gentle, the bravest of the brave, yet, when *one* topic was introduced, he became straightway insane; his eyes glared, his voice screamed, his hand vibrated frenzy.' But Mr. Gilfillan is entirely in the wrong when he countenances the notion that harsh treatment had any concern in riveting the fanaticism of Shelley. On the contrary, he met with an indulgence to the first manifestation of his anti-Christian madness, better suited to the goodness of the lunatic than to the pestilence of his lunacy. It was at Oxford that this earliest explosion of Shelleyism occurred; and though, with respect to secrets of prison-houses, and to discussions that proceed 'with closed doors,' there is always a danger of being misinformed, I believe, from the uniformity of such accounts as have reached myself, that the following *brief* of the matter may be relied on. Shelley, being a venerable sage of sixteen, or rather less, came to a resolution that he would convert, and that it was his solemn duty to convert, the universal Christian church to Atheism or to Pantheism, no great matter *which.* But, as such large undertakings require time, twenty months, suppose, or even two years, — for you know, reader, that a railway requires on an average little less, — Shelley was determined to obey no impulse of youthful rashness. Oh no! Down with presumption, down with levity, down with boyish precipitation! Changes of religion are awful things: people must have time to think. He would move slowly and discreetly. So first he wrote a pamphlet, clearly and satisfactorily explaining the necessity of being an atheist; and, with his usual exemplary courage, (for, seriously, he was the least *false* of human creatures,) Shelley put his name to the pamphlet, and the name of his college. His ultimate object was to accomplish a general apostasy in the Christian church of whatever name. But for one six months, it was quite enough if he caused a revolt in the Church of England. And as, before a great naval action, when the enemy is approaching, you throw a long shot or two by way of trying his range, — on that principle Shelley had thrown out his tract in Oxford. Oxford formed the advanced squadron of the English Church; and, by way of a *coup d'essai*, though in itself a bagatelle, what if he should begin with converting Oxford? To make any beginning at all is one half the battle; or, as a writer in this magazine [June 1845] suggests, a good deal more. To speak seriously, there is something even thus far in the boyish presumption of Shelley, not altogether without nobility. He affronted the armies of Christendom. Had it been possible for *him* to be jesting, it would *not* have been noble. But here, even in the most monstrous of his undertakings, here, as always, he was perfectly sincere and single-minded. Satisfied that Atheism was the sheet anchor of the world, he was not the person to speak by halves. Being a boy, he attacked those [upon a point the most sure to irritate] who were gray; having no station in society, he flew at the throats of none but those who *had;* weaker than an infant for the purpose before him, he planted his fist in the face of a giant, saying, 'Take *that*, you devil, and *that*, and *that*.'... The pamphlet had been published; and though an undergraduate of Oxford is not (technically speaking) a member of the university as a responsible corporation, still he bears a near relation to it. And the heads of colleges felt a disagreeable summons to an extra-meeting. There are in Oxford five-and-twenty colleges, to say nothing of halls. Frequent and full the heads assembled in Golgotha, a well-known Oxonian chamber, which, being interpreted, (as scripturally we know,) is 'the place of a skull,' and must, therefore, naturally be the place of a head. There the heads met to deliberate. What was to be done? Most of them were inclined to mercy: to proceed at all — was to proceed to extremities; and, (generally speaking,) to expel a man from Oxford, is to ruin his prospects in any of the liberal professions. Not, therefore, from consideration for Shelley's position in society, but on the kindest motives of forbearance towards one so young, the heads decided for declining all notice of the pamphlet. Levelled *at* them, it was not specially addressed *to* them; and, amongst the infinite children born every morning from that mightiest of mothers, the press, why should Golgotha be supposed to have known anything, officially, of this little brat? That evasion might suit some people, but not Percy Bysshe Shelley. There was a flaw (was there?) in his process; his pleading could not, regularly, come up before the court. Very well — he would heal that defect immediately. So he sent his pamphlet, with five-and-twenty separate letters, addressed to the five-and-twenty heads of colleges in Golgotha assembled; courteously 'inviting' all and every of them to notify, at his earliest convenience, his adhesion to the enclosed unanswerable arguments for Atheism. Upon this, it is undeniable that Golgotha looked black; and, after certain formalities, 'invited' P. B. Shelley to consider himself expelled from the University of Oxford. But, if this were harsh, how would Mr. Gilfillan have had them to proceed? Already they had done, perhaps, too much in the way of forbearance. There were many men in Oxford who knew the standing of Shelley's family. Already it was whispered that any man of obscure connections would have been visited for his Atheism, whether writing to Golgotha or not. And this whisper would have strengthened, had any further neglect been shown to formal letters, which requested a formal answer. The authorities of Oxford, deeply responsible to the nation in a matter of so much peril, could not have acted otherwise than they did. They were not severe. The severity was *extorted* and imposed by

Shelley. But, on the other hand, in some palliation of Shelley's conduct, it ought to be noticed that he is unfairly placed, by the undistinguishing, on the manly station of an ordinary Oxford student. The undergraduates of Oxford and Cambridge are not 'boys,' as a considerable proportion must be, for good reasons, in other universities, — the Scottish universities, for instance, of Glasgow and St. Andrews, and many of those on the continent. Few of the English students even *begin* their residence before eighteen; and the larger proportion are at least twenty. Whereas Shelley was *really* a boy at this era, and no man. He had entered on his sixteenth year, and he was still in the earliest part of his academic career, when his obstinate and reiterated attempt to inoculate the university with a disease that he fancied indispensable to their mental health, caused his expulsion.

I imagine that Mr. Gilfillan will find himself compelled, hereafter, not less by his own second thoughts, than by the murmurs of some amongst his readers, to revise that selection of memorial traits, whether acts or habits, by which he seeks to bring Shelley, as a familiar presence, within the field of ocular apprehension. The acts selected, unless characteristic, — the habits selected, unless representative, — must be absolutely impertinent to the true identification of the man; and most of those rehearsed by Mr. Gilfillan, unless where they happen to be merely accidents of bodily constitution, are such as all of us would be sorry to suppose naturally belonging to Shelley. To 'rush out of the room in terror, as his wild imagination painted to him a pair of eyes in a lady's breast,' is not so much a movement of poetic frenzy, as of typhus fever — to 'terrify an old lady out of her wits,' by assuming, in a stage-coach, the situation of a regal sufferer from Shakspeare, is not eccentricity so much as painful discourtesy — and to request of Rowland Hill, a man most pious and sincere, 'the use of Surrey chapel,' as a theatre for publishing infidelity, would have been so thoroughly the act of a heartless coxcomb, that I, for one, cannot bring myself to believe it an authentic anecdote. Not that I doubt of Shelley's violating at times his own better nature, as every man is capable of doing, under youth too fervid, wine too potent, and companions too misleading; but it strikes me that, during Shelley's very earliest youth, the mere accident of Rowland Hill's being a man well-born and aristocratically connected, yet sacrificing these advantages to what he thought the highest of services, spiritual service on behalf of poor laboring men, would have laid a pathetic arrest upon any impulse of fun in one who, with the very same advantages of birth and position, had the same deep reverence for the rights of the poor. Willing, at all times, to forget his own pretensions in the presence of those who seemed powerless — willing in a degree that seems sublime — Shelley could not but have honored the same nobility of feeling in another. And Rowland Hill, by his guileless simplicity, had a separate hold upon a nature so childlike as Shelley's. He was full of love to man; so was Shelley. He was full of humility; so was Shelley. Difference of creed, however vast the interval which it created between the men, could not have hid from Shelley's eye the close approximation of their natures. Infidel by his intellect, Shelley was a Christian in the tendencies of his heart. As to his 'lying asleep on the hearth-rug, with his small round head thrust almost into the very fire,' this, like his 'basking in the hottest beams of an Italian sun,' illustrates nothing but his physical temperament. That he should be seen 'devouring large pieces of bread amid his profound abstractions,' simply recalls to my eye some hundred thousands of children in the streets of great cities, Edinburgh, Glasgow, London, whom I am daily detecting in the same unaccountable practice; and yet, probably, with very little abstraction to excuse it; whilst his 'endless cups of tea,' in so tea-drinking a land as ours, have really ceased to offer the attractions of novelty which, eighty years ago, in the reign of Dr. Johnson, and under a higher price of tea, they might have secured. Such habits, however, are inoffensive, if not particularly mysterious, nor particularly significant. But that, in defect of a paper boat, Shelley should launch upon the Serpentine a fifty pound bank note, seems to my view an act of childishness, or else (which is worse) an act of empty ostentation, not likely to proceed from one who generally exhibited in his outward deportment a sense of true dignity. He who, through his family,[3] connected himself with that 'spirit without spot,' (as Shelley calls him in the 'Adonais,') Sir Philip Sidney, (a man how like in gentleness, and in faculties of mind, to himself!) —he that, by consequence, connected himself with that later descendant of Penshurst, the noble martyr of freedom, Algernon Sidney, could not have degraded himself by a pride so mean as any which roots itself in wealth. On the other hand, in the anecdote of his repeating Dr. Johnson's benign act, by 'lifting a poor houseless outcast upon his back, and carrying her to a place of refuge,' I read so strong a character of internal probability, that it would be gratifying to know upon what external testimony it rests.

The life of Shelley, according to the remark of Mr. Gilfillan, was 'among the most romantic in literary story.' Everything was romantic in his short career; everything wore a tragic interest. From his childhood he moved through a succession of afflictions. Always craving for love, loving and seeking to be loved, always he was destined to reap hatred from those with whom life had connected him. If in the darkness he raised up images of his departed hours, he would behold his family disowning him, and the home of his infancy knowing him no more; he would behold his magnificent university, that under happier circumstances would have gloried in his genius, rejecting him for ever; he would behold his first wife, whom once he had loved passionately, through calamities arising from himself, called away to an early and a tragic death. The peace after which his heart panted for ever, in what dreadful contrast it stood to the eternal contention upon which his restless intellect or accidents of position threw him like a passive victim! It seemed as if not any choice of his, but some sad doom of opposition from without, forced out, as by a magnet, struggles of frantic resistance from *him,* which as gladly he would have evaded, as ever victim of epilepsy yearned to evade his convulsions! Gladly he would have slept in eternal seclusion, whilst eternally the trumpet summoned him to battle. In storms unwillingly created by himself, he lived; in a storm, cited by the finger of God, he died.

It is affecting, — at least it is so for any one who believes in the profound sincerity of Shelley, a man (however erring) whom neither fear, nor hope, nor vanity, nor hatred, ever seduced into falsehood, or even into dissimulation, — to read the account which he gives of a revolution occurring in his own mind at school: so early did his struggles begin! It is in verse, and forms part of those beautiful stanzas addressed to his second wife, which he prefixed to 'The Revolt of Islam.' Five or six of these stanzas may be quoted with a certainty of pleasing many readers, whilst they throw light on the early condition of Shelley's feelings, and of his early anticipations with regard to the promises and the menaces of life.

'Thoughts of great deeds were mine, dear friend, when first
The clouds which wrap this world, from youth did pass.
I do remember well the hour which burst
My spirit's sleep; a fresh May-dawn it was,
When I walk'd forth upon the glittering grass,
And wept — I knew not why; until there rose,
From the near school-room, voices that, alas!
Were but one echo from a world of woes —
The harsh and grating strife of tyrants and of foes.

And then I clasp'd my hands, and look'd around —
(But none was near to mock my streaming eyes,
Which pour'd their warm drops on the sunny ground,)
So without shame I spake — I will be wise,
And just, and free, and mild, if in me lies

Such power: for I grow weary to behold
The selfish and the strong still tyrannize
Without reproach or check. I then controll'd
My tears; my heart grew calm; and I was meek and bold.

And from that hour did I with earnest thought
Heap knowledge from forbidden mines of lore:
Yet nothing, that my tyrants knew or taught,
I cared to learn; but from that secret store
Wrought linked armor for my soul, before
It might walk forth to war among mankind:
Thus power and hope were strengthen'd more and more
Within me, till there came upon my mind
A sense of loneliness, a thirst with which I pined.

Alas, that love should be a blight and snare
To those who seek all sympathies in one! —
Such once I sought in vain; then black despair,
The shadow of a starless night, was thrown
Over the world in which I moved alone: —
Yet never found I one not false to me,
Hard hearts and cold, like weights of icy stone
Which crush'd and wither'd mine, that could not be
Aught but a lifeless clog, until revived by thee.

Thou, friend, whose presence on my wintry heart
Fell, like bright spring upon some herbless plain;
How beautiful and calm and free thou wert
In thy young wisdom, when the mortal chain
Of Custom[4] thou didst burst and rend in twain,
And walk'd as free as light the clouds among,
Which many an envious slave then breathed in vain
From his dim dungeon, and my spirit sprung
To meet thee from the woes which had begirt it long.

No more alone through the world's wilderness,
Although I trod the paths of high intent,
I journey'd now: no more companionless,
Where solitude is like despair, I went.

. . . .

Now has descended a serener hour ;
And, with inconstant fortune, friends return :
Though suffering leaves the knowledge and the power
Which says — Let scorn be not repaid with scorn.
And from thy side two gentle babes are born
To fill our home with smiles ; and thus are we
Most fortunate beneath life's beaming morn ;
And these delights and thou have been to me
The parents of the song I consecrate to thee.' . . .

My own attention was first drawn to Shelley by the report of his Oxford labors as a missionary in the service of infidelity. Abstracted from the absolute sincerity and simplicity which governed that boyish movement, qualities which could not be known to a stranger, or even suspected in the midst of so much extravagance, there was nothing in the Oxford reports of him to create any interest beyond that of wonder at his folly and presumption in pushing to such extremity what, naturally, all people viewed as an elaborate jest. Some curiosity, however, even at that time, must have gathered about his name; for I remember seeing, in London, a little Indian ink sketch of him in the academic costume of Oxford. The sketch tallied pretty well with a verbal description which I had heard of him in some company, viz., that he looked like an elegant and slender flower, whose head drooped from being surcharged with rain. This gave, to the chance observer, an impression that he was tainted, even in his external deportment, by some excess of sickly sentimentalism, from which I believe that, in all stages of his life, he was remarkably free. Between two and three years after this period, which was that of his expulsion from Oxford, he married a beautiful girl named Westbrook. She was respectably connected; but had not moved in a rank corresponding to Shelley's; and that accident brought him into my own neighborhood. For his family, already estranged from him, were now thoroughly irritated by what they regarded as a *mesalliance*, and withdrew, or greatly reduced, his pecuniary allowances. Such, at least, was the story current. In this embarrassment, his wife's father made over to him an annual income of £200; and, as economy had become important, the youthful pair — both, in fact, still children — came down to the Lakes, supposing this region of Cumberland and Westmoreland to be a sequestered place, which it *was*, for eight months in the year, and also to be a cheap place — which it was *not*. Another motive to this choice arose with the then Duke of Norfolk. He was an old friend of Shelley's family, and generously refused to hear a word of the young man's errors, except where he could do anything to relieve him from their consequences. His grace possessed the beautiful estate of Gobarrow Park on Ulleswater, and other estates of greater extent in the same two counties;[5] his own agents he had directed to furnish any accommodations that might meet Shelley's views; and he had written to some gentlemen amongst his agricultural friends in Cumberland, requesting them to pay such neighborly attentions to the solitary young people as circumstances might place in their power. This bias, being impressed upon Shelley's wanderings, naturally brought him to Keswick as the most central and the largest of the little towns dispersed amongst the lakes.

Southey, made aware of the interest taken in Shelley by the Duke of Norfolk, with his usual kindness immediately called upon him ; and the ladies of Southey's family subsequently made an early call upon Mrs. Shelley. One of them mentioned to me as occurring in this first visit an amusing expression of the youthful matron, which, four years later, when I heard of her gloomy end, recalled with the force of a pathetic contrast, that icy arrest then chaining up her youthful feet for ever. The Shelleys had been induced by one of their new friends to take part of a house standing about half a mile out of Keswick, on the Penrith road ; more, I believe, in that friend's intention for the sake of bringing them easily within his hospitalities, than for any beauty in the place. There was, however, a pretty garden attached to it. And whilst walking in this, one of the Southey party asked Mrs. Shelley if the garden had been let with *their* part of the house. 'Oh, no,' she replied, 'the garden is not ours; but then, you know, the people let us run about in it whenever Percy and I are tired of sitting in the house.' The *naïveté* of this expression 'run about,' contrasting so picturesquely with the intermitting efforts of the girlish wife at supporting a matron-like gravity, now that she was doing the honors of her house to married ladies, caused all the party to smile. And *me* it caused profoundly to sigh, four years later, when the gloomy death of this young creature, now frozen in a distant grave, threw back my remembrance upon her fawn-like playfulness, which, unconsciously to herself, the girlish phrase of *run about* so naturally betrayed.

At that time I had a cottage myself in Grasmere, just thirteen miles distant from Shelley's new abode. As he had then written nothing of any interest, I had no motive for calling upon him, except by way of showing any little attentions in my power to a brother Oxonian, and to a man of letters. These attentions, indeed, he might have claimed simply in the character of a neighbor. For as men living on the coast of Mayo or Galway are apt to consider the dwellers on the sea-board of North America in the light of next-door neighbors, divided only by a party-wall of crystal, — and what if accidentally three thousand miles thick? — on the same principle we amongst the slender population of this lake region, and wherever no ascent intervened between two parties higher than Dunmail Raise and the spurs of Helvellyn, were apt to take with each other the privileged tone of neighbors. Some neighborly advantages I might certainly have placed at Shelley's disposal — Grasmere, for instance, itself, which tempted at that time[6] by a beauty that had not been sullied; Wordsworth, who then lived in Grasmere; Elleray and Professor Wilson, nine miles further; finally, my own library, which, being rich in the wickedest of German speculations, would naturally have been more to Shelley's taste than the Spanish library of Southey.

But all these temptations were negatived for Shelley by his sudden departure. Off he went in a hurry: but *why* he went, or *whither* he went, I did not inquire; not guessing the interest which he would create in my mind, six years later, by his 'Revolt of Islam.' A life of Shelley, in a continental edition of his works, says that he went to Edinburgh and to Ireland. Some time after, we at the lakes heard that he was living in Wales. Apparently he had the instinct within him of his own Wandering Jew for eternal restlessness. But events were now hurrying upon his heart of hearts. Within less than ten years the whole arrear of his life was destined to revolve. Within that space, he had the whole burden of life and death to exhaust; he had all his suffering to suffer, and all his work to work.

In about four years his first marriage was dissolved by the death of his wife. She had brought to Shelley two children. But feuds arose between them, owing to incompatible habits of mind. They parted. And it is one chief misery of a beautiful young woman, separated from her natural protector, that her desolate situation attracts and stimulates the calumnies of the malicious. Stung by these calumnies, and oppressed (as I have understood) by the loneliness of her abode, perhaps also by the delirium of fever, she threw herself into a pond, and was drowned. The name under which she first enchanted all eyes, and sported as the most playful of nymph-like girls, is now forgotten amongst men; and that other name, for a brief period her ambition and her glory, is inscribed on her gravestone as the name under which she wept and she despaired,—suffered and was buried,—turned away even from the faces of her children, and sought a hiding-place in darkness.

After this dreadful event, an anonymous life of Shelley asserts that he was for some time deranged. Pretending to no private and no circumstantial acquaintance with the case, I cannot say how that really was. There is a great difficulty besetting all sketches of lives so steeped in trouble as was Shelley's. If you have a confidential knowledge of the case, as a dear friend privileged to stand by the bed-side of raving grief, how base to use such advantages of position for the gratification of a fugitive curiosity in strangers! If you have no such knowledge, how little qualified you must be for tracing the life with the truth of sympathy, or for judging it with the truth of charity! To me it appears, from the peace of mind which Shelley is reported afterwards to have recovered for a time, that he could not have had to reproach himself with any harshness or neglect as contributing to the shocking catastrophe. Neither ought any reproach to rest upon the memory of this first wife, as respects her relation to Shelley. Nonconformity of tastes might easily arise between two parties, without much blame to either, when one of the two had received from nature an intellect and a temperament so dangerously eccentric, and constitutionally carried, by delicacy so exquisite of organization, to eternal restlessness and irritability of nerves, if not absolutely at times to lunacy.

About three years after this tragic event, Shelley, in company with his second wife, the daughter of Godwin, and Mary Wollstonecraft, passed over for a third time to the Continent, from which he never came back. On Monday, July 8, 1822, being then in his twenty-ninth year, he was returning from Leghorn to his home at Lerici, in a schooner-rigged boat of his own, twenty-four feet long, eight in the beam, and drawing four feet water. His companions were only two, — Mr. Williams, formerly of the Eighth Dragoons, and Charles Vivian, an English seaman in Shelley's service. The run homewards would not have occupied more than six or eight hours. But the Gulf of Spezia is peculiarly dangerous for small craft in bad weather; and unfortunately a squall of about one hour's duration came on, the wind at the same time shifting so as to blow exactly in the teeth of the course to Lerici. From the interesting narrative drawn up by Mr. Trelawney, well known at that time for his connection with the Greek Revolution, it seems that for eight days the fate of the boat was unknown; and during that time couriers had been dispatched along the whole line of coast between Leghorn and Nice, under anxious hopes that the voyagers might have run into some creek for shelter. But at the end of the eight days this suspense ceased. Some articles belonging to Shelley's boat had previously been washed ashore: these might have been thrown overboard; but finally the two bodies of Shelley and Mr. Williams came on shore near Via Reggio, about four miles apart. Both were in a state of advanced decomposition, but were fully identified. Vivian's body was not recovered for three weeks. From the state of the two corpses, it had become difficult to remove them; and they were therefore burned by the seaside, on funeral pyres, with the classic rites of paganism, four English gentlemen being present, — Capt. Shenley of the navy, Mr. Leigh Hunt, Lord Byron, and Mr. Trelawney. A circumstance is added by Mr. Gilfillan, which previous accounts do not mention, viz., that Shelley's heart remained unconsumed by the fire; but this is a phenomenon that has repeatedly occurred at judicial deaths by fire. The remains of Mr. Williams, when collected from the fire, were conveyed to England; but Shelley's were buried in the Protestant burying-ground at Rome, not far from a child of his own, and Keats the poet. It is remarkable that Shelley, in the preface to his Adonais, dedicated to the memory of that young poet, had spoken with delight of this cemetery, — as 'An open space among the ruins' (of ancient Rome,) 'covered in winter with violets and daisies;' adding, 'It might make one in love with death, to think that one should be buried in so sweet a place.'

I have allowed myself to abridge the circumstances as reported by Mr. Trelawney and Mr. Hunt, partly on the consideration that three-and-twenty years have passed since the event, so that a new generation has had time to grow up — not feeling the interest of *contemporaries* in Shelley, and generally, therefore, unacquainted with the case; but partly for the purpose of introducing the following comment of Mr. Gilfillan on the striking points of a catastrophe, 'which robbed the world of this strange and great spirit,' and which secretly tempts men to superstitious feelings, even whilst they are denying them: —

'Everybody knows that, on the arrival of Leigh Hunt in Italy, Shelley hastened to meet him. During all the time he spent in Leghorn, he was in brilliant spirits — to him ever a sure prognostic of coming evil.' [That is, in the Scottish phrase, he was *fey*.] 'On his return to his home and family, his skiff was overtaken by a fearful hurricane, and all on board perished. To a gentleman, who, at the time, was with a glass surveying the sea, the scene of his drowning assumed a very striking appearance. A great many vessels were visible, and among them one small skiff, which attracted his particular attention. Suddenly a dreadful storm, attended by thunder and columns of lightning, swept over the sea and eclipsed the prospect. When it had passed, he looked again. The larger vessels were all safe, riding upon the swell; the skiff only had gone down for ever. And in that skiff was Alastor![7] Here he had met his fate. Wert thou, oh religious sea, only avenging on his head the cause of thy denied and insulted Deity? Were ye, ye elements, in your courses, commissioned to destroy him? Ah! there is no reply. The surge is silent; the elements have no voice. In the eternal councils the secret is hid of the reason of the man's death. And there, too, rests the still more tremendous secret of the character of his destiny.'[8]

The last remark possibly pursues the scrutiny too far; and, conscious that it tends beyond the limits of charity, Mr. Gilfillan recalls himself from the attempt to fathom the unfathomable. But undoubtedly the temptation is great, in minds the least superstitious, to read a significance, and a silent personality in such a fate applied to such a defier of the Christian heavens. As a shepherd by his dog fetches out one of his flock from amongst five hundred, so did the holy hurricane seem to fetch out from the multitude of sails *that* one which carried him that hated the hopes of the world; and the sea, which swelled and ran down within an hour, was present at the audit. We are reminded forcibly of the sublime storm in the wilderness, (as given in the fourth book of 'Paradise Regained,') and the remark upon it made by the mysterious tempter —

> 'This tempest at this desert most was bent,
> Of men at thee.'

Undoubtedly, I do not understand Mr. Gilfillan, more than myself, to read a 'judgment' in this catastrophe. But there is a solemn appeal to the thoughtful, in a death of so much terrific grandeur following upon defiances of such unparalleled audacity. Æschylus acknowledged the same sense of mysterious awe, and all antiquity acknowledged it, in the story of Amphiaraus.[9]

Shelley, it must be remembered, carried his irreligion to a point beyond all others. Of the darkest beings we are told, that they 'believe and tremble:' but Shelley believed and *hated;* and his defiances were meant to show that he did *not* tremble. Yet, has he not the excuse of something like *monomania* upon this subject? I firmly believe it. But a superstition, old as the world, clings to the notion, that words of deep meaning, uttered even by lunatics or by idiots, execute themselves; and that also, when uttered in presumption, they bring round their own retributive chastisements.

On the other hand, however shocked at Shelley's obstinate revolt from all religious sympathies with his fellow-men, no man is entitled to deny the admirable qualities of his moral nature, which were as striking as his genius. Many people remarked something seraphic in the expression of his features; and something seraphic there was in his nature. No man was better qualified to have loved Christianity; and to no man, resting under the shadow of that one darkness, would Christianity have said more gladly — *talis cum sis, utinam noster esses!* Shelley would, from his earliest manhood, have sacrificed all that he possessed to any comprehensive purpose of good for the race of man. He dismissed all injuries and insults from his memory. He was the sincerest and the most truthful of human creatures. He was also the purest. If he denounced marriage as a vicious institution, *that* was but another phasis of the partial lunacy which affected him: for to no man were purity and fidelity more essential elements in his idea of real love. I agree, therefore, heartily with Mr. Gilfillan, in protesting against the thoughtless assertion of some writer in *The Edinburgh Review* — that Shelley at all selected the story of his 'Cenci' on account of its horrors, or that he has found pleasure in dwelling on those horrors. So far from it, he has retreated so entirely from the most shocking feature of the story, viz., the incestuous violence of Cenci the father, as actually to leave it doubtful whether the murder were in punishment of the last outrage committed, or in repulsion of a menace continually repeated. The true motive of the selection of such a story was — not its darkness, but (as Mr. Gilfillan, with so much penetration, perceives,) the light which fights with the darkness: Shelley found the whole attraction of this dreadful tale in the angelic nature of Beatrice, as revealed in the portrait of her by Guido. Everybody who has read with understanding the 'Wallenstein' of Schiller, is aware of the repose and the divine relief arising upon a background of so much darkness, such a tumult of ruffians, bloody intriguers, and assassins, from the situation of the two lovers, Max. Piccolomini and the princess Thekla, both yearning so profoundly after peace, both so noble, both so young, and both destined to be so unhappy. The same fine relief, the same light shining in darkness, arises here from the touching beauty of Beatrice, from her noble aspirations after deliverance, from the remorse which reaches her in the midst of real innocence, from her meekness, and from the agitation of her inexpressible affliction. Even the murder, even the parricide, though proceeding from herself, do but deepen that background of darkness, which throws into fuller revelation the glory of that suffering face immortalized by Guido.

Something of a similar effect arises to myself when reviewing the general abstract of Shelley's life, — so brief, so full of agitation, so full of strife. When one thinks of the early misery which he suffered, and of the insolent infidelity which, being yet so young, he wooed with a lover's passion, then the darkness of midnight begins to form a deep, impenetrable background, upon which the phantasmagoria of all that is to come may arrange itself in troubled phosphoric streams, and in sweeping processions of wo. Yet, again, when one recurs to his gracious nature, his fearlessness, his truth, his purity from all fleshliness of appetite, his freedom from vanity, his diffusive love and tenderness, — suddenly out of the darkness reveals itself a morning of May, forests and thickets of roses advance to the foreground, from the midst of them looks out 'the eternal child,' cleansed from his sorrow, radiant with joy, having power given him to forget the misery which he suffered, power given him to forget the misery which he caused, and leaning with his heart upon that dove-like faith against which his erring intellect had rebelled.

NOTES.

Note 1. Page 40.

'Transact:'—this word, used in this Roman sense, illustrates the particular mode of Milton's liberties with the English language: liberties which have never yet been properly examined, collated, numbered, or appreciated. In the Roman law, *transigere* expressed the case, where each of two conflicting parties conceded something of what originally he had claimed as the rigor of his right; and *transactio* was the technical name for a legal compromise. Milton has here introduced no new word into the English language, but has given a new and more learned sense to an old one. Sometimes, it is true, as in the word *sensuous,* he introduces a pure coinage of his own, and a very useful coinage: but generally to re-endow an old foundation is the extent of his innovations. M. de Tocqueville is therefore likely to be found wrong in saying, that 'Milton alone introduced more than six hundred words into the English language, almost all derived from the Latin, the Greek, or the Hebrew.' The passage occurs in the 16th chapter of his 'Democracy in America,' Part II., where M. de Tocqueville is discussing the separate agencies through which democratic life on the one hand, or aristocratic on the other, affects the changes of language. His English translator, Mr. H. Reeve, an able and philosophic annotator, justly views this bold assertion as 'startling and probably erroneous.'

NOTE 2. Page 41.

Since the boyish period in which these redressing corrections occurred to me, I have seen some reason (upon considering the oriental practice of placing live coals in a pan upon the head, and its meaning as still in use amongst the Turks) to alter the whole interpretation of the passage. It would too much interrupt the tenor of the subject to explain this at length: but, if right, it would equally harmonize with the spirit of Christian morals.

NOTE 3. Page 51.

'Family:' *i. e.*, The *gens* in the Roman sense, or collective house. Shelley's own immediate branch of the house did not, in a legal sense, represent the family of Penshurst, because the *rights* of the lineal descent had settled upon another branch. But *his* branch had a collateral participation in the glory of the Sidney name, and might, by accidents possible enough, have come to be its sole representative.

NOTE 4. Page 54.

'Of Custom:' — This alludes to a theory of Shelley's, on the subject of marriage as a vicious institution, and an attempt to realize his theory by way of public example; which attempt there is no use in noticing more particularly, as it was subsequently abandoned. Originally he had derived his theory from the writings of Mary Wollstonecraft, the mother of his second wife, whose birth in fact had cost that mother her life. But by the year 1812, (the year following his first marriage,) he had so fortified, from other quarters, his previous opinions upon the wickedness of all nuptial ties consecrated by law or by the church, that he apologized to his friends for having submitted to the marriage ceremony as for an offence; but an offence, he pleaded, rendered necessary by the vicious constitution of society, for the comfort of his female partner.

Note 5. Page 56.

'*Two* counties:'—the frontier line between Westmoreland and Cumberland, traverse obliquely the Lake of Ulleswater, so that the banks on both sides lie partly in both counties.

Note 6. Page 58.

'At *that* time!'—the reader will say, who happens to be aware of the mighty barriers which engirdle Grasmere, Fairfield, Arthur's Chair, Seat Sandal, Steil Fell, &c. (the lowest above two thousand, the higher above *three* thousand feet high,)—'what then? do the mountains change, and the mountain tarns?' Perhaps not: but, if they do not change in substance or in form, they 'change countenance' when they are disfigured from below. One cotton-mill, planted by the side of a torrent, disenchants the scene, and banishes the ideal beauty even in the case where it leaves the physical beauty untouched: a truth which, many years ago, I saw illustrated in the little hamlet of Church Coniston. But is there any cotton-mill in Grasmere? Not that I have heard: But if no water has been filched away from Grasmere, there is one water too much which has crept lately into that loveliest of mountain chambers; and *that* is the 'water-cure,' which has built unto itself a sort of residence in that vale; whether a rustic nest, or a lordly palace, I do not know. Meantime, in honesty it must be owned, that many years ago the vale was half ruined by an insane substruction carried along the eastern margin of the lake as a basis for a mail-coach road. This infernal mass of solid masonry swept away the loveliest of sylvan recesses, and the most absolutely charmed against intrusive foot or angry echoes. It did worse: it swept away the stateliest of Flora's daughters, and swept away, at the same time, the birth-place of a well known verse, describing that stately plant, which is perhaps (as a separate line) the most exquisite that the poetry of earth can show. The plant was the *Osmunda regalis*;

'Plant lovelier in its own recess
Than Grecian Naiad seen at earliest dawn

Tending her fount, or *lady of the lake*
Sole-sitting by the shores of old romance.'

It is this last line and a half which some have held to ascend in beauty as much beyond any single line known to literature, as the Osmunda ascends in luxury of splendor above other ferns. I have restored the original word *lake*, which the poet himself under an erroneous impression had dismissed for *mere*. But the line rests no longer on an earthly reality — the recess, which suggested it, is gone: the Osmunda has fled; and a vile causeway, such as Sin and Death build in Milton over Chaos, fastening it with 'asphaltic slime' and 'pins of adamant,' having long displaced the loveliest chapel (as I may call it) in the whole cathedral of Grasmere, I have since considered Grasmere itself a ruin of its former self.

Note 7. Page 63.

'Alastor,' *i. e.* Shelley. Mr. Gilfillan names him thus from the designation, self-assumed by Shelley, in one of the least intelligible amongst his poems.

Note 8. Page 63.

The immediate cause of the catastrophe was supposed to be this: — Shelley's boat had reached a distance of four miles from the shore, when the storm suddenly arose, and the wind suddenly shifted: 'from excessive smoothness,' says Mr. Trelawney, all at once the sea was 'foaming, breaking, and getting up into a very heavy swell.' After one hour the swell went down; and towards evening it was almost a calm. The circumstances were all adverse: the gale, the current setting into the gulf, the instantaneous change of wind, acting upon an undecked boat, having all the sheets fast, overladen, and no expert hands on board but one, made the foundering as sudden as it was inevitable. The boat is supposed to have filled to leeward, and (carrying two tons of ballast) to have gone down like a shot. A book found in the pocket of Shelley, and the unaltered state of the dress on all the corpses when washed on shore, sufficiently indicated that not a moment's preparation for meeting the danger had been possible.

NOTE 9. Page 64.

See 'The Seven against Thebes' of Æschylus.

NOTE 10. Page 67.

'The eternal child:' — this beautiful expression, so true in its application to Shelley, I borrow from Mr. Gilfillan; and I am tempted to add the rest of his eloquent parallel between Shelley and Lord Byron, so far as it relates to their external appearance: — 'In the forehead and head of Byron there is more massive power and breadth: Shelley's has a smooth, arched, spiritual expression; wrinkle there seems none on his brow; it is as if perpetual youth had there dropped its freshness. Byron's eye seems the focus of pride and lust; Shelley's is mild, pensive, fixed on you, but seeing you through the mist of his own idealism. Defiance curls on Byron's nostril, and sensuality steeps his full large lips: the lower features of Shelley's face are frail, feminine, flexible. Byron's head is turned upwards; as if, having risen proudly above his contemporaries, he were daring to claim kindred, or to demand a contest, with a superior order of beings: Shelley's is half bent, in reverence and humility, before some vast vision seen by his own eye alone. Misery erect, and striving to cover its retreat under an aspect of contemptuous fury, is the permanent and pervading expression of Byron's countenance: — sorrow, softened and shaded away by hope and habit, lies like a "holier day" of still moonshine upon that of Shelley. In the portrait of Byron, taken at the age of nineteen, you see the unnatural age of premature passion; his hair is young, his dress is youthful; but his face is old: — in Shelley you see the eternal child, none the less that his hair is gray, and that "sorrow seems half his immortality."'

JOHN KEATS.

Mr. Gilfillan * introduces this section with a discussion upon the constitutional peculiarities ascribed to men of genius; such as nervousness of temperament, idleness, vanity, irritability, and other disagreeable tendencies ending in *ty* or in *ness;* one of the *ties* being 'poverty;' which disease is at least not amongst those morbidly cherished by the patients. All that can be asked from the most penitent man of genius is, that he should humbly confess his own besetting infirmities, and endeavor to hate them; and, as respects this one infirmity at least, I never heard of any man (however eccentric in genius) who did otherwise. But what special relation has such a preface to Keats? His whole article occupies twelve pages; and six of these are allotted to this preliminary discussion, which perhaps equally concerns every other man in the household of literature. Mr. Gilfillan seems to have been acting here on celebrated precedents. The '*Omnes homines qui sese student præstare cæteris animalibus*' has long been 'smoked' by a wicked posterity as an old hack of Sallust's fitted on with paste and scissors to the Catilinarian conspiracy.

---

* 'Gallery of Literary Portraits.'

Cicero candidly admits that he kept in his writing-desk an assortment of movable prefaces, beautifully fitted (by means of avoiding all questions but 'the general question') for parading, *en grand costume*, before any conceivable book. And Coleridge, in his early days, used the image of a man's 'sleeping under a manchineel tree,' alternately with the case of Alexander's killing his friend Clitus, as resources for illustration which Providence had bountifully made inexhaustible in their applications. No emergency could by possibility arise to puzzle the poet, or the orator, but one of these similes (please Heaven!) should be made to meet it. So long as the manchineel continued to blister with poisonous dews those who confided in its shelter, so long as Niebuhr should kindly forbear to prove that Alexander of Macedon was a hoax, and his friend Clitus a myth, so long was Samuel Taylor Coleridge fixed and obdurate in his determination that one or other of these images should come upon duty whenever, as a youthful writer, he found himself on the brink of insolvency.

But it is less the generality of this preface, or even its disproportion, which fixes the eye, than the questionableness of its particular statements. In that part which reviews the *idleness* of authors, Horace is given up as too notoriously indolent; the thing, it seems, is past denying; but 'not so Lucretius.' Indeed! and how shall this be brought to proof? Perhaps the reader has heard of that barbarian prince, who sent to Europe for a large map of the world accompanied by the best of English razors; and the clever use which he made of his importation was, that, first cutting out with exquisite accuracy the whole ring-fence of his own dominions, and then doing the same office, with the same equity, (barbarous or barber-ous,) for the dominions of a hostile neighbor, next he proceeded to weigh off the rival segments against each other in a pair of gold scales; after which, of course, he arrived at a satisfactory algebraic equation between himself and his enemy. Now, upon this principle of comparison, if we should take any *common* edition (as the *Delphin* or the *Variorum*) of Horace and Lucretius, strictly shaving away all notes, prefaces, editorial absurdities, &c., all 'flotsom' and 'jetsom' that may have gathered like barnacles about the two weather-beaten hulks; in that case we should have the two old files undressed, and *in puris naturalibus;* they would be prepared for being weighed; and, going to the nearest grocer's, we might then settle the point at once, as to which of the two had been the idler man. I back Horace for *my* part; and it is my private opinion that, in the case of a quarto edition, the grocer would have to throw at least a two ounce weight into the scale of Lucretius, before he could be made to draw against the other. Yet, after all, this would only be a collation of quantity against quantity; whilst, upon a second collation of quality against quality, (I do not mean quality as regards the final merit of the composition, but quality as regards the difficulties in the process of composition,) the difference in amount of labor would appear to be as between the weaving of a blanket and the weaving of an exquisite cambric. The *curiosa felicitas* of Horace in his lyric compositions, the elaborate delicacy of workmanship in his thoughts and in his style, argue a scale of labor that, as against any equal number of lines in Lucretius, would measure itself by months against days. There are single odes in Horace that must have cost him a six weeks' seclusion from the wickedness of Rome. Do I then question the extraordinary power of Lucretius? On the contrary, I admire him as the first of demoniacs; the frenzy of an earth-born or a hell-born inspiration; divinity of stormy music sweeping round us in eddies, in order to prove that for us there could be nothing divine; the grandeur of a prophet's voice rising in angry gusts, by way of convincing us that prophets were swindlers; oracular scorn of oracles; frantic efforts, such as might seem reasonable in one who was scaling the heavens, for the purpose of degrading all things, making man to be the most abject of necessities as regarded his causes, to be the blindest of accidents as regarded his expectations; these fierce antinomies expose a mode of insanity, but of an insanity affecting a sublime intellect.[1] One would suppose him partially mad by the savagery of his headlong manner. And most people who read Lucretius at all, are aware of the traditional story current in Rome, that he did actually write in a delirious state; not under any figurative disturbance of brain, but under a real physical disturbance caused by philters administered to him without his own knowledge. But this kind of supernatural *afflatus* did not deliver into words and metre by lingering oscillations, and through processes of self-correction: it threw itself forward, and precipitated its own utterance, with the hurrying and bounding of a cataract. It was an *œstrum*, a rapture, the bounding of a mœnad, by which the muse of Lucretius lived and moved. So much is known by the impression about him current among his contemporaries: so much is evident in the characteristic manner of his poem, if all anecdotes had perished. And, upon the whole, let the proportions of power between Horace and Lucretius be what they may, the proportions of labor are absolutely incommensurable: in Horace the labor was *directly* as the power, in Lucretius *inversely* as the power. Whatsoever in Horace was best — had been obtained by *most* labor; whatsoever in Lucretius was best — by *least*. In Horace, the exquisite skill co-operated with the exquisite nature; in Lucretius, the powerful nature disdained the skill, which, indeed, would not have been applicable to *his* theme, or to *his* treatment of it, and triumphed by means of mere precipitation of volume, and of headlong fury.

Another paradox of Mr. Gilfillan's, under this head, is, that he classes Dr. Johnson as indolent; and it is the more startling, because he does not utter it as a careless opinion upon which he might have been thrown by inconsideration, but as a concession extorted from him reluctantly: he had sought to evade it, but could not. Now, that Dr. Johnson had a morbid predisposition to decline labor from his scrofulous habit of body,[2] is probable. The question for us, however, is, not what nature prompted him to do, but what he did. If he had an extra difficulty to fight with in attempting to labor, the more was his merit in the known result, that he *did* fight with that difficulty, and that he conquered it. This is undeniable. And the attempt to deny it presents itself in a comic shape, when one imagines some ancient shelf in a library, that has groaned for nearly a century under the weight of the doctor's works, demanding, 'How say you? Is this Sam Johnson, whose Dictionary alone is a load for a camel, one of those authors whom you call idle? Then Heaven preserve us poor oppressed book-shelves from such as you will consider active.' George III., in a compliment as happily turned as if it had proceeded from Louis XIV., expressed his opinion upon this question of the doctor's industry by saying, that he also should join in thinking Johnson too voluminous a contributor to literature, were it not for the extraordinary merit of his contributions. Now it would be an odd way of turning the royal praise into a reproach, if we should say; 'Sam, had you been a pretty good writer, we, your countrymen, should have held you to be also an industrious writer: but, because you are a *very* good writer, therefore we pronounce you a lazy vagabond.'

Upon other points in this discussion there is some room to differ from Mr. Gilfillan. For instance, with respect to the question of the comparative happiness enjoyed by men of genius, it is not necessary to argue, nor does it seem possible to prove, even in the case of any one individual poet, that, on the whole, he was either more happy or less happy than the average mass of his fellow-men: far less could this be argued as to the whole class of poets. What seems *really* open to proof, is, that men of genius have a larger *capacity* of happiness, which capacity, both from within and from without, may be defeated in ten thousand ways. This seems involved in the very word *genius.* For, after all the pretended and hollow attempts to distinguish genius from talent, I shall continue to think (what heretofore I have explained) that no distinction in the case is tenable for a moment but this: viz. that genius is that mode of intellectual power which moves in alliance with the *genial* nature, *i. e.* with the capacities of pleasure and pain; whereas talent has no vestige of such an alliance, and is perfectly independent of all human sensibilities. Consequently, genius is a voice or breathing that represents the *total* nature of man; whilst, on the contrary, talent represents only a single function of that nature. Genius is the language which interprets the synthesis of the human spirit with the human intellect, each acting through the other; whilst talent speaks only from the insulated intellect. And hence also it is that, besides its relation to suffering and enjoyment, genius always implies a deeper relation to virtue and vice: whereas talent has no shadow of a relation to *moral* qualities, any more than it has to vital sensibilities. A man of the highest talent is often obtuse and below the ordinary standard of men in his feelings; but no man of genius can unyoke himself from the society of moral perceptions that are brighter, and sensibilities that are more tremulous, than those of men in general.

As to the examples[3] by which Mr. Gilfillan supports his prevailing views, they will be construed by any ten thousand men in ten thousand separate modes. The objections are so endless, that it would be abusing the reader's time to urge them; especially as every man of the ten thousand will be wrong, and will also be right, in all varieties of proportion. Two only it may be useful to notice as examples, involving some degree of error, viz. Addison and Homer. As to the first, the error, if an error, is one of fact only. Lord Byron had said of Addison, that he 'died drunk.' This seems to Mr. Gilfillan a 'horrible statement;' for which he supposes that no authority can exist but 'a rumor circulated by an inveterate gossip,' meaning Horace Walpole. But gossips usually go upon some foundation, broad or narrow; and, until the rumor had been authentically put down, Mr. Gilfillan should not have pronounced it a 'malignant calumny.' Me this story caused to laugh exceedingly; not at Addison, whose fine genius extorts pity and tenderness towards his infirmities; but at the characteristic misanthropy of Lord Byron, who chuckles as he would do over a glass of nectar, on this opportunity for confronting the old solemn legend about Addison's sending for his step-son, Lord Warwick, to witness the peaceful death of a Christian, with so rich a story as this, that he, the said Christian, 'died drunk.' Supposing that he *did*, the mere physical fact of inebriation, in a stage of debility where so small an excess of stimulating liquor (though given medicinally) sometimes causes such an appearance, would not infer the moral blame of drunkenness; and if such a thing were ever said by any person *present* at the bed-side, I should feel next to certain that it was said in that spirit of exaggeration to which most men are tempted by circumstances unusually fitted to impress a startling picturesqueness upon the statement. But, without insisting on Lord Byron's way of putting the case,

I believe it is generally understood that, latterly, Addison gave way to habits of intemperance. He suffered, not only from his wife's dissatisfied temper, but also (and probably much more) from *ennui*. He did not walk one mile a day, and he ought to have walked ten. Dyspepsy was, no doubt, the true ground of his unhappiness: and he had nothing to hope for. To remedy these evils, I have always understood that every day (and especially towards night) he drank too much of that French liquor, which, calling itself *water of life*, nine times in ten proves the water of death. He lived latterly at Kensington, viz. in Holland House, the well-known residence of the late Lord Holland; and the tradition attached to the gallery in that house, is, that duly as the sun drew near to setting, on two tables, one at each end of the long *ambulachrum*, the right honorable Joseph placed, or caused to be placed, two tumblers of brandy, somewhat diluted with water; and those, the said vessels, then and there did alternately to the lips of him, the aforesaid Joseph, diligently apply, walking to and fro during the process of exhaustion, and dividing his attention between the two poles, arctic and antartic, of his evening *diaulos*, with the impartiality to be expected from a member of the Privy Council. How often the two 'blessed bears,' northern and southern, were replenished, entered into no *affidavit* that ever reached *me*. But so much I have always understood, that in the gallery of Holland House, the ex-secretary of state caught a decided hiccup, which never afterwards subsided. In all this there would have been little to shock people, had it not been for the sycophancy which ascribed to Addison a religious reputation such as he neither merited nor wished to claim. But one penal reaction of mendacious adulation, for him who is weak enough to accept it, must ever be, to impose restraints upon his own conduct, which otherwise he would have been free to decline. How lightly would Sir Roger de Coverley have thought of a little sotting in any honest gentleman of right politics! And Addison would not, in that age, and as to that point, have carried his scrupulosity higher than his own Sir Roger. But such knaves as he who had complimented Addison with the praise of having written 'no line which, dying, he could wish to blot,'. whereas, in fact, Addison started in life by publishing a translation of Petronius Arbiter, had painfully coerced his free agency. This knave, I very much fear, was Tickell the first; and the result of his knavery was, to win for Addison a disagreeable sanctimonious reputation that was, 1st, founded in lies; 2d, that painfully limited Addison's free agency; and, 3dly, that prepared insults to his memory, since it pointed a censorious eye upon those things viewed as the acts of a demure pretender to piety, which would else have passed without notice as the most venial of frailties in a layman.

Something I had to say also upon Homer, who mingles amongst the examples cited by Mr. Gilfillan, of apparent happiness connected with genius. But, for want of room,[4] I forbear to go further, than to lodge my protest against imputing to Homer as any personal merit, what belongs altogether to the stage of society in which he lived. 'They,' says Mr. Gilfillan, speaking of the 'Iliad' and the 'Odyssey,' 'are the healthiest of works. There are in them no sullenness, no querulous complaint, not one personal allusion.' No; but how *could* there have been? Subjective poetry had not an existence in those days. Not only the powers for introverting the eye upon the *spectator*, as himself, the *spectaculum*, were then undeveloped and inconceivable, but the sympathies did not exist to which such an innovation could have appealed. Besides, and partly from the same cause, even as objects, the human feelings and affections were too broadly and grossly distinguished, had not reached even the infancy of that stage in which the passions begin their processes of intermodification, nor *could* have reached it, from the simplicity of social life, as well as from the barbarism of the Greek religion. The author of the 'Iliad,' or even of the 'Odyssey,' (though doubtless a product of a later period,) could not have been 'unhealthy,' or 'sullen,' or 'querulous,' from any cause, except *psora* or *elephantiasis*, or scarcity of beef, or similar afflictions with which it is quite impossible to inoculate poetry. The metrical romances of the middle ages have the same shivering character of starvation, as to the inner life of man; and, if *that* constitutes a meritorious distinction, no man ought to be excused for wanting what it is so easy to obtain by simple neglect of culture. On the same principle, a cannibal, if truculently indiscriminate in his horrid diet, might win sentimental praises for his temperance; others were picking and choosing, miserable epicures! but he, the saint upon earth, cared not what he ate; any joint satisfied *his* moderate desires; shoulder of man, leg of child; anything, in fact, that was nearest at hand, so long as it was good, wholesome human flesh; and the more plainly dressed the better.

But these topics, so various and so fruitful, I touch only because they are introduced, amongst many others, by Mr. Gilfillan. Separately viewed, some of these would be more attractive than any merely personal interest connected with Keats. His biography, stripped of its false coloring, offers little to win attention: for he was not the victim of any systematic malignity, as has been represented. He met, as I have understood, with unusual kindness from his liberal publishers, Messrs. Taylor and Hessey. He met with unusual severity from a cynical reviewer, the late Mr. Gifford, then editor of *The Quarterly Review*. The story ran, that this article of Mr. G.'s had killed Keats; upon which, with natural astonishment, Lord Byron thus commented, in the 11th canto of Don Juan: —

> John Keats who was kill'd off by one critique,
>   Just as he really promised something great,
> If not intelligible, — without Greek,
>   Contrived to talk about the gods of late,
> Much as they might have been supposed to speak.
>   Poor fellow! his was an untoward fate:
> 'T is strange the mind, that very fiery particle,
> Should let itself be snuff'd out by an Article.

Strange, indeed! and the friends, who honor Keats's memory, should not lend themselves to a story so degrading. He died, I believe, of pulmonary consumption; and would have died of it, probably, under any circumstances of prosperity as a poet. Doubtless, in a condition of languishing decay, slight causes of irritation act powerfully. But it is hardly conceivable that one ebullition of splenetic bad feeling, in a case so proverbially open to revision as the pretensions of a poet, could have overthrown any masculine life, unless where that life had already been *irrecoverably* undermined by sickness. As a man, and viewed in relation to social objects, Keats was nothing. It was as mere an affectation when he talked with apparent zeal of liberty, or human rights, or human prospects, as is the hollow enthusiasm which many people profess for music, or most poets for external nature. For these things Keats fancied that he cared; but in reality he cared not at all. Upon them, or any of their aspects, he had thought too little, and too indeterminately, to feel for them as personal concerns. Whereas Shelley, from his earliest days, was mastered and shaken by the great moving realities of life, as a prophet is by the burden of wrath or of promise which he has been commissioned to reveal. Had there been no such thing as literature, Keats would have dwindled into a cipher. Shelley, in the same event, would hardly have lost one plume from his crest. It is in relation to literature, and to the boundless questions as to the true and the false arising out of literature and poetry, that Keats challenges a fluctuating interest; sometimes an interest of strong disgust, sometimes of deep admiration. There is not, I believe, a case on record throughout European literature, where feelings so repulsive of each other have centred in the same individual.

The very midsummer madness of affectation, of false vapory sentiment, and of fantastic effeminacy, seemed to me combined in Keats's *Endymion*, when I first saw it near the close of 1821. The Italian poet, Marino, had been reputed the greatest master of gossamery affectation in Europe. But *his* conceits showed the palest of rosy blushes by the side of Keats's bloody crimson. Naturally, I was discouraged from looking further. But about a week later, by pure accident, my eye fell upon his *Hyperion*. The first feeling was that of incredulity that the two poems could, under change of circumstances or lapse of time, have emanated from the same mind. The *Endymion* displays absolutely the most shocking revolt against good sense and just feeling, that all literature does now, or ever *can*, furnish. The *Hyperion*, as Mr. Gilfillan truly says, 'is the greatest of poetical torsos.' The first belongs essentially to the vilest collections of wax-work filagree, or gilt gingerbread. The other presents the majesty, the austere beauty, and the simplicity of Grecian temples enriched with Grecian sculpture. . . .

We have in this country a word, viz. the word *Folly*, which has a technical appropriation to the case of fantastic buildings. Any building is called 'a folly,'[5] which mimics purposes incapable of being realized, and makes a promise to the eye which it cannot keep to the experience. The most impressive illustration of this idea, which modern times have seen, was, undoubtedly, the ice-palace of the Empress Elizabeth[6] —

'That most magnificent and mighty freak,'

which, about eighty years ago, was called up from the depths of winter by

'The imperial mistress of the fur-clad Russ.'

Winter and the Czarina were, in this architecture, fellow-laborers. She, by her servants, furnished the blocks of ice, hewed them, dressed them, laid them: winter furnished the cement, by freezing them together. The palace has long melted back into water; and the poet who described it best, viz. Cowper, is not so much read in this age, except by the religious. It will, therefore, be a sort of resurrection for both the palace and the poet, if I cite his description of this gorgeous folly. It is a passage in which Cowper assumes so much of a Miltonic tone, that, of the two, it is better to have read his lasting description, than to have seen, with bodily eyes, the fleeting reality. The poet is apostrophizing the Empress Elizabeth.

——— 'No forest fell,
When *thou* wouldst build: no quarry sent its stores
To enrich thy walls: but thou didst hew the floods,
And make thy marble of the glassy wave.

. . . .

Silently as a dream the fabric rose:
No sound of hammer or of saw was there:
Ice upon ice, the well-adjusted parts
Were soon conjoin'd, nor other cement ask'd
Than water interfus'd to make them one.
Lamps gracefully disposed, and of all hues,
Illumin'd every side; a watery light
Gleam'd through the clear transparency, that seem'd
Another moon new-risen:———

. . . .

——— Nor wanted aught within
That royal residence might well befit
For grandeur or for use. Long weavy wreaths
Of flowers, that feared no enemy but warmth,
Blush'd on the panels. Mirror needed none,
Where all was vitreous: but in order due
Convivial table and commodious seat
(What *seem'd* at least commodious seat) were there;
Sofa, and couch, and high-built throne august.
The same lubricity was found in all,
And all was moist to the warm touch; a scene
Of evanescent glory, once a stream,
And soon to slide into a stream again.'

The poet concludes by viewing the whole as an unintentional stroke of satire by the Czarina,

——— 'On her own estate,
On human grandeur, and the courts of kings.
'T was transient in its nature, as in show
'T was durable; as worthless, as it seem'd
Intrinsically precious: to the foot
Treacherous and false, — it smiled, and it was cold.'

Looking at this imperial plaything of ice in the month of March, and recollecting that in May all its crystal arcades would be weeping away into vernal brooks, one would have been disposed to mourn over a beauty so frail, and to marvel at a frailty so elaborate. Yet still there was some proportion observed: the saloons were limited in number, though *not* limited in splendor. It was a *petit Trianon.* But what if, like Versailles, this glittering bauble, to which all the science of Europe could not have secured a passport into June, had contained six thousand separate rooms? A 'folly' on so gigantic a scale would have moved every man to indignation. For all that could be had, the beauty to the eye, and the gratification to the fancy, in seeing water tortured into every form of solidity, resulted from two or three suites of rooms, as fully as from a thousand.

Now, such a folly, as *would* have been the Czarina's, if executed upon the scale of Versailles, or of the new palace at St. Petersbugh, *was* the Endymion: a gigantic edifice (for its tortuous enigmas of thought multiplied every line of the four thousand into fifty) reared upon a basis slighter and less apprehensible than moonshine. As reasonably, and as hopefully in regard to human sympathies, might a man undertake an epic poem upon the loves of two butterflies. The modes of existence in the two parties to the love-fable of the Endymion, their relations to each other and to us, their prospects finally, and the obstacles to the *instant* realization of these prospects, — all these things are more vague and incomprehensible than the reveries of an oyster. Still the unhappy subject, and its unhappy expansion, must be laid to the account of childish years and childish inexperience. But there is another fault in Keats, of the first magnitude, which youth does not palliate, which youth even aggravates. This lies in the most shocking abuse of his mother-tongue. If there is one thing in this world that, next after the flag of his country and its spotless honor, should be wholly in the eyes of a young poet, — it is the *language* of his country. He should spend the third part of his life in studying this language, and cultivating its total resources. He should be willing to pluck out his right eye, or to circumnavigate the globe, if by such a sacrifice, if by such an exertion, he could attain to greater purity, precision, compass, or idiomatic energy of diction. This if he were even a Kalmuck Tartar, who by the way *has* the good feeling and patriotism to pride himself upon his beastly language.[7] But Keats was an Englishman; Keats had the honor to speak the language of Chaucer, Shakspeare, Bacon, Milton, Newton. The more awful was the obligation of his allegiance. And yet upon this mother tongue, upon this English language, has Keats trampled as with the hoofs of a buffalo. With its syntax, with its prosody, with its idiom, he has played such fantastic tricks as could enter only into the heart of a barbarian, and for which only the anarchy of Chaos could furnish a forgiving audience. Verily it required the *Hyperion* to weigh against the deep treason of these unparalleled offences.

NOTES.

Note 1. Page 78.

There is one peculiarity about Lucretius which, even in the absence of all anecdotes to that effect, would have led an observing reader to suspect some unsoundness in his brain. It is this, and it lies in his manner. In all poetic enthusiasm, however grand and sweeping may be its compass, so long as it is healthy and natural, there is a principle of self-restoration in the opposite direction: there is a counter state of repose, a compensatory state, as in the tides of the sea, which tends continually to re-establish the equipoise. The lull is no less intense than the fury of commotion. But in Lucretius there is no lull. Nor would there *seem* to be any, were it not for two accidents: 1st, the occasional pause in his raving tone enforced by the interruption of an episode; 2dly, the restraints (or at least the suspensions) imposed upon him by the difficulties of *argument conducted in verse.* To dispute metrically, is as embarrassing as to run or dance when knee-deep in sand. Else, and apart from these counteractions, the motion of the style is not only stormy, but self-kindling and continually accelerated.

Note 2. Page 79.

'*Habit of body:*' but much more from mismanagement of his body. Dr. Johnson tampered with medical studies, and fancied himself learned enough to prescribe for his female correspondents. The affectionateness with which he sometimes did this is interesting; but his ignorance of the subject is not the less apparent. In his own case he had the merit of one heroic self-conquest; he weaned himself from wine, having once become convinced that it was injurious. But he never brought himself to take regular exercise. He ate too much at all times of his life. And in another point, he betrayed a thoughtlessness, which (though really common as laughter) is yet extravagantly childish. Every body knows that Dr. Johnson was all his life reproaching himself with lying too long in bed. Always he was sinning, (for he thought it a sin;) always he was repenting; always he was vainly endeavoring to reform. But why vainly? Cannot a resolute man in six weeks bring himself to rise at *any* hour of the twenty-four? Certainly he can; but not without appropriate means. Now the Doctor rose about eleven, A. M. This, he fancied, was shocking; he was determined to rise at eight, or at seven. Very well; why not? But will it be credited that the one sole change occuring to the Doctor's mind, was to take a flying leap backwards from eleven to eight, without any corresponding leap at the other terminus of his sleep. To rise at eight instead of eleven, presupposes that a man goes off to bed at twelve instead of three. Yet this recondite truth, never to his dying day dawned on Dr. Johnson's mind. The conscientious man continued to offend; continued to repent; continued to pave a disagreeable place with good intentions, and daily resolutions of amendment; but at length died full of years, without having once seen the sun rise, except in some Homeric description, written [as Mr. Fynes Clifton makes it probable] thirty centuries before. The fact of the sun's rising at all, the Doctor adopted as a point of faith, and by no means of personal knowledge, from an insinuation to that effect in the most ancient of Greek books.

NOTE 3. Page 81.

One of these examples is equivocal, in a way that Mr. Gilfillan is apparently not aware of. He cites Tickell, 'whose very name' [he says] 'savors of laughter,' as being, 'in fact, a very happy fellow.' In the first place, Tickell would have been likly to 'square' at Mr. Gilfillan for that liberty taken with his name; or might even, in Falstaff's language, have tried to 'tickle his catastrophe.' It is a ticklish thing to lark with honest men's names. But, secondly, *which* Tickell? For there are two at the least in the field of English literature: and if one of them was 'very happy,' the chances are, according to D. Bernoulli and De Moivre, that the other was particularly miserable. The first Tickell, who may be described as Addison's Tickell, never tickled anything, that I know of, except Addison's vanity. But Tickell the second, who came into working order about fifty years later, was really a very pleasant fellow. In the time of Burke he diverted the whole nation by his poem of '*Anticipation*,' in which he anticipated and dramatically rehearsed the course of a whole Parliamentary debate, (on the king's speech,) which did not take place till a week or two afterwards. Such a mimicry was easy enough: but *that* did not prevent its fidelity and characteristic truth from delighting the political world.

Note 4. Page 84.

For the same reason, I refrain from noticing the pretensions of Savage. Mr. Gilfillan gives us to understand, that not from want of room, but of time, he does not (which else he *could*) prove him to be the man he pretended to be. For my own part, I believe Savage to have been the vilest of swindlers; and in these days, under the surveillance of an active police, he would have lost the chance which he earned of being hanged, by having long previously been transported to the Plantations. How can Mr. Gilfillan allow himself, in a case of this nature, to speak of 'universal impression' (if it had really existed) as any separate ground of credibility for Savage's tale? When the public have no access at all to sound means of judging, what matters it in which direction their 'impression' lies, or how many thousands swell the belief, for which not one of all these thousands has anything like a reason to offer?

NOTE 5. Page 88.

'*A folly.*' We English limit the application of this term to buildings: but the idea might as fitly be illustrated in other objects. For instance, the famous galley presented to one of the Ptolemies, which offered the luxurious accommodations of capital cities, but required a little army of four thousand men to row it, whilst its draught of water was too great to allow of its often approaching the shore; this was 'a folly' in our English sense. So again was the Macedonian phalanx: the Roman legion could form upon *any* ground: it was a true working tool. But the phalanx was too fine and showy for use. It required for its manœuvring a sort of opera stage, or a select bowling-green, such as few fields of battle offered.

NOTE 6. Page 88.

I had written the 'Empress *Catherine;*' but, on second thoughts, it occurred to me that the 'mighty freak' was, in fact, due to the Empress Elizabeth. There is, however, a freak connected with ice, not quite so 'mighty,' but quite as autocratic, and even more feminine in its caprice, which belongs exclusively to the Empress Catherine. A lady had engaged the affections of some young noblemen, who was regarded favorably by the imperial eye. No pretext offered itself for interdicting the marriage; but, by way of freezing it a little at the outset, the Czarina coupled with her permission this condition — that the wedding night should be passed by the young couple on a mattress of *her* gift. The mattress turned out to be a block of ice, elegantly cut, by the court upholsterer, into the likeness of a well-stuffed Parisian mattress. One pities the poor bride, whilst it is difficult to avoid laughing in the midst of one's sympathy. But it is to be hoped that no *ukase* was issued against spreading seven Turkey carpets, by way of under-blankets, over this amiable nuptial present. Amongst others who have noticed the story, is Captain Colville Frankland, of the navy.

NOTE 7. Page 92.

Bergmann, the German traveller, in his account of his long rambles and residence amongst the Kalmucks, makes us acquainted with the delirious vanity which possesses these demi-savages. Their notion is, that excellence of every kind, perfection in the least things as in the greatest, is briefly expressed by calling it *Kalmuckish*. Accordingly, their hideous language, and their vast national poem, [doubtless equally hideous,] they hold to be the immediate gifts of inspiration: and for this I honor them, as each generation learns both from the lips of their mothers. This great poem, by the way, measures (if I remember) seventeen English miles in length; but the most learned man amongst them, in fact a monster of erudition, never read farther than the eighth mile-stone. What he could repeat by heart was little more than a mile and a half; and, indeed, *that* was found too much for the choleric part of his audience. Even the Kalmuck face, which to us foolish Europeans looks so unnecessarily flat and ogre-like, these honest Tartars have ascertained to be the pure classical model of human beauty, — which, in fact, it *is*, upon the principle of those people who hold that the chief use of a face is — to frighten one's enemy.

OLIVER GOLDSMITH.*

THIS book accomplishes a retribution which the world has waited for through seventy and odd years. Welcome at any rate by its purpose, it is trebly welcome by its execution, to all hearts that linger indulgently over the frailties of a national favorite once wickedly exaggerated — to all hearts that brood indignantly over the powers of that favorite once maliciously undervalued.

A man of original genius, shown to us as revolving through the leisurely stages of a biographical memoir, lays open, to readers prepared for sympathy, two separate theatres of interest: one in his personal career; the other in his works and his intellectual development. Both unfold together: and each borrows a secondary interest from the other: the life from the recollection of the works — the works from the joy and sorrow of the life. There have, indeed, been authors whose great creations, severely preconceived in a region of thought transcendent to all impulses of earth, would have been pretty nearly what they are under any possible changes in the

* The Life and Adventures of Goldsmith, by John Forster.

dramatic arrangement of their lives. Happy or not happy — gay or sad — these authors would equally have fulfilled a mission too solemn and too stern in its obligations to suffer any warping from chance, or to bend before the accidents of life, whether dressed in sunshine or in wintry gloom. But generally this is otherwise. Children of Paradise, like the Miltons of our planet, have the privilege of stars — to 'dwell apart.' But the children of flesh, whose pulses beat too sympathetically with the agitations of mother-earth, cannot sequester themselves in that way. They walk in no such altitudes, but at elevations easily reached by ground-winds of humble calamity. And from that cup of sorrow, which upon all lips is pressed in some proportion, they must submit, by the very tenure on which they hold their gifts, to drink, if not more profoundly than others, yet always with more peril to the accomplishment of their earthly mission.

Amongst this household of children too tremulously associated to the fluctuations of earth, stands forward conspicuously Oliver Goldsmith. And there is a belief current — that he was conspicuous, not only in the sense of being constitutionally flexible to the impressions of sorrow and adversity, in case they had happened to occur, but also that he really *had* more than his share of those afflictions. We are disposed to think that this was not so. Our trust is, that Goldsmith lived upon the whole a life which, though troubled, was one of average enjoyment. Unquestionably, when reading at midnight, and in the middle watch of a century which *he* never reached, this record of one so amiable, so guileless, so upright, or seeming to be otherwise for a moment only in the eyes of those who did not know his difficulties, nor could have understood them; when recurring also to his admirable genius, to the sweet natural gaiety of his oftentimes pathetic humor, and to the varied accomplishments from talent or erudition, by which he gave effect to endowments so fascinating — one cannot but sorrow over the strife which he sustained, and over the wrong by which he suffered. A few natural tears one sheds at the rehearsal of so much contumely from fools, which he stood under unresistingly as one bareheaded under a hail-storm;[1] and worse to bear than the scorn of fools, was the imperfect sympathy and jealous self-distrusting esteem which he received to the last from friends. Doubtless he suffered much wrong; but so, in one way or other, do most men: he suffered also this special wrong, that in his lifetime he never was fully appreciated by any one friend — something of a counter-movement ever mingled with praise for *him* — he never saw himself enthroned in the heart of any young and fervent admirer, and he was always overshadowed by men less deeply genial, though more showy than himself: but these things happen, and *have* happened to myriads amongst the benefactors of earth. Their names ascend in songs of thankful commemoration, but not until the ears are deaf that would have thrilled to the music. And these were the heaviest of Goldsmith's afflictions: what are likely to be thought such, viz. the battles which he fought for his daily bread, we do not number amongst them. To struggle is not to suffer. Heaven grants to few of us a life of untroubled prosperity, and grants it least of all to its favorites. Charles I. carried, as it was thought by a keen Italian judge of physiognomy, a predestination to misery written in his features. And it is probable that if any Cornelius Agrippa had then been living, to show him in early life the strife, the bloodshed, the triumphs of enemies, the treacheries of friends, the separation for ever from the familiar faces of his hearth, which darkened the years from 1642 to 1649, he would have said—'Prophet of wo! if I bear to live through this vista of seven years, it is because at the further end of it thou showest me the consolation of a scaffold.' And yet our persuasion is, that in the midst of its deadly agitations and its torments of suspense, probably enough by the energies of hope, or even of anxiety which exalted it, that period of bitter conflict was found by the king a more ennobling life than he *would* have found in the torpor of a prosperity too profound. To be cloyed perpetually is a worse fate than sometimes to stand within the vestibule of starvation; and we need go no further than the confidential letters of the court ladies of this and other countries to satisfy ourselves how much worse in its effects upon happiness than any condition of alarm and peril, is the lethargic repose of luxury too monotonous, and of security too absolute. If, therefore, Goldsmith's life *had* been one of continual struggle, it would not follow that it had therefore sunk below the standard of ordinary happiness. But the life-struggle of Goldsmith, though severe enough (after all allowances) to challenge a feeling of tender compassion, was not in such a degree severe as has been represented.[2] He enjoyed two great immunities from suffering that have been much overlooked ; and *such* immunities that, in our opinion, four in five of all the people ever connected with Goldsmith's works, as publishers, printers, compositors (that is, men taken at random), have very probably suffered more, upon the whole, than he. The immunities were these : — 1st, From any *bodily* taint of low spirits. He had a constitutional gaiety of heart ; an elastic hilarity ; and, as he himself expresses it, 'a knack of hoping' — which knack could not be bought with Ormus and with Ind, nor hired for a day with the peacock-throne of Delhi. How easy was it to bear the brutal affront of being to his face described as '*Doctor minor*,' when one hour or less would dismiss the *Doctor major*, so invidiously contradistinguished from himself, to a struggle with scrofulous melancholy ; whilst *he*, if returning to solitude and a garret, was returning also to habitual cheerfulness. *There* lay one immunity, beyond all price, from a mode of strife to which others, by a large majority, are doomed — strife with bodily wretchedness. Another immunity he had of almost equal value, and yet almost equally forgotten by his biographers, viz., from the responsibilities of a family. Wife and children he had not. They it is that, being a man's chief blessings, create also for him the deadliest of his anxieties, that stuff his pillow with thorns, that surround his daily path with snares. Suppose the case of a man who has helpless dependents of this class upon himself summoned to face some sudden failure of his resources : how shattering to the power of exertion, and, above all, of exertion by an organ so delicate as the creative intellect, dealing with subjects so coy as those of imaginative sensibility, to know that instant ruin attends his failure. Success in such paths of literature might at the best be doubtful; but success is impossible, with any powers whatever, unless in a genial state of those powers; and this geniality is to be sustained in the case supposed, whilst the eyes are fixed upon the most frightful of abysses yawning beneath his feet. He is to win his inspiration for poetry or romance from the prelusive cries of infants clamoring for daily bread. Now, on the other hand, in the case of an extremity equally sudden alighting on the head of a man in Goldsmith's position, having no burden to support but the trivial one of his own personal needs, the resources are endless for gaining time enough to look around. Suppose him ejected from his lodgings; let him walk into the country, with a pencil and a sheet of paper; there sitting under a hay-stack for one morning, he may produce what will pay his expenses for a week: a day's labor will carry the sustenance of ten days. Poor may be the trade of authorship, but it is as good as that of a slave in Brazil, whose one hour's work will defray the twenty-four hours' living. As a reader, or corrector of proofs, a good Latin and French scholar (like Goldsmith) would always have enjoyed a preference, we presume, at any eminent printing-office. This again would have given him time for looking round; or, he might perhaps have obtained the same advantage for deliberation from some confidential friend's hospitality. In short, Goldsmith enjoyed the two privileges, one subjective — the other objective —

which, when uniting in the same man, would prove more than a match for all difficulties that *could* arise in a literary career to him who was at once a man of genius so popular, of talents so versatile, of reading so various, and of opportunities so large for still more extended reading. The subjective privilege lay in his buoyancy of animal spirits; the objective in his freedom from responsibilities. Goldsmith wanted very little more than Diogenes: now Diogenes *could* only have been robbed of his tub:[3] which perhaps was about as big as most of poor Goldsmith's sitting-rooms, and far better ventilated. So that the liability of these two men, cynic and non-cynic, to the kicks of fortune, was pretty much on a par; whilst Goldsmith had the advantage of a better temper for bearing them, though certainly Diogenes had the better climate for soothing his temper.

But it may be imagined, that if Goldsmith were thus fortunately equipped for authorship, on the other hand, the position of literature, as a money-making resource, was in Goldsmith's days less advantageous than ours. We are not of that opinion; and the representation by which Mr. Forster endeavors to sustain it seems to us a showy but untenable refinement. The outline of his argument is, that the aristocratic patron had, in Goldsmith's day, by the progress of society, disappeared; he belonged to the past — that the mercenary publisher had taken his place — he represented the ugly present — but that the great reading public (that true and equitable patron, as some fancy) had not yet matured its means of effectual action upon literature: this reading public virtually, perhaps, belonged to the future. All this we steadfastly resist. No doubt the old full-blown patron, *en grand costume*, with his heraldic bearings emblazoned at the head of the Dedication, was dying out, like the golden pippin. But he still lingered in sheltered situations. And part of the machinery by which patronage had ever moved, viz. using influence for obtaining subscriptions, was still in capital working order — a fact which we know from Goldsmith himself (see the *Enquiry*); for he tells us that a popular mode of publication amongst bad authors, and certainly it needed no publisher's countersign, was by means of subscription papers: upon which, as we believe, a considerable instalment was usually paid down when as yet the book existed only by way of title-page, supposing that the whole sum were not even paid *up*. Then as to the publisher (a nuisance, we dare say, in all stages of his Natural History), *he* could not have been a weed first springing up in Goldsmith's time, but must always have been an indispensable broker or middleman between the author and the world. In the days even of Horace and Martial the book-*seller* (bibliopola) clearly acted as book-*publisher*. Amongst other passages proving this, and showing undeniably that Martial at least had sold the copyright of his work to *his* publisher, is one arguing pretty certainly that the price of a gay drawing-room copy must have been hard upon £1. 11*s*. 6*d*. Did ever any man hear the like? A New York newspaper would have been too happy to pirate the whole of Martial had he been three times as big, and would have engaged to drive the bankrupt publisher into a madhouse for twopence. Now, it cannot be supposed that Martial, a gay light-hearted fellow, willing to let the public have his book for a shilling, or perhaps for love, had been the person to put that ridiculous price upon it. We may conclude that it was the publisher. As to the public, *that* respectable character must always have presided over the true and final court of appeal, silently defying alike the *prestige* of patronage and the intriguing mysteries of publishing. Lordly patronage might fill the sails of one edition, and masterly publishing of three. But the books that ran contagiously through the educated circles, or that lingered amongst them for a generation, must have owed their success to the unbiassed feelings of the reader — not overawed by authority, not mystified by artifice. Varying, however, in whatever proportion as to power, the three possible parties to an act of publication will always be seen intermittingly at work — the voluptuous self-indulging public, and the insidious publisher, of course; but even the brow-beating patron still exists in a new *avatar*. Formerly he made his descent upon earth in the shape of Dedicatee; and it is true that this august being, to whom dedications burned incense upon an altar, withdrew into sunset and twilight during Goldsmith's period; but he still revisits the glimpses of the moon in the shape of author. When the *auctoritas* of a peer could no longer sell a book by standing at the head of a dedication, it lost none of its power when standing on the title-page as the author. Vast catalogues might be composed of books and pamphlets that have owed a transient success to no other cause on earth than the sonorous title, or the distinguished position of those who wrote them. Ceasing to patronize other people's books, the grandee has still power to patronize his own. All *celebrities* have this form of patronage. And, for instance, had the boy Jones[4] (otherwise called Inigo Jones) possessed enough of book-making skill to forge a plausible curtain-lecture, as overheard by himself when concealed in Her Majesty's bed-room, ten steam-presses working day and night would not have supplied the public demand; and even Her Majesty must herself have sent for a large-paper copy, were it only to keep herself *au courant* of English literature. In short, first, the extrinsic patronage of books; secondly, the self-patronage of books in right of their merits; and thirdly, the artificial machineries for diffusing the knowledge of their existence, are three forces in current literature that ever *have* existed and must exist, in some imperfect degree. Horace recognises them in his

'Non Dî, non homines, non concessere columnæ.'

The *Dî* are the paramount public, arbitrating finally on the fates of books, and generally on some just ground of judgment, though it may be fearfully exaggerated on the scale of importance. The *homines* are the publishers; and a sad *homo* the publisher sometimes is, particularly when he commits insolvency. But the *columnæ* are those pillars of state, the grandees of our own age, or any other patrons, that support the golden canopy of our transitory pomps, and thus shed an alien glory of colored light from above upon the books falling within that privileged area.

We are not therefore of Mr. Forster's opinion, that Goldsmith fell upon an age less favorable to the expansion of literary powers, or to the attainment of literary distinction, than any other. The patron might be a tradition — but the public was not therefore a prophecy. My lord's trumpets had ceased to sound, but the *vox populi* was not therefore muffled. The means indeed of diffusive advertisement and of rapid circulation, the combinations of readers into reading societies, and of roads into iron net-works, were as yet imperfectly developed. These gave a potent stimulus to periodic literature. And a still more operative difference between ourselves and them is — that a new class of people has since then entered our reading public, viz. — the class of artisans and of all below the gentry, which (taken generally) was in Goldsmith's day a cipher as regarded any real encouragement to literature. In our days, if *The Vicar of Wakefield* had been published as a Christmas tale, it would have produced a fortune to the writer. In Goldsmith's time, few below the gentry were readers on any large scale. So far there really *was* a disadvantage. But it was a disadvantage which applied chiefly to novels. The new influx of readers in our times, the collateral affluents into the main stream from the mechanic and provincial sections of our population, which have centupled the volume of the original current, cannot be held as telling favorably upon literature, or telling at all, except in the departments of popularized science, of religion, of fictitious tales, and of journalism. To be a reader, is no longer as once it was, to be of a meditative turn. To be a *very* popular author is no longer that honorary distinction which once it might have been amongst a more elevated because more select body of readers. We do not say this invidiously, or with any special reference. But it is evident that writers and readers must often act and reäct for reciprocal degradation. A writer of this day, either in France or England, to be *very* popular, must be a story-teller; which is a function of literature neither very noble in itself, nor, secondly, tending to permanence. All novels whatever, the best equally with the worst, have faded almost with the generation that produced them. This is a curse written as a superscription above the whole class. The modes of combining characters, the particular objects selected for sympathy, the diction, and often the manners,[5] hold up an imperfect mirror to any generation that is not their own. And the reader of novels belonging to an obsolete era, whilst acknowledging the skill of the groupings, or the beauty of the situations, misses the echo to that particular revelation of human nature which has met him in the social aspects of his own day; or too often he is perplexed by an expression which, having dropped into a lower use, disturbs the unity of the impression, or is revolted by a coarse sentiment, which increasing refinement has made unsuitable to the sex or to the rank of the character. How bestial and degrading at this day seem many of the scenes in Smollett! How coarse are the ideals of Fielding! — his odious Squire Western, his odious Tom Jones! What a gallery of histrionic masqueraders is thrown open in the novels of Richardson, powerful as they were once found by the two leading nations of the earth. A popular writer, therefore, who, *in order* to be popular, must speak through novels, speaks to what is least permanent in human sensibilities. That is already to be self-degraded. *Secondly*, because the novel-reading class is by far the most comprehensive one, and being such, must count as a large majority amongst its members those who are poor in capacities of thinking, and are passively resigned to the instinct of immediate pleasure — to these the writer must chiefly humble himself: he must study *their* sympathies, must assume them, must give them back. In our days, he must give them back even their own street slang; so servile is the modern novelist's dependence on his *canaille* of an audience. In France, amongst the Sues, &c., it has been found necessary to give back even the closest portraits of obscene atrocities that shun the light, and burrow only in the charnel-houses of vast manufacturing towns. Finally, the very principle of commanding attention only by the interest of a tale, which means the interest of a momentary curiosity that is to vanish for ever in a sense of satiation, and of a momentary suspense that, having once collapsed, can never be rekindled, is in itself a confession of reliance upon the meaner offices of the mind. The result from all which is — that to be popular in the most extensive walk of popularity, that is, as a novelist, a writer must generally be in a very considerable degree self-degraded by sycophancy to the lowest order of minds, and cannot (except for mercenary purposes) think himself advantageously placed.

To have missed, therefore, this enormous expansion of the reading public, however unfortunate for Goldsmith's purse, was a great escape for his intellectual purity. Every man has two-edged tendencies lurking within himself, pointing in one direction to what will expand the elevating principles of his nature, pointing in another to what will tempt him to its degradation. A mob is a dreadful audience for chafing and irritating the latent vulgarisms of the human heart. Exaggeration and caricature, before such a tribunal, become inevitable, and sometimes almost a duty. The genial but not very delicate humor of Goldsmith would in such circumstances have slipped, by the most natural of transitions, into buffoonery; the unaffected pathos of Goldsmith would, by a monster audience, have been debauched into theatrical sentimentality. All the motions of Goldsmith's nature moved in the direction of the true, the natural, the sweet, the gentle. In the quiet times, politically speaking, through which his course of life travelled, he found a musical echo to the tenor of his own original sensibilities — in the architecture of European history, as it unfolded its proportions along the line of his own particular experience, there was a symmetry with the proportions of his own unpretending mind. Our revolutionary age would have unsettled his brain. The colossal movements of nations, from within and from without; the sorrow of the times, which searches so deeply; the grandeur of the times, which aspires so loftily; these forces, acting for the last fifty years by secret sympathy upon our fountains of thinking and impassioned speculation, have raised them from depths never visited by our fathers, into altitudes too dizzy for *their* contemplating. This generation and the last, with their dreadful records, would have untuned Goldsmith for writing in the key that suited him; and *us* they would have untuned for understanding his music, had we not learned to understand it in childhood, before the muttering hurricanes in the upper air had begun to reach our young ears, and forced them away to the thundering overhead, from the carolling of birds amongst earthly bowers.

Goldsmith, therefore, as regards the political aspects of his own times, was fortunately placed; a thrush or a nightingale is hushed by the thunderings which are awakening to Jove's eagle. But an author stands in relation to other influences than political; and some of these are described by Mr. Forster as peculiarly unfavorable to comfort and respectability at the era of Goldsmith's novitiate in literature. Will Mr. Forster excuse us for quarrelling with his whole doctrine upon this subject — a subject and a doctrine continually forced upon our attention in these days, by the extending lines of our own literary order, and continually refreshed in warmth of coloring by the contrast as regards *social* consideration, between our literary body and the corresponding order in France. The questions arising have really a general interest, as well as a special one, in connection with Goldsmith; and therefore we shall stir them a little, not with any view of exhausting the philosophy that is applicable to the case, but simply of amusing some readers (since Pliny's remark on history is much more true of literature or literary gossip, viz., that '*quoquo* modo scripta delectat;') and with the more ambitious purpose of recalling some other readers from precipitate conclusions upon a subject where nearly all that is most plausible happens to be most untrue.

Mr. Forster, in his views upon the *social* rights of literature, is rowing pretty nearly in the same boat as Mr. Carlyle in *his* views upon the rights of labor. Each denounces, or by implication denounces, as an oppression and a nuisance, what *we* believe to be a necessity inalienable from the economy and structure of our society. Some years ago Mr. Carlyle offended us all (or all of us that were interested in social philosophy) by enlarging on a social affliction, which few indeed needed to see exposed, but most men would have rejoiced to see remedied, if it were but on paper, and by way of tentative suggestion. Precisely at that point, however, where his aid was invoked, Mr. Carlyle halted. So does Mr. Forster with regard to *his* grievance; he states it, and we partly understand him — as ancient Pistol says — 'We hear him with ears;' and when we wait for him to go on, saying — 'Well, here's a sort of evil in life, how would you redress it? you've shown, or you've made another hole in the tin-kettle of society; how do you propose to tinker it?' — behold! he is suddenly almost silent. But this cannot be allowed. The right to insist upon a well known grievance cannot be granted to that man (Mr. Carlyle, for instance, or Mr. Forster) who uses it as matter of blame and denunciation, unless, at the same time, he points out the methods by which it could have been prevented. He that simply bemoans an evil has a right to his moan, though he should make no pretensions to a remedy; but he that criminates, that imputes the evil as a fault, that charges the evil upon selfishness or neglect lurking in some alterable arrangements of society, has no right to do so, unless he can instantly sketch the remedy ; for the very first step by which he could have learned that the evil involved a blame, the first step that could have entitled him to denounce it as a wrong, must have been that step which brought him within the knowledge (wanting to everybody else) that it admitted of a cure. A wrong it could not have been even in *his* eyes, so long as it was a necessity, nor a ground of complaint until the cure appeared to him a possibility. And the overriding motto for these parallel speculations of Messrs. Carlyle and Forster, in relation to the frailties of our social system, ought to have been — '*Sanabilibus ægrotamus malis.*' Unless with this watchword they had no right to commence their crusading march. *Curable* evils justify clamorous complaints ; the incurable justify only prayers.

Why it was that Mr. Carlyle, in particular, halted so steadily at the point where his work of love was first beginning, it is not difficult to guess. As the 'Statutes at large' have not one word against the liberty of unlicensed hypothesis, it is conceivable that Mr. C. might have indulged a little in that agreeable pastime : but this, he was well aware, would have brought him in one moment under the fire of Political Economy, from the whole vast line of its modern batteries. These gentlemen, the economists, would have torn to ribbons, within fifteen minutes, any *positive* speculation for amending the evil. It was better, therefore, to keep within the trenches of the blank negative, pointing to everything as *wrong* — horribly wrong, but never hinting at the mysterious *right:* which, to this day, we grieve to say, remains as mysterious as ever.[6]

Passing to Mr. Forster, who (being capable of a splendor so original) disappoints us most when he reminds us of Mr. Carlyle, by the most disagreeable of that gentleman's phraseological forms; and, in this instance, by a speculation twin-sister to the economic one just noticed; we beg to premise that in anything here said, it is far from our wish to express disaffection to the cause of our literary brothers. We grudge them nothing that they are ever likely to get. We wish even that the House of Commons would see cause for creating *majorats* in behalf of us all; only whispering in the ear of that honorable House to appoint a Benjamin's portion to ourselves, as the parties who suggested the idea. But what is the use of benevolently bequeathing larks for dinner to all literary men, in all time coming, if the sky must fall before they can bag our bequest? We shall discuss Mr. Forster's views, not perhaps according to any arrangement of his, but according to the order in which they come back to our own remembrance.

Goldsmith's period, Mr. F. thinks, was bad — not merely by the transitional misfortune (before noticed) of coming too late for the patron, and too soon for the public, (which is the compound ill-luck of being a day after one fair, and a month too soon for the next,) — but also by some co-operation in this evil destiny through misconduct on the part of authors themselves (p. 70.) Not 'the circumstances' only of authors were damaged, but the 'literary character' itself.

We are sorry to hear *that.* But, as long as they did not commit murder, we have a great indulgence for the frailties of authors. If ever the 'benefit of clergy' could be fairly pleaded, it might have been by Grub Street for petty larceny. The 'clergy' they surely could have pleaded; and the call for larceny was so audible in their condition, that in *them* it might be called an instinct of self-preservation, which surely was not implanted in man to be disobeyed. One word allow us to say on these three topics: — 1. The condition of the literary body in its hard-working section at the time when Goldsmith belonged to it. 2. Upon the condition of that body in England as compared with that of the corresponding body in France. 3. Upon the condition of the body in relation to patronage purely *political.*

1. The pauperized (or Grub Street) section of the literary body, at the date of Goldsmith's taking service amongst it, was (in Mr. Forster's estimate) at its very lowest point of depression. And one comic presumption in favor of that notion we ourselves remember; viz. that Smart, the prose translator of Horace, and a well-built scholar, actually *let* himself out to a monthly journal on a regular lease of ninety-nine years.[7] What could move the rapacious publisher to draw the lease for this monstrous term of years, we cannot conjecture. Surely the villain might have been content with threescore years and ten. But think, reader, of poor Smart two years after, upon another publisher's applying to him vainly for contributions, and angrily demanding what possible objection could be made to offers so liberal, being reduced to answer — 'No objec-

tion, sir, whatever, except an unexpired term of ninety-seven years yet to run.' The bookseller saw that he must not apply again in *that* century; and, in fact, Smart could no longer let himself, but must be sublet (if let at all) by the original lessee. Query now — was Smart entitled to vote as a freeholder, and Smart's children (if any were born during the currency of the lease) would they be serfs, and *ascripti prelo*? Goldsmith's own terms of self-conveyance to Griffiths — the terms we mean on which he 'conveyed' his person and free-agency to the uses of the said Griffiths (or his assigns?) — do not appear to have been much more dignified than Smart's in the quality of the *conditions,* though considerably so in the duration of the *term;* Goldsmith's lease being only for one year, and not for ninety-nine, so that he had (as the reader perceives) a clear ninety-eight years at his own disposal. We suspect that poor Oliver, in his guileless heart, never congratulated himself on having made a more felicitous bargain. Indeed, it was not so bad, if everything be considered; Goldsmith's situation at the time was bad; and for that very reason the lease (otherwise monstrous) was *not* bad. He was to have lodging, board, and 'a small salary,' *very* small, we suspect; and in return for all these blessings, he had nothing to do, but to sit still at a table, to work hard from an early hour in the morning until 2 P. M. (at which elegant hour we presume that the parenthesis of dinner occurred,) but also — which, not being an article in the lease, might have set aside, on a motion before the King's Bench — to endure without mutiny the correction and revisal of all his MSS. by *Mrs.* Griffiths, wife to Dr. G. the lessee. This affliction of Mrs. *Dr.* G. surmounting his shoulders, and controlling his pen, seems to us not at all less dreadful than that of Sinbad when indorsed with the old man of the sea; and we, in Goldsmith's place, should certainly have tried how far Sinbad's method of abating the nuisance had lost its efficacy by time, viz. the tempting our oppressor to get drunk once or twice a day, and then suddenly throwing Mrs. Dr. G. off her perch. From that 'bad eminence,' which she had audaciously usurped, what harm could there be in thus dismounting this 'old *woman* of the sea?' And as to an occasional thump or so on the head, which Mrs. Dr. G. might have caught in tumbling, that was *her* look-out; and might besides have improved her style. For really now if, the candid reader will believe us, we know a case, odd certainly but very true, where a young man, an author by trade,[8] who wrote pretty well, happening to tumble out of a first-floor in London, was afterwards observed to grow very perplexed and almost unintelligible in his style; until some years later, having the good fortune (like Wallenstein at Vienna) to tumble out of a two-pair of stairs window, he slightly fractured his skull, but on the other hand, recovered the brilliancy of his long fractured style. Some people there are of our acquaintance who would need to tumble out of the attic story before they could seriously improve their style.

Certainly these conditions — the hard work, the being chained by the leg to the writing-table, and above all the having one's pen chained to that of Mrs. Dr. Griffiths, *do* seem to countenance Mr. F.'s idea, that Goldsmith's period was the purgatory of authors. And we freely confess — that excepting Smart's ninety-nine years' lease, or the contract between the Devil and Dr. Faustus, we never heard of a harder bargain driven with any literary man. Smart, Faustus, and Goldsmith, were clearly overreached. Yet after all, was this treatment in any important point (excepting as regards Dr. Faustus) worse than that given to the whole college of Grub Street, in the days of Pope? The first edition of the Dunciad dates from 1727: Goldsmith's matricalculation in Grub Street dates from 1757 — just thirty years later; which is one generation. And it is important to remember that Goldsmith, at this time in his twenty-ninth year, was simply an usher at an obscure boarding-school; had never practised writing for the press; and had not even himself any faith at all in his own capacity for writing. It is a singular fact, which we have on Goldsmith's own authority, that until his thirtieth year (that is, the year he spent with Dr. and Mrs. Griffiths) it never entered into his head that literature was his natural vocation. That vanity, which has been so uncandidly and sometimes so falsely attributed to Goldsmith, was compatible, we see, if at all it existed, with the humblest estimate of himself. Still, however much this deepens our regard for a man of so much genius united with so much simplicity and unassumingness, humility would not be likely to raise his salary; and we must not forget that his own want of self-esteem would reasonably operate on the terms offered by Griffiths. A man, who regarded himself as little more than an amanuensis, could not expect much better wages than an under-gardener, which perhaps he had. And, weighing all this, we see little to have altered in the lease — that was fair enongh ; only as regarded the execution of the lease, we really must have protested, under any circumstances, against Mrs. Doctor Griffiths. That woman would have broken the back of a camel, which must be supposed tougher than the heart of an usher. There we should have made a ferocious stand ; and should have struck for much higher wages, before we could have brought our mind to think of capitulation. It is remarkable, however, that this year of humble servitude was not only (or, as if by accident) the epoch of Goldsmith's intellectual development, but also the occasion of it. Nay, if all were known, perhaps it may have been to Mrs. Doctor Griffiths in particular, that we owe that revolution in his self-estimation which made Goldsmith an author by deliberate choice. Hag-ridden every day, he must have plunged and kicked violently to break loose from this harness ; but, not impossibly, the very effort of contending with the hag, when brought into collision with his natural desire to soothe the hag, and the inevitable counter-impulse in any continued practice of composition, towards the satisfaction at the same time of his own reason and taste, must have furnished a most salutary *palæstra* for the education of his literary powers. When one lives at Rome, one must do as they do at Rome : when one lives with a hag, one must accommodate oneself to haggish caprices ; besides, that once in a month the hag might be right ; or if not, and supposing her *always* in the wrong, which perhaps is too much to assume even of Mrs. Dr. G., *that* would but multiply the difficulties of reconciling *her* demands with the demands of the general reader and of Goldsmith's own judgment. And in the pressure of these difficulties would lie the very value of this rough Spartan education. Rope-dancing cannot be very agreeable in its elementary lessons; but it must be a capital process for calling out the agilities that slumber in a man's legs.

Still, though these hardships turned out so beneficially to Goldsmith's intellectual interests, and, consequently, so much to the advantage of all who have since delighted in his works, not the less on that account they *were* hardships, and hardships that imposed heavy degradation. So far, therefore, they would seem to justify Mr. Forster's characterization of Goldsmith's period by comparison with Addison's period[9] on the one side, and our own on the other. But, on better examination, it will be found that this theory is sustained only by an unfair selection of the antithetic objects in the comparison. Compare Addison's age *generally* with Goldsmith's — authors, prosperous or unprosperous, in each age taken indiscriminately — and the two ages will be found to offer 'much of a muchness.' But, if you take the paupers of one generation to contrast with the grandees of another, how is there any justice in the result? Goldsmith at starting was a penniless man. Except by random accidents, he had not money enough to buy a rope, in case he had fancied himself in want of such a thing. Addison, on the contrary, was the son of a tolerably rich man; lived gaily at a most aristocratic college (Magdalen), in a most aristocratic university; formed early and brilliant connections with the political party that were magnificently preponderant until the last four years of

Queen Anne; travelled on the Continent, not as a pedestrian mendicant, housing with owls, and thankful for the bounties of a village fair, but with the appointments and introduction of a young nobleman; and became a secretary of statè, not by means of his 'delicate humor,' as Mr. Forster chooses to suppose, but through splendid patronage, and (speaking *Hibernicé*) through a 'strong back.' His bad verses, his Blenheim, his Cato, in later days, and other rubbish, had been the only part of his works that aided his rise; and even these would have availed him little, had he not originally possessed a *locus standi*, from which he could serve his artilleries of personal flatteries with commanding effect, and could *profit* by his successes. As to the really exquisite part of his writings, *that* did him no yeoman's service at all, nor *could* have done; for he was a made man, and had almost received notice to quit this world of prosperous whiggery, before he had finished those exquisite prose miscellanies. Pope, Swift, Gay, Prior, &c. all owed their social positions to early accidents of good connections and sometimes of luck, which would not indeed, have supplied the place of personal merit, but which gave lustre and effect to merit where it existed in strength. There were authors quite as poor as Goldsmith in the Addisonian age; there were authors quite as rich as Pope, Steele, &c. in Goldsmith's age, and having the same social standing. Goldsmith struggled with so much distress, not because his period was more inauspicious, but because his connections and starting advantages were incomparably less important. His profits were so trivial, because his capital was next to none.

So far, as regards the comparison between Goldsmith's age and the one immediately before it. But now, as regards the comparison with our own, removed by two generations — can it be said truly that the literary profession has risen in estimation, or is rising? There is a difficulty in making such an appraisement; and from different minds there would proceed very different appraisements; and even from the same mind, surveying the case at different stations. For, on the one hand, if a greater breadth of social respectability catches the eye on looking carelessly over the body of our modern literati, which may be owing chiefly to the large increase of gentlemen that in our day have entered the field of literature; on the other hand, the hacks and *handicraftsmen* whom the shallow education of newspaper journalism has introduced to the press, and whom poverty compels to labors not meriting the name of literature, are correspondingly expanding their files. There is, however, one reason from analogy, which may incline us to suppose that a higher consideration is now generally conceded to the purposes of literature, and, consequently, a juster estimate made of the persons who minister to those purposes. Literature — provided we use that word not for the mere literature of knowledge, but for the literature of power — using it for literature as it speaks to what is genial in man, viz. — to the human *spirit*, and *not* for literature (falsely so called) as it speaks to the meagre understanding — is a fine art; and not only so, it is the supreme of the fine arts; nobler, for instance, potentially, than painting, or sculpture, or architecture. Now *all* the fine arts, *that popularly are called such*, have risen in esteem within the last generation. The most aristocratic of men will now ask into his own society an artist, whom fifty years ago he would have transferred to the house-steward's table. And why? Not simply because more attention having been directed to the arts, more notoriety has gathered about the artist; for that sort of *éclat* would not work any durable change; but it is because the interest in the arts having gradually become much more of an enlightened interest, the public has been slowly trained to fix its attention upon the *intellect* which is presupposed in the arts, rather than upon the offices of *pleasure* to which they minister. The fine arts have now come to be regarded, rather as powers that are to mould, than as luxuries that are to embellish. And it has followed that artists are valued more by the elaborate agencies which they guide, than by the fugitive sensations of wonder or sympathy which they evoke.

Now this is a change honorable to both sides. The public has altered its estimate of certain men; and yet has not been able to do so, without previously enlarging its idea of the means through which those men operate. It could not elevate the men, without previously elevating itself. But, if so, then, in correcting their appreciation of the fine arts, the public must simultaneously have corrected their appreciation of literature; because whether men have or have not been in the habit of regarding literature as a fine art, this they must have felt, viz., that literature, in its more genial functions, works by the very same organs as the liberal arts, speaks to the same heart, operates through the same compound nature, and educates the same deep sympathies with mysterious ideals of beauty. *There* lies the province of the arts usually acknowledged as fine or liberal: *there* lies the province of fine or liberal literature. And with justifiable pride a *littérateur* may say — that *his* fine art wields a sceptre more potent than any other; literature is more potent than other fine arts, because *deeper* in its impressions according to the usual tenor of human sensibilities; because more *extensive*, in the degree that books are more diffused than pictures or statues; because more *durable*, in the degree that language is durable beyond marble or canvas, and in the degree that vicarious powers are opened to books for renewing their phœnix immortality through unlimited translations: powers denied to painting except through copies that are feeble, and denied to sculpture except to casts that are costly.

We infer that, as the fine arts have been rising, literature (on the secret feeling that essentially it moves by the same powers) must also have been rising; that, as the arts will continue to rise, literature will continue to rise; and that, in both cases, the men, the ministers, must ascend in social consideration as the things, the ministrations, ascend. But there is another form, in which the same result offers itself to our notice; and this should naturally be the last paragraph in this section 1, but, as we have little room to spare, it may do equally well as the first paragraph in section 2, viz., on the condition of our own literary body by comparison with the same body in France.

2. Who were the people amongst ourselves, that, throughout the eighteenth century, chiefly came forward as undervaluers of literature? They belonged to two very different classes — the aristocracy and the commercial body, who agreed in the thing, but on very different impulses. To the mercantile man, the author was an object of ridicule, from natural poverty; *natural*, because there was no regular connection between literature and any mode of money-making. By accident the author might *not* be poor, but professionally, or according to any obvious opening for an income, he *was*. Poverty was the badge of all his tribe. Amongst the aristocracy, the instinct of contempt, or at least of slight regard towards literature, was supported by the irrelation of literature to the *state*. Aristocracy itself was the flower and fruitage of the state; a nobility was possible only in the ratio of the grandeur and magnificence developed for *social* results; so that a poor and unpopulous nation cannot create a great aristocracy: the flower and foliation must be in relation to the stem and the radix out of which they germinate. Inevitably, therefore, a nobility so great as the English — that not in pride, but in the mere logic of its political relations, felt its order to be a sort of heraldic shield, charged with the trophies and ancestral glories of the nation — could not but in its *public* scale of appreciation estimate every profession and rank of men by the mode of their natural connection with the state. Law and arms, for instance, were honored, not because any capricious precedent had been established of a title to public honor in favor of those professions, but because, through their essential functions,

they opened for themselves a permanent necessity of introsusception into the organism of the state. A great law officer, a great military leader, a popular admiral, is already, by virtue of his functions, a noble in men's account, whether you gave or refused him a title ; and in such cases it has always been the policy of an aristocratic state to confer, or even impose the title, lest the disjunction of the virtual nobility from the titular should gradually disturb the estimate of the latter. But literature, by its very grandeur, is degraded socially ; for its relations are essentially cosmopolitan, or, speaking more strictly, not cosmopolitan, which might mean to all other peoples considered as national states, whereas literature has no relation to any sections or social schisms amongst men — its relations are to the race. In proportion as any literary work rises in its pretensions; for instance, if it works by the highest forms of passion, its *nisus*, its natural effort is to address the race, and not any individual nation. That it found a bar to this *nisus*, in a limited language, was but an accident: the essential relations of every great intellectual work are to those capacities in man by which he tends to brotherhood, and not to those by which he tends to alienation. Man is ever coming nearer to agreement, ever narrowing his differences, notwithstanding that the interspace may cost an eternity to traverse. Where the agreement is, not where the difference is, in the centre of man's affinities, not of his repulsions, *there* lies the magnetic centre towards which all poetry that is potent, and all philosophy that is faithful, are eternally travelling by natural tendency. Consequently, if indirectly literature may hold a patriotic value as a gay plumage in the cap of a nation, directly, and, by a far deeper tendency, literature is essentially alien. A poet, a book, a system of religion, belongs to the nation best qualified for appreciating their powers, and not to the nation that, perhaps by accident, gave them birth. How, then, is it wonderful that an intense organ of the social principle in a nation, viz., a nobility, should fail, in their professional character, to rate highly, or even to recognise, as having any proper existence, a fine art which is by tendency anti-social (anti-social in this sense, that what it seeks, it seeks by transcending all social barriers and separations)? Yet it is remarkable that in England, where the aristocracy for three centuries (16th, 17th, 18th) paid so little honor, in their public or corporate capacity, to literature, privately they honored it with a rare courtesy. That same grandee, who would have looked upon Camden, Ben Jonson, Selden, or Hobbes, as an audacious intruder, if occupying any prominent station at a state festival, would have received him with a kind of filial reverence in his own mansion; for in this place, as having no national reference, as sacred to hospitality, which regards the human tie, and not the civic tie, he would be at liberty to regard the man of letters in his cosmopolitan character. And on the same instinct, a prince in the very meanest State, would, in a state-pageant commemorating the national honors, assign a distinguished place to the national high admiral, though he were the most stupid of men, and would utterly neglect the stranger Columbus. But in his own palace, and at his own table, he would perhaps invert this order of precedency, and would place Columbus at his own right hand.

Some such principle, as is here explained, did certainly prevail in the practice (whether consciously perceived or not in the philosophy) of that England, which extended through the sixteenth and seventeenth centuries. First, in the eighteenth century all honor to literature, under *any* relation, began to give way. And why? Because expanding politics, expanding partisanship, and expanding journalism, then first called into the field of literature an inferior class of laborers. Then first it was that, from the noblest of professions, literature became a trade. Literature it was that gave the first wound to literature; the hack scribbler it was that first degraded the lofty literary artist. For a century and a half we have lived under the shade of this fatal revolution. But, however painful such a state of things may be to the keen sensibilities of men pursuing the finest of vocations — carrying forward as inheritors from past generations the eternal chase after truth, and power, and beauty — still we must hold that the dishonor to literature has issued from internal sources proper to herself, and not from without. The nobility of England have, for three and a half centuries, personally practised literature as an elevated accomplishment: our royal and noble authors are numerous; and they would have continued the same cordial attentions to the literary body, had that body maintained the same honorable composition. But a *littérateur*, simply *as* such, it is no longer safe to distinguish with favor; once, but not now, he was liable to no misjudgment. Once he was pretty sure to be a man of some genius, or, at the least, of unusual scholarship. Now, on the contrary, a mob of traitors have mingled with the true men; and the loyal perish with the disloyal, because it is impossible in a mob, so vast and fluctuating, for the artillery of avenging scorn to select its victims.

All this, bitter in itself, has become *more* bitter from the contrast furnished by France. We know that literature has long been misappreciated amongst ourselves. In France it has long been otherwise appreciated — more advantageously appreciated. And we infer that therefore it is in France more wisely appreciated. But this does not follow. We have ever been of opinion that the valuation of literature in France, or at least of current literature, and as it shows itself in the treatment of literary men, is unsound, extravagant, and that it rests upon a basis originally false. Simply to have been the translator from the English of some prose book, a history or a memoir, neither requiring nor admitting any display of mastery over the resources of language, conferred, throughout the eighteenth century, so advantageous a position in society upon one whom we English should view as a literary scrub or mechanic drudge, that we really had a right to expect the laws of France and the court ceremonies to reflect this feature of public manners. Naturally, for instance, any man honored so preposterously ought in law to have enjoyed, in right of his book, the *jus trium liberorum*, and perpetual immunity from taxes. Or again, as regards ceremonial honors, on any fair scale of proportions, it was reasonable to expect that to any man who had gone into a fourth edition, the royal sentinels should present arms; that to the author of a successful tragedy, the guard should everywhere turn out; and that an epic poet, if ever such a difficult birth should make its epiphany in Paris, must look to have his approach towards a *soirée* announced by a salvo of a hundred and one guns.

Our space will not allow us to go into the illustrative details of this monstrous anomaly in French society. We confine ourselves to its cause — as sufficiently explaining why it is that no imitation of such absurdities can or ought to prosper in England. The same state of things, under a different modification, takes place in Germany; and from the very same cause. Is it not monstrous, or *was* it not until within recent days, to find every German city drawing the pedantic materials, and the pedantic interest of its staple conversation from the systems and the conflicts of a few rival academic professors? Generally these paramount lords of German conversation, that swayed its movements this way or that, as a lively breeze sways a cornfield, were metaphysicians; Fichte, for instance, and Hegel. These were the arid sands that bibulously absorbed all the perennial gushings of German enthusiasm. France of the last century and the modern Germany were, as to this point, on the same level of foolishness. But France had greatly the advantage in point of liberality. For general literature furnishes topics a thousand times more graceful and fitted to blend with social pleasure, than the sapless problems of ontological systems meant only for scholastic use.

But what then was the cause of this social deformity? Why was literature allowed eventually to disfigure itself by disturbing the natural currents of conversation, to make itself odious by usurpation, and thus virtually to operate as a mode of pedantry? It was because in neither land had the people any power of free discussion. It was because every question growing out of religion, or connecting itself with laws, or with government, or with governors, with political interests or political machineries, or with judicial courts, was an interdicted theme. The mind sought in despair for some free area wide enough to allow of boundless openings for individualities of sentiment — human enough to sustain the interests of festive discussion. That open area was found in books. In Paris to talk of politics was to talk of the king; *l'état c'est moi;* to talk of the king in any spirit of discussion, to talk of that *Jupiter optimus maximus*, from whom all fountains flowed of good and evil things, before whom stood the two golden urns, one filled with *lettres de cachet* — the other with crosses, pensions, offices, what was it but to dance on the margin of a volcano, or to swim cotillons in the suction of a maelstrom? Hence it was that literature became the only safe colloquial subject of a general nature in old France; hence it was that literature furnished the only 'open questions;' and hence it *is* that the mode and the expression of honor to literature in France has continued to this hour tainted with false and histrionic feeling, because originally it grew up from spurious roots, prospered unnaturally upon deep abuses in the system, and at this day (so far as it still lingers) memorializes the political bondage of the nation. Cleanse therefore — is our prayer — cleanse, oh, unknown Hercules, this Augéan stable of our English current literature, rich in dunghills, rich therefore in precipitate mushroom and fraudulent fungus, yet rich also (if we may utter our real thoughts) — rich pre-eminently at this hour in seed-plots of immortal growths, and in secret vegetations of volcanic strength; — cleanse it (oh coming man!) but not by turning through it any river of Lethe, such as for two centuries swept over the literature of France. Purifying waters were these in one sense; they banished the accumulated depositions of barbarism; they banished Gothic tastes; yes, but they did this by laying asleep the nobler activities of a great people, and reconciling them to forgetfulness of all which commanded them as duties, or whispered to them as rights.

If, therefore, the false homage of France towards literature still survives, it is no object for imitation amongst *us;* since it arose upon a vicious element in the social composition of that people. Partially it *does* survive, as we all know by the experience of the last twenty years, during which authors, and *as* authors (not like Mirabeau or Talleyrand in spite of authorship), have been transferred from libraries to senates and privy councils. This has done no service to literature, but, on the contrary, has degraded it by seducing the children of literature from their proper ambition. It is the glory of literature to rise as if on wings into an atmosphere nobler than that of political intrigue. And the whole result to French literature has been, — that some ten or twelve of the leading literati have been tempted away by bribes from their appropriate duties, while some five thousand have been made envious and discontented.

At this point, when warned suddenly that the hour-glass is running out, which measures our residuum of flying minutes, we first perceive on looking round, that we have actually been skirmishing with Mr. Forster, from the beginning of our paper to this very line; and thus we have left ourselves but a corner for the main purpose (to which our other purpose of 'argle-bargling' was altogether subordinate) of expressing emphatically our thanks to him for this successful labor of love in restoring a half-subverted statue to its upright position. We are satisfied that many thousands of readers will utter the same thanks to him, with equal fervor and with the same sincerity. Admiration for the versatile ability with which he has pursued his object is swallowed up for the moment in gratitude for his perfect success. It might have been imagined, that exquisite truth of household pathos, and of humor, with happy graces of style plastic as the air or the surface of a lake to the pure impulses of nature, sweeping them by the motions of her eternal breath, were qualities authorized to justify themselves before the hearts of men, in defiance of all that sickly scorn or the condescension of masquerading envy could avail for their disturbance. And so they are: and left to plead for themselves at such a bar as unbiassed human hearts, they could not have their natural influences intercepted. But in the case of Goldsmith, literary traditions have *not* left these qualities to their natural influences. It is a fact that up to this hour the contemporary falsehoods at Goldsmith's expense, and (worse perhaps than those falsehoods) the malicious constructions of incidents partly true, having wings lent to them by the levity and amusing gossip of Boswell, continue to obstruct the full ratification of Goldsmith's pretensions. To this hour the scorn from many of his own age, runs side by side with the misgiving sense of his real native power. A feeling still survives, originally derived from his own age, that the 'inspired idiot,' wherever he succeeded, ought *not* to have succeeded,—having owed his success to accident, or even to some inexplicable perverseness in running counter to his own nature. It was by shooting awry that he had hit the mark; and, when most he came near to the bull's eye, most of all 'by rights' he ought to have missed it. He had blundered into the Traveller, into Mr. Croaker, into Tony Lumkin; and not satisfied with such dreadful blunders as these, he had consummated his guilt by blundering into the Vicar of Wakefield, and the Deserted Village; atrocities over which, in effect, we are requested to drop the veil of human charity; since the more gem-like we may choose to think these works, the more unnatural, audacious, and indeed treasonable, it was in an idiot to produce them.

In this condition of Goldsmith's traditionary character, so injuriously disturbing to the natural effect of his inimitable works, (for in its own class each of his best works *is* inimitable,) Mr. Forster steps forward with a three-fold exposure of the falsehood inherent in the anecdotes upon which this traditional character has arisen. Some of these anecdotes he challenges as *literally* false; others as virtually so; they are true, perhaps, but under such a version of their circumstances as would altogether take out the sting of their offensive interpretation. For others again, and this is a profounder service, he furnishes a most just and philosophic explanation, that brings them at once within the reader's toleration, nay, sometimes within a deep reaction of pity. As a case, for instance, of downright falsehood, we may cite the well known story told by Boswell,—that, when Goldsmith travelled in France with some beautiful young English women (meaning the Miss Hornecks), he was seriously uneasy at the attentions which they received from the gallantry of Frenchmen, as intruding upon his own claims. Now this story, in logical phrase, proves too much. For the man who *could* have expressed such feelings in such a situation, must have been ripe for Bedlam. Coleridge mentions a man who entertained so exalted an opinion of himself, and of his own right to apotheosis, that he never uttered that great pronoun '*I*,' without solemnly taking off his hat. Even to the oblique case '*me*,' which no compositor ever honors with a capital *M*, and to the possessive pronoun *my* and *mine*, he held it a duty to kiss his hand. Yet this bedlamite would not have been a competitor with a lady for the attentions paid to her in right of her sex. In Goldsmith's case, the whole allegation was dissipated in the most decisive way. Some years after Goldsmith's death, one of the sisters personally concerned in the case, was unaffectedly shocked at the printed story when coming to her knowledge, as a gross calumny; her sorrow made it evident that the whole had been a malicious distortion of some light-hearted gaiety uttered by Goldsmith. There is little doubt that the story of the bloom-colored coat, and of the puppet-show, rose on a similar basis — the calumnious perversion of a jest.

But in other cases, where there really *may* have been some fretful expression of self-esteem, Mr. Forster's explanation transfers the foible to a truer and a more pathetic station. Goldsmith's own precipitancy, his overmastering defect in proper reserve, in self-control, and in presence of mind, falling in with the habitual undervaluation of many amongst his associates, placed him at a great disadvantage in animated conversation. His very truthfulness, his simplicity, his frankness, his hurry of feeling, all told against him. They betrayed him into inconsiderate expressions that lent a color of plausibility to the malicious ridicule of those who disliked him the more, from being compelled, after all, to respect him. His own understanding oftentimes sided with his disparagers. He *saw* that he had been in the wrong; whilst secretly he *felt* that his meaning — if properly explained — had been right. Defrauded in this way, and by his own co-operation, of distinctions that naturally belonged to him, he was driven unconsciously to attempt some restoration of the balance, by claiming for a moment distinctions to which he had no real pretensions. The whole was a trick of sorrow, and of sorrowing perplexity: he felt that no justice had been done to him, and that he himself had made an opening for the wrong: the result he saw, but the process he could not disentangle; and, in the confusion of his distress, natural irritation threw him upon blind efforts to recover his ground by unfounded claims, when claims so well founded had been maliciously disallowed.

But a day of accounting comes at last, — a day of rehearing for the cause, and of revision for the judgment. The longer this review has been delayed, the more impressive it becomes in the changes which it works. Welcome is the spectacle when, after three-fourths of a century have passed away, a writer — qualified for such a task, by ample knowledge of things and persons, by great powers for a comprehensive estimate of the case, and for a splendid exposition of its results, with deep sensibility to the merits of the man chiefly concerned in the issue, enthusiastic, but without partisanship — comes forward to unsettle false verdicts, to recombine misarranged circumstances, and to explain anew misinterpreted facts. Such a man wields the authority of heraldic marshals. Like the Otho of the Roman theatre, he has power to raise or to degrade — to give or to take away precedency. But, like this Otho, he has so much power, because he exercises it on known principles, and without caprice. To the man of true genius, like Goldsmith, when seating himself in humility on the lowest bench, he says, — 'Go thou up to a higher place. Seat thyself above those proud men, that once trampled thee in the dust. Be thy memorial upon earth, — not (as of some who scorned thee) "the whistling of a name." Be thou remembered amongst men by tears of tenderness, by happy laughter untainted with malice, and by the benedictions of those that, reverencing man's nature, see gladly its frailties brought within the gracious smile of human charity, and its nobilities levelled to the apprehension of simplicity and innocence.'

Over every grave, even though tenanted by guilt and shame, the human heart, when circumstantially made acquainted with its silent records of suffering or temptation, yearns in love or in forgiveness to breathe a solemn *Requiescat!* how much more, then, over the grave of a benefactor to the human race! But it is a natural feeling, with respect to such a prayer, that, however fervent and sincere, it has no perfect faith in its own validity, so long as any unsettled feud from ancient calumny hangs over the buried person. The undressed wrong seems to haunt the sepulchre in the shape of a perpetual disturbance to its rest. First of all, when this wrong has been adjudicated and expiated, is the *Requiescat* uttered with a perfect faith in itself. By a natural confusion we then transfer our own feelings to the occupant of the grave. The tranquillization to our own wounded sense of justice seems like an atonement to *his*: the peace for *us* transforms itself under a fiction of tenderness into a peace for *him*: the reconciliation between the world that did the wrong and the grave that seemed to suffer it, is accomplished; the reconciler, in such a case, whoever he may be, seems a double benefactor — to *him* that endured the injury — to *us* that resented it; and in the particular case now before the public, we shall all be ready to agree that this reconciling friend, who might have entitled his work *Vindiciæ Oliverianæ*, has, by the piety of his service to a man of exquisite genius, so long and so foully misrepresented, earned a right to interweave for ever his own cipher and cognisance in filial union with those of OLIVER GOLDSMITH.

NOTES.

NOTE 1. Page 101.

WE do not allude chiefly to his experience in childhood, when he is reported to have been a general butt of mockery for his ugliness and his supposed stupidity; since as regarded the latter reproach, he could not have suffered very long, having already at a childish age vindicated his intellectual place by the verses which opened to him an academic destination. We allude to his mature life, and the supercilious condescension with which even his reputed friends doled out their praises to *him*.

NOTE 2. Page 102.

We point this remark, not at Mr. Forster, who, upon the whole, shares our opinion as to the tolerable comfort of Goldsmith's life; he speaks indeed elsewhere of Goldsmith's depressions; but the question still remains — were they of frequent recurrence, and had they any constitutional settlement? We are inclined to say *no* in both cases.

NOTE 3. Page 105.

Which tub the reader may fancy to have been only an old tar barrel; if so, he is wrong. Isaac Casaubon, after severe researches into the nature of that tub, ascertained to the general satisfaction of Christendom that it was not of wood, or within the restorative powers of a cooper, but of earthenware, and once shattered by a horse's kick, quite past repair. In fact, it was a large oil jar, such as the remnant of the forty thieves lurked in, when waiting for their captain's signal from Ali Baba's house; and in Attica, it must have cost fifteen shillings, supposing that the philosopher did not steal it. Consequently a week's loss of house-room and credit to Oliver Goldsmith, at the rate of living then prevalent in Grub street, was pretty much the same thing in money value as the loss to Diogenes of his crockery house by burglary, or in any nocturnal lark of young Attic wine-bibbers. The underwriters would have done an insurance upon either man at pretty much the same premium.

Note 4. Page 108.

It may be necessary to explain, for the sake of the many persons who have come amongst the reading public since the period of the incident referred to, that this was a boy called Jones, who was continually entering Buckingham Palace clandestinely, was as regularly ejected by the police, but with respectable pertinacity constantly returned, and on one occasion effected a lodgment in the royal bedchamber. Some happy wit, in just admiration of such perseverance and impudence, christened him *In-I-go Jones.*

Note 5. Page 110.

Often, but not so uniformly (the reader will think) as the diction, because the manners are sometimes not those of the writer's own age, being ingenious adaptations to meet the modern writer's conjectural ideas of ancient manners. These, however, (even in Sir Walter Scott,) are precisely the most mouldering parts in the entire architecture, being always (as, for instance, in Ivanhoe) fantastic, caricatured, and betraying the true modern ground gleaming through the artificial tarnish of antiquity. All novels, in every language, are hurrying to decay; and hurrying by *internal* changes, were those all; but, in the meantime, the everlasting life and fertility of the human mind is for ever accelerating this hurry by *superseding* them, *i. e.* by an external change. Old forms, fading from the interest, or even from the apprehension, have no chance at all as against new forms embodying the same passions. It is only in the grander passions of poetry, allying themselves with forms more abstract and permanent, that such a conflict of the old with the new is possible.

Note 6. Page 116.

It ought, by this time, to be known equally amongst governments and philosophers — that for the State to promise with sincerity the absorption of surplus labor, as fast as it accumulates, cannot be postulated as a duty, until it can first be demonstrated as a possibility. This was forgotten, however, by Mr. C., whose vehement complaints, that the arable field, without a ploughman, should be in one county, whilst in another county was the stout ploughman without a field; and sometimes (which was worse still) that the surplus ploughmen should far outnumber the surplus fields, certainly proceeded on the secret assumption that all this was within the remedial powers of the state. The same doctrine was more openly avowed by various sections of our radicals, who (in their occasionally insolent petitions to parliament) many times asserted that one main use and function of a government was, to find work for everybody. At length (February and March, 1848) we see this doctrine solemnly adopted by a French body of rulers, self-appointed, indeed, or perhaps appointed by their wives, and so far sure, in a few weeks, to be answerable for nothing; but, on the other hand, adopting it as a practical *undertaking*, in the lawyer's sense, and by no means as a mere gaiety of rhetoric. Meantime, they themselves will be 'broken' before they will have had time for being reproached with broken promises; though neither fracture is likely to require much above the length of a quarantine.

Note 7. Page 117.

When writing this passage, we were not aware (as we now are) that Mr. Forster had himself noticed the case.

NOTE 8. Page 119.

His name began with A, and ended with N; there are but three more letters in the name, and if doubt arises upon our story, in the public mind, we shall publish them.

NOTE 9. Page 122.

If Addison died (as we think he did) in 1717, then because Goldsmith commenced authorship in 1757, there would be forty years between the two periods. But, as it would be fairer to measure from the centre of Addison's literary career, *i. e.* from 1707, the difference would be just half a century.

ALEXANDER POPE.*

Every great classic in our native language should from time to time be reviewed anew; and especially if he belongs in any considerable extent to that section of the literature which connects itself with manners; and if his reputation originally, or his style of composition, is likely to have been much influenced by the transient fashions of his own age. The withdrawal, for instance, from a dramatic poet, or a satirist, of any false lustre which he has owed to his momentary connection with what we may call the *personalities* of a fleeting generation, or of any undue shelter to his errors which may have gathered round them from political bias, or from intellectual infirmities amongst his partisans, will sometimes seriously modify, after a century or so, the fairest *original* appreciation of a fine writer. A window, composed of Claude Lorraine glasses, spreads over the landscape outside a disturbing effect, which not the most practised eye can evade. The *eidola theatri* affect us all. No man escapes the contagion from his contemporary bystanders. And the reader may see further

* The Works of Pope, by Roscoe.

on, that, had Pope been merely a satiric poet, he must in these times have laid down much of the splendor which surrounds him in our traditional estimate of his merit. Such a renunciation would be a forfeit — not always to errors in himself — but sometimes to errors in that stage of English society, which forced the ablest writer into a collusion with its own meretricious tastes. The antithetical prose 'characters,' as they were technically termed, which circulated amongst the aristocracy in the early part of the last century, the style of the dialogue in such comedy as was then popular, and much of the occasional poetry in that age, expose an immoderate craving for glittering effects from contrasts too harsh to be natural, too sudden to be durable, and too fantastic to be harmonious. To meet this vicious taste, from which (as from any diffusive taste) it is vain to look for *perfect* immunity in any writer lying immediately under its beams, Pope sacrificed, in *one* mode of composition, the simplicities of nature and sincerity; and had he practised no other mode, we repeat that *now* he must have descended from his pedestal. To some extent he is degraded even as it is; for the reader cannot avoid whispering to himself — what quality of thinking must *that* be which allies itself so naturally (as will be shown) with distortions of fact or of philosophic truth? But, had his whole writings been of that same cast, he must have been degraded altogether, and a star would have fallen from our English galaxy of poets.

We mention this particular case as a reason generally for renewing by intervals the examination of great writers, and liberating the verdict of their contemporaries from the casual disturbances to which every age is liable in its judgments, and in its tastes. As books multiply to an unmanageable excess, selection becomes more and more a necessity for readers, and the power of selection more and more a desperate problem for the busy part of readers. The possibility of selecting wisely is becoming continually more hopeless, as the necessity for selection is becoming continually more crying. Exactly as the growing weight of books overlays and stifles the power of comparison, *pari passu* is the call for comparison the more clamorous; and thus arises a duty correspondingly more urgent, of searching and revising until everything spurious has been weeded out from amongst the Flora of our highest literature; and until the waste of time for those who have so little at their command, is reduced to a *minimum*. For, where the good cannot be read in its twentieth part, the more requisite it is that no part of the bad should steal an hour of the available time; and it is not to be endured that people without a minute to spare, should be obliged first of all to read a book before they can ascertain whether it was at all *worth* reading. The public cannot read by proxy as regards the good which it is to appropriate, but it *can* as regards the poison which is to escape. And thus, as literature expands, becoming continually more of a household necessity, the duty resting upon critics (who are the vicarious readers for the public) becomes continually more urgent — of reviewing all works that may be supposed to have benefited too much or too indiscriminately by the superstition of a name. The *prægustatores* should have tasted of every cup, and reported its quality, before the public call for it; and, above all, they should have done this in all cases of the higher literature — that is, of literature properly so called.

What is it that we mean by *literature*? Popularly, and amongst the thoughtless, it is held to include everything that is printed in a book. Little logic is required to disturb *that* definition; the most thoughtless person is easily made aware that in the idea of *literature* one essential element is, — some relation to a general and common interest of man, so that what applies only to a local, or professional, or merely personal interest, even though presenting itself in the shape of a book, will not belong to literature. So far the definition is easily narrowed; and it is as easily expanded. For not only is much that takes a station in books not literature; but inversely, much that really *is* literature never reaches a station in books. The weekly sermons of Christendom, that vast pulpit literature which acts so extensively upon the popular mind — to warn, to uphold, to renew, to comfort, to alarm, does not attain the sanctuary of libraries in the ten thousandth part of its extent. The drama again, as for instance, the finest of Shakspeare's plays in England, and all leading Athenian plays in the noontide of the Attic stage, operated as a literature on the public mind, and were (according to the strictest letter of that term) *published* through the audiences that witnessed [1] their representation some time before they were published as things to be read; and they were published in this scenical mode of publication with much more effect than they could have had as books, during ages of costly copying or of costly printing.

Books, therefore, do not suggest an idea co-extensive and interchangeable with the idea of literature; since much literature, scenic, forensic, or didactic, (as from lecturers and public orators,) may never come into books; and much that *does* come into books, may connect itself with no literary interest. But a far more important correction, applicable to the common vague idea of literature, is to be sought — not so much in a better definition of literature, as in a sharper distinction of the two functions which it fulfils. In that great social organ, which collectively we call literature, there may be distinguished two separate offices that may blend and often *do* so, but capable severally of a severe insulation, and naturally fitted for reciprocal repulsion. There is first the literature of *knowledge*, and secondly, the literature of *power*. The function of the first is — to *teach;* the function of the second is — to *move:* the first is a rudder, the second an oar or a sail. The first speaks to the *mere* discursive understanding; the second speaks ultimately, it may happen, to the higher understanding or reason, but always *through* affections of pleasure and sympathy. Remotely, it may travel towards an object seated in what Lord Bacon calls *dry* light; but proximately it does and must operate, else it ceases to be a literature of *power*, on and through that *humid* light which clothes itself in the mists and glittering *iris* of human passions, desires, and genial emotions. Men have so little reflected on the higher functions of literature, as to find it a paradox if one should describe it as a mean or subordinate purpose of books to give information. But this is a paradox only in the sense which makes it honorable to be paradoxical. Whenever we talk in ordinary language of seeking information or gaining knowledge, we understand the words as connected with something of absolute novelty. But it is the grandeur of all truth which *can* occupy a very high place in human interests, that it is never absolutely novel to the meanest of minds: it exists eternally by way of germ or latent principle in the lowest as in the highest, needing to be developed but never to be planted. To be capable of transplantation is the immediate criterion of a truth that ranges on a lower scale. Besides which, there is a rarer thing than truth, namely, power or deep sympathy with truth. What is the effect, for instance, upon society, of children? By the pity, by the tenderness, and by the peculiar modes of admiration, which connect themselves with the helplessness, with the innocence, and with the simplicity of children, not only are the primal affections strengthened and continually renewed, but the qualities which are dearest in the sight of heaven — the frailty, for instance, which appeals to forbearance, the innocence which symbolizes the heavenly, and the simplicity which is most alien from the worldly, are kept up in perpetual remembrance, and their ideals are continually refreshed. A purpose of the same nature is answered by the higher literature, viz., the literature of power. What do you learn from Paradise Lost? Nothing at all. What do you learn from a cookery-book? Something new, something that you did not know before, in every paragraph. But would you therefore put the wretched cookery-book on a higher level of estimation than the divine poem? What you owe to Milton is not any knowledge, of which a million separate items are still but a million of advancing steps on the same earthly level; what you owe, is *power*, that is, exercise and expansion to your own latent capacity of sympathy with the infinite, where every pulse and each separate influx is a step upwards — a step ascending as upon a Jacob's ladder from earth to mysterious altitudes above the earth. *All* the steps of knowledge, from first to last, carry you further on the same plane, but could never raise you one foot above your ancient level of earth: whereas, the very *first* step in power is a flight — is an ascending into another element where earth is forgotten.

Were it not that human sensibilities are ventilated and continually called out into exercise by the great phenomena of infancy, or of real life as it moves through chance and change, or of literature as it recombines these elements in the mimicries of poetry, romance, &c., it is certain that, like any animal power or muscular energy falling into disuse, all such sensibilities would gradually droop and dwindle. It is in relation to these great *moral* capacities of man that the literature of power, as contradistinguished from that of knowledge, lives and has its field of action. It is concerned with what is highest in man: for the Scriptures themselves never condescended to deal by suggestion or co-operation, with the mere discursive understanding: when speaking of man in his intellectual capacity, the Scriptures speak not of the understanding, but of '*the understanding heart*,' — making the heart, *i. e.* the great *intuitive* (or non-discursive) organ, to be the interchangeable formula for man in his highest state of capacity for the infinite. Tragedy, romance, fairy tale, or epopee, all alike restore to man's mind the ideals of justice, of hope, of truth, of mercy, of retribution, which else (left to the support of daily life in its realities) would languish for want of sufficient illustration. What is meant, for instance, by *poetic justice?* — It does not mean a justice that differs by its object from the ordinary justice of human jurisprudence; for then it must be confessedly a very bad kind of justice; but it means a justice that differs from common forensic justice by the degree in which it *attains* its object, a justice that is more omnipotent over its own ends, as dealing — not with the refractory elements of earthly life — but with elements of its own creation, and with materials flexible to its own purest preconceptions. It is certain that, were it not for the literature of power, these ideals would often remain amongst us as mere arid national forms; whereas, by the creative forces of man put forth in literature, they gain a vernal life of restoration, and germinate into vital activities. The commonest novel by moving in alliance with human fears and hopes, with human instincts of wrong and right, sustains and quickens those affections. Calling them into action, it rescues them from torpor. And hence the preeminency over all authors that merely *teach*, of the meanest that *moves;* or that teaches, if at all, indirectly *by* moving. The very highest work that has ever existed in the literature of knowledge, is but a *provisional* work: a book upon trial and sufferance, and *quamdiu bene se gesserit.* Let its teaching be even partially revised, let it be but expanded, nay, even let its teaching be but placed in a better order, and instantly it is superseded. Whereas the feeblest works in the literature of power, surviving at all, survive as finished and unalterable amongst men. For instance, the *Principia* of Sir Isaac Newton was a book *militant* on earth from the first. In all stages of its progress it would have to fight for its existence: 1st, as regards absolute truth; 2dly, when that combat is over, as regards its form or mode of presenting the truth. And as soon as a La Place, or anybody else, builds higher upon the foundations laid by this book, effectually he throws it out of the sunshine into decay and darkness; by weapons won from this book he superannuates and destroys this book, so that soon the name of Newton remains, as a mere *nominis umbra*, but his book, as a living power, has transmigrated into other forms. Now, on the contrary, the Iliad, the Prometheus of Æschylus, — the Othello or King Lear, — the Hamlet or Macbeth, — and the Paradise Lost, are not militant but triumphant for ever as long as the languages exist in which they speak or can be taught to speak. They never *can* transmigrate into new incarnations. To reproduce *these* in new forms, or variations, even if in some things they should be improved, would be to plagiarize. A good steam-engine is properly superseded by a better. But one lovely pastoral valley is not superseded by another, nor a statue of Praxiteles by a statue of Michael Angelo. These things are not separated by imparity, but by disparity. They are not thought of as unequal under the same standard, but as different in *kind*, and as equal under a different standard. Human works of immortal beauty and works of nature in one respect stand on the same footing: they never absolutely repeat each other; never approach so near as not to differ; and they differ not as better and worse, or simply by more and less: they differ by undecipherable and incommunicable differences, that cannot be caught by mimicries, nor be reflected in the mirror of copies, nor become ponderable in the scales of vulgar comparison.

Applying these principles to Pope, as a representative of fine literature in general, we would wish to remark the claim which he has, or which any equal writer has, to the attention and jealous winnowing of those critics in particular who watch over public morals. Clergymen, and all the organs of public criticism put in motion by clergymen, are more especially concerned in the just appreciation of such writers, if the two canons are remembered, which we have endeavored to illustrate, viz., that all works in this class, as opposed to those in the literature of knowledge, 1st, work by far deeper agencies; and, 2dly, are more permanent; in the strictest sense they are κτήματα ἐς ἀεὶ: and what evil they do, or what good they do, is commensurate with the national language, sometimes long after the nation has departed. At this hour, five hundred years since their creation, the tales of Chaucer,[2] never equalled on this earth for their tenderness, and for life of picturesqueness, are read familiarly by many in the charming language of their natal day, and by others in the modernizations of

Dryden, of Pope, and Wordsworth. At this hour, one thousand eight hundred years since their creation, the Pagan tales of Ovid, never equalled on this earth for the gaiety of their movement and the capricious graces of their narrative, are read by all Christendom. This man's people and their monuments are dust: but *he* is alive: he has survived them, as he told us that he had it in his commission to do, by a thousand years; and *shall* a thousand more.'

All the literature of knowledge builds only ground-nests, that are swept away by floods, or confounded by the plough; but the literature of power builds nests in aërial altitudes of temples sacred from violation, or of forests inaccessible to fraud. *This* is a great prerogative of the *power* literature; and it is a greater which lies in the mode of its influence. The *knowledge* literature, like the fashion of this world, passeth away. An Encyclopædia is its abstract; and, in this respect, it may be taken for its speaking symbol — that, before one generation has passed, an Encyclopædia is superannuated; for it speaks through the dead memory and unimpassioned understanding, which have not the *rest* of higher faculties, but are continually enlarging and varying their phylacteries. But all literature, properly so called — literature *κατ᾽ ἐξοχήν*, for the very same reason that it is so much more durable than the literature of knowledge, is (and by the very same proportion it is) more intense and electrically searching in its impressions. The directions in which the tragedy of this planet has trained our human feelings to play, and the combinations into which the poetry of this planet has thrown our human passions of love and hatred, of admiration and contempt, exercise a power bad or good over human life, that cannot be contemplated, when stretching through many generations, without a sentiment allied to awe.[3] And of this let every one be assured — that he owes to the impassioned books which he has read, many a thousand more of emotions than he can consciously trace back to them. Dim by their origination, these emotions yet arise in him, and mould him through life like the forgotten incidents of childhood.

In making a revaluation of Pope as regards some of his principal works, we should have been glad to examine more closely than we shall be able to do, some popular errors affecting his whole intellectual position; and especially these two, *first*, That he belonged to what is idly called the *French* School of our literature; *secondly*, That he was specially distinguished from preceding poets by *correctness*. The first error has infected the whole criticism of Europe. The Schlegels, with all their false airs of subtlety, fall into this error in discussing every literature of Christendom. But, if by a mere accident of life any poet *had* first turned his thoughts into a particular channel on the suggestion of some French book, *that* would not justify our classing what belongs to universal nature, and what *inevitably* arises at a certain stage of social progress, under the category of a French creation. Somebody must have been first in point of time upon every field; but this casual precedency establishes no title whatever to authority, or plea of original dominion over fields that lie within the inevitable line of march upon which nations are moving. Had it happened that the first European writer on the higher geometry was a Græco-Sicilian, *that* would not have made it rational to call geometry the Græco-Sicilian Science. In *every* nation first comes the higher form of passion, next the lower. This is the mere order of nature in governing the movements of human intellect, as connected with social evolution; this is therefore the universal order, that in the earliest stages of literature, men deal with the great elementary grandeurs of passion, of conscience, of the will in self-conflict; they deal with the capital struggle of the human race in raising empires, or in overthrowing them — in vindicating their religion (as by crusades), or with the more mysterious struggles amongst spiritual races allied to our own, that have been dimly revealed to us. We have an Iliad, a Jerusalem Delivered, a Paradise Lost. These great subjects exhausted, or exhausted in their more inviting manifestations, inevitably by the mere endless motion of society, there succeeds a lower key of passion. Expanding social intercourse in towns, multiplied and crowded more and more, banishes those gloomier and grander phases of human history from literature. The understanding is quickened; the lower faculties of the mind — fancy, and the habit of minute distinction, are applied to the contemplation of society and manners. Passion begins to wheel in lower flights, and to combine itself with interests that in part are addressed to the insulated understanding — observing, refining, reflecting. This may be called the *minor* key of literature in opposition to the *major*, as cultivated by Shakspeare, Spenser, Milton. But this key arises spontaneously in *every* people, and by a necessity as sure as any that moulds the progress of civilization. Milton and Spenser were *not* of any Italian school. Their Italian studies were the result and not the cause of the determination given to their minds by nature working in conjunction with their social period. It is equally childish to say of Dryden and Pope, that they belonged to any French school. That thing which they did, they *would* have done though France had been at the back of China. The school to which they belonged, was a school developed at a certain stage of progress in all nations alike by the human heart as modified by the human understanding: it is a school depending on the peculiar direction given to the sensibilities by the reflecting faculty, and by the new phases of society. Even as a fact, (though a change as to the fact could not make any change at all in the philosophy of the case,) it is not true that either Dryden or Pope was influenced by French literature. Both of them had a very imperfect acquaintance with the French language. Dryden ridiculed French literature; and Pope, except for some purposes connected with his Homeric translations, read as little of it as convenience would allow. But, had this been otherwise, the philosophy of the case stands good; that, after the primary formations of the fermenting intellect, come everywhere — in Thebes or Athens, France or England, the secondary; that, after the creating passion comes the reflecting and recombining passion; that after the solemnities and cloistral grandeurs of life — solitary and self-conflicting, comes the recoil of a self-observing and self-dissecting stage, derived from life social and gregarious. After the

Iliad, but doubtless many generations after, comes a Batrachomyomachia: after the gorgeous masque of our forefathers came always the anti-masque, that threw off echoes as from some devil's laughter in mockery of the hollow and transitory pomps that went before.

It is an error equally gross, and an error in which Pope himself participated, that his plume of distinction from preceding poets consisted in *correctness*. Correctness in what? Think of the admirable qualifications for settling the scale of such critical distinctions which that man must have had who turned out upon this vast world the single oracular word 'correctness' to shift for itself, and explain its own meaning to all generations. Did he mean logical correctness in maturing and connecting thoughts? But of all poets that have practised reasoning in verse, Pope is the one most inconsequential in the deduction of his thoughts, and the most severely distressed in any effort to effect or to explain the dependency of their parts. There are not ten consecutive lines in Pope unaffected by this infirmity. All his thinking proceeded by insulated and discontinuous jets; and the only resource for *him*, or chance of even seeming correctness, lay in the liberty of stringing his aphoristic thoughts like pearls, having no relation to each other but that of contiguity. To *set* them like diamonds was for Pope to risk distraction; to systematize was ruin. On the other hand, if this elliptical word *correctness* is to be understood with such a complimentary qualification as would restrict it to Pope's use of *language*, that construction is even more untenable than the other — more conspicuously untenable — for many are they who have erred by illogical thinking, or by distracted evolution of thoughts: but rare is the man amongst classical writers in any language who has disfigured his meaning more remarkably than Pope by imperfect expression. We do not speak of plebeian phrases, of exotic phrases, of slang, from which Pope was not free, though *more* free than many of his contemporaries. From vulgarism indeed he was shielded, though imperfectly, by the aristocratic society he kept: *they* being right, *he* was right: and he erred only in the cases where they misled him; for even the refinement of that age was oftentimes coarse and vulgar. His grammar, indeed, is often vicious: preterites and participles he constantly confounds, and registers this class of blunders for ever by the cast-iron index of rhymes that never *can* mend. But worse than this mode of viciousness is his syntax, which is so bad as to darken his meaning at times, and at other times to defeat it. But these were errors cleaving to his times; and it would be unfair to exact from Pope a better quality of diction than belonged to his contemporaries. Still it is indisputable that a better model of diction and of grammar prevailed a century before Pope. In Spenser, in Shakspeare, in the Bible of King James's reign, and in Milton, there are very few grammatical errors.[4] But Pope's defect in language was almost peculiar to himself. It lay in an inability, nursed doubtless by indolence, to carry out and perfect the expression of the thought he wishes to communicate. The language does not realize the idea: it simply suggests or hints it. Thus, to give a single illustration: —

'Know, God and Nature only are the same:
In man the judgment shoots at flying game.'

The first line one would naturally construe into this: that God and Nature were in harmony, whilst all other objects were scattered into incoherency by difference and disunion. Not at all; it means nothing of the kind; but that God and Nature only are exempted from the infirmities of change. *They* only continue uniform and self-consistent. This might mislead many readers; but the second line *must* do so: for who would not understand the syntax to be, that the judgment, as it exists in man, shoots at flying game? But, in fact, the meaning is, that the judgment, in aiming its calculations at man, aims at an object that is still on the wing, and never for a moment stationary. We give this as a specimen of a fault in diction, the very worst amongst all that are possible; to write bad grammar or colloquial slang does not necessarily obscure the sense; but a fault like this is a treachery, and hides the true meaning under the cloud of a conundrum: nay worse; for even a conundrum has fixed conditions for determining its solution, but this sort of mutilated expression is left to the solutions of conjecture.

There are endless varieties of this fault in Pope, by which he sought relief for himself from half-an-hour's labor, at the price of utter darkness to his reader.

One editor distinguishes amongst the epistles that which Pope addressed to Lord Oxford some years after his fall, as about the most '*correct*, musical, dignified, and affecting' that the poet has left. Now, even as a specimen of vernacular English, it is conspicuously bad: the shocking gallicism, for instance, of '*attend*,' for 'wait his leisure,' in the line 'For *him*, *i. e.* on his behalf, thou oft hast bid the world attend,' would alone degrade the verses. To bid the world attend — is to bid the world listen attentively; whereas what Pope means is, that Lord Oxford bade the world wait in his ante-chamber, until he had leisure from his important conferences with a poet, to throw a glance upon affairs so trivial as those of the human race. This use of the word *attend* is a shocking violation of the English idiom; and even the slightest would be an unpardonable blemish in a poem of only forty lines, which ought to be polished as exquisitely as a cameo. It is a still worse disfiguration of the very same class, viz. a silent confession of defeat, in a regular wrestling match with the difficulties of a metrical expression, that the poem terminates thus —

'Nor fears to tell that *Mortimer* is he;'

why *should* he fear? Really there is no very desperate courage required for telling the most horrible of secrets about Mortimer. Had Mortimer even been so wicked as to set the Thames on fire, safely it might have been published by Mortimer's bosom friend to all magistrates, sheriffs and constables; for not a man of them would have guessed in what hiding-place to look for Mortimer, or who Mortimer might be. True it is, that a secondary earldom, conferred by Queen Anne upon Robert Harley, was that of Mortimer; but it lurked unknown to the public ear; it was a coronet that lay hid under the beams of *Oxford* — a title so long familiar to English ears, when descending through six-and-twenty generations of de Veres. Quite as reasonable it would be in a birth-day ode to the Prince of Wales, if he were addressed as my Lord of Chester, or Baron of Renfrew, or your Grace of Cornwall. To express a thing in cipher may do for a conspirator; but a poet's *correctness* is shown in his intelligibility.

Amongst the early poems of Pope, the 'ELOISA TO ABELARD' has a special interest of a double order: first, it has a *personal* interest as the poem of Pope, because indicating the original destination of Pope's intellect, and the strength of his native vocation to a class of poetry in deeper keys of passion than any which he systematically cultivated. For itself also, and abstracting from its connection with Pope's natural destination, this poem has a *second* interest, an intrinsic interest, that will always make it dear to impassioned minds. The self-conflict — the flux and reflux of the poor agitated heart — the spectacle of Eloisa now bending penitentially before the shadowy austerities of a monastic future, now raving upon the remembrances of the guilty past — one moment reconciled by the very anguish of her soul to the grandeurs of religion and of prostrate adoration, the next moment revolting to perilous retrospects of her treacherous happiness — the recognition by shining gleams through the very storm and darkness evoked by her earthly sensibilities, of a sensibility deeper far in its ground, and that trembled towards holier objects — the lyrical tumult of the changes, the hope, the tears, the rapture, the penitence, the despair — place the reader in tumultuous sympathy with the poor distracted nun.

Exquisitely imagined, among the passages towards the end, is the introduction of a voice speaking to Eloisa from the grave of some sister nun, that, in long-forgotten years, once had struggled and suffered like herself,

> 'Once (like herself) that trembled, wept, and prayed,
> Love's victim then, though now a sainted maid.'

Exquisite is the passage in which she prefigures a visit yet to come from Abelard to herself — no more in the character of a lover, but as a priest, ministering by spiritual consolations to her dying hours, pointing her thoughts to heaven, presenting the Cross to her through the mists of death, and fighting for her as a spiritual ally against the torments of flesh. That anticipation was not gratified. Abelard died long before her; and the hour never arrived for *him* of which with such tenderness she says, —

> 'It will be *then* no crime to gaze on me.'

But another anticipation *has* been fulfilled in a degree that she could hardly have contemplated; the anticipation, namely, —

> 'That ages hence, when all her woes were o'er,
> And that rebellious heart should beat no more,'

wandering feet should be attracted from afar

> 'To Paraclete's white walls and silver springs,'

as the common resting-place and everlasting marriage-bed of Abelard and Eloisa; that the eyes of many that had been touched by their story, by the memory of their extraordinary accomplishments in an age of darkness, and by the calamitous issue of their attachment, should seek, first and last, for the grave in which the lovers trusted to meet again in peace; and should seek it with interest so absorbing, that even amidst the ascent of hosannahs from the choir, amidst the grandeurs of high mass, the raising of the host, and 'the pomp of dreadful sacrifice,' sometimes these wandering eyes should steal aside to the solemn abiding-place of Abelard and his Eloisa, offering so pathetic a contrast, by its peaceful silence, to the agitations of their lives; and that there, amidst thoughts which by right were all due and dedicated

'to heaven,
One *human* tear should drop and be forgiven.'

We may properly close this subject of Abelard and Eloisa, by citing, in English, the solemn Latin inscription placed in the last century, six hundred years after their departure from earth, over their common remains. They were buried in the same grave, Abelard dying first by a few weeks more than twenty-one years; his tomb was opened again to admit the coffin of Eloisa; and the tradition at Quincey, the parish near Nogent-sur-Seine, in which the monastery of the Paraclete is situated, was, that at the moment of interment Abelard opened his arms to receive the impassioned creature that once had loved *him* so frantically, and whom *he* had loved with a remorse so memorable. The epitaph is singularly solemn in its brief simplicity, considering that it came from Paris, and from academic wits: 'Here, under the same marble slab, lie the founder of this monastery, Peter

Abelard, and its earliest Abbess, Heloisa — once united in studies, in love, in their unhappy nuptial engagements, and in penitential sorrow; but now, our hope is, reünited for ever in bless.'

The Satires of Pope, and what under another name *are* satires, viz. his Moral Epistles, offer a second variety of evidence to his voluptuous indolence. They offend against philosophic truth more heavily than the Essay on Man; but not in the same way. The Essay on Man sins chiefly by want of central principle, and by want therefore of all coherency amongst the separate thoughts. But taken *as* separate thoughts, viewed in the light of fragments and brilliant aphorisms, the majority of the passages have a mode of truth; not of truth central and coherent, but of truth angular and splintered. The Satires, on the other hand, were of false origin. They arose in a sense of talent for caustic effects, unsupported by any satiric heart. Pope had neither the malice (except in the most fugitive form) which thirsts for leaving wounds, nor, on the other hand, the deep moral indignation which burns in men whom Providence has from time to time armed with scourges for cleansing the sanctuaries of truth or justice. He was contented enough with society as he found it: bad it might be, but it was good enough for *him:* and it was the merest self-delusion if at any moment the instinct of glorying his satiric mission (the *magnificabo apostolatum meum*) persuaded him that in *his* case it might be said — *Facit indignatio versum.* The indignation of Juvenal was not always very noble in its origin, or pure in its purpose: it was sometimes mean in its quality, false in its direction, extravagant in its expression: but it was tremendous in the roll of its thunders, and as withering as the scowl of a Mephistopheles. Pope having no such internal principle of wrath boiling in his breast, being really (if one must speak the truth) in the most pacific and charitable frame of mind towards all scoundrels whatever, except such as might take it into their heads to injure a particular Twickenham grotto, was unavoidably a hypocrite of the first magnitude when he affected (or sometimes really conceited himself) to be in a dreadful passion with offenders as a body. It provokes fits of laughter, in a man who knows Pope's real nature, to watch him in the process of brewing the storm that spontaneously will not come; whistling, like a mariner, for a wind to fill his satiric sails; and pumping up into his face hideous grimaces in order to appear convulsed with histrionic rage. Pope should have been counselled never to write satire, except on those evenings when he was suffering horribly from indigestion. By this means the indignation would have been ready-made. The rancor against all mankind would have been sincere; and there would have needed to be no extra expense in getting up the steam. As it is, the short puffs of anger, the uneasy snorts of fury in Pope's satires, give one painfully the feeling of a steam-engine with unsound lungs. Passion of any kind may become in some degree ludicrous, when disproportioned to its exciting occasions. But it is never entirely ludicrous, until it is self-betrayed as counterfeit. Sudden collapses of the manufactured wrath, sudden oblivion of the criminal, announce Pope's as *always* counterfeit.

Meantime insincerity is contagious. One falsehood

draws on another. And having begun by taking a station of moral censorship, which was in the uttermost degree a self-delusion, Pope went on to other self-delusions in reading history the most familiar, or in reporting facts the most notorious. Warburton had more to do with Pope's satires as an original suggester,[5] and not merely as a commentator, than with any other section of his works. Pope and he hunted in couples over this field: and those who know the absolute craziness of Warburton's mind, the perfect frenzy and *lymphaticus error* which possessed him for leaving all high-roads of truth and simplicity, in order to trespass over hedge and ditch after coveys of shy paradoxes, cannot be surprised that Pope's good sense should often have quitted him under such guidance.——There is, amongst the earliest poems of Wordsworth, one which has interested many readers by its mixed strain of humor and tenderness. It describes two thieves who act in concert with each other. One is a very aged man, and the other is his great-grandson of three years old:

> 'There are ninety good years of fair and foul weather
> Between them, and both go a stealing together.'

What reconciles the reader to this social iniquity, is the imperfect accountability of the parties; the one being far advanced in dotage, and the other an infant. And thus

> 'Into what sin soever the couple may fall,
> *This* child but half-knows it, and *that* not at all.'

Nobody besides suffers from their propensities: since the child's mother makes good in excess all their depredations ; and nobody is duped for an instant by their gross attempts at fraud ; for

> 'Wherever they carry their plots and their wiles,
> Every face in the village is dimpled with smiles.'

There was not the same disparity of years between Pope and Warburton as between old Daniel and his descendant in the third generation: Warburton was but ten years younger. And there was also this difference, that in the case of the two thieves neither was official ringleader: on the contrary, they took it turn about; great-grandpapa was ringleader to day, and the little great-grandson to-morrow :

> 'Each in his turn was both leader and led :'

whereas, in the connection of the two literary accomplices, the Doctor was latterly always the instigator to any outrage on good sense ; and Pope, from mere habit of deference to the Doctor's theology and theological wig, as well as from gratitude for the Doctor's pugnacity in his defence, (since Warburton really was as good as a bull-dog in protecting Pope's advance or retreat,) followed with docility the leading of his reverend friend into any excess of folly. It is true, that oftentimes in earlier days Pope had run into scrapes from his own heedlessness: and the Doctor had not the merit of suggesting the *escapade*, but only of defending it ; which he always does (as sailors express it) 'with a will:' for he never shows his teeth so much, or growls so ferociously, as when he suspects the case to be desperate. But in the satires, although the original absurdity comes forward in the text of Pope, and the Warburtonian note in defence is a pparently no more than an afterthought of the good Doctor, in his usual style of threatening to cudgel anybody who disputes his friend's assertion; yet sometimes the thought expressed and adorned by the poet had been prompted by the divine. This only can account for the savage crotchets, paradoxes, and conceits, which disfigure Pope's later edition of his satires.

Truth, even of the most appreciable order, truth of history, goes to wreck continually under the perversities of Pope's satire applied to celebrated men; and as to the higher truth of philosophy, it was still less likely to survive amongst the struggles for striking effects and startling contrasts. But worse are Pope's satiric sketches of women, as carrying the same outrages on good sense to a far greater excess; and as these expose the false principles on which he worked more brightly, and have really been the chief ground of tainting Pope's memory with the reputation of a woman-hater, (which he was *not*,) they are worthy of separate notice.

It is painful to follow a man of genius through a succession of inanities descending into absolute nonsense, and of vulgarities sometimes terminating in brutalities. These are harsh words, but not harsh enough by half as applied to Pope's gallery of female portraits. What is the key to his failure? It is simply that, throughout this whole satiric section, not one word is spoken in sincerity of heart, or with any vestige of self-belief. The case was one of those so often witnessed, where either the indiscretion of friends, or some impulse of erring vanity in the writer, had put him upon undertaking a task in which he had too little natural interest to have either thought upon it with originality, or observed upon it with fidelity. Sometimes the mere coercion of system drives a man into such a folly. He treats a subject which branches into A, B, and C. Having discussed A and B, upon which he really *had* something to offer, he thinks it necessary to integrate his work by going forward to C, on which he knows nothing at all, and, what is even worse, for which in his heart he cares nothing at all. Fatal is all falsehood. Nothing is so sure to betray a man into the abject degradation of self-exposure as pretending to a knowledge which he has not, or to an enthusiasm which is counterfeit. By whatever mistake Pope found himself pledged to write upon the characters of women, it was singularly unfortunate that he had begun by denying to women any characters at all.

'Matter too soft a lasting mark to bear,
And best distinguished by black, brown, or fair.'

Well for *him* if he had stuck to that liberal doctrine: 'Least said, soonest mended.' And *much* he could not easily have said upon a subject that he had pronounced all but a nonentity. In Van Troil's work, or in Horrebow's, upon Iceland, there is a well known chapter regularly booked in the index — *Concerning the Snakes of Iceland.* This is the title, the running rubric; and the body of the chapter consists of these words — 'There *are* no snakes in Iceland.' That chapter is soon studied, and furnishes very little opening for foot-notes or supplements. Some people have thought that Mr. Van T. might with advantage have amputated this unsnaky chapter on snakes; but at least nobody can accuse him of forgetting his own extermination of snakes from Iceland, and proceeding immediately to describe such horrible snakes as eye had never beheld amongst the afflictions of the island. Snakes there are none, he had protested; and, true to his word, the faithful man never wanders into any description of Icelandic snakes. Not so our satiric poet. He, with Mahometan liberality, had denied characters, *i. e.* souls, to women. 'Most women,' he says, 'have no character at all;'[6] yet, for all that, finding himself pledged to treat this very subject of female characters, he introduces us to a museum of monsters in that department, such as few fancies could create, and no logic can rationally explain. What was he to do? He had entered upon a theme concerning which, as the result has shown, he had not one solitary thought — good, bad, or indifferent. Total bankruptcy was impending. Yet he was aware of a deep interest connected with this section of his satires; and, to meet this interest, he invented what was pungent, when he found nothing to record which was true.

It is a consequence of this desperate resource — this plunge into absolute fiction — that the true objection to Pope's satiric sketches of the other sex ought not to arise amongst women, as the people that suffered by his malice, but amongst readers generally, as the people that suffered by his fraud. He has promised one thing, and done another. He has promised a chapter in the zoology of nature, and he gives us a chapter in the fabulous zoology of the herald's college. A tigress is not much within ordinary experience, still there *is* such a creature; and in default of a better choice, that is, of a choice settling on a more familiar object, we are content to accept a good description of a tigress. We are reconciled; but we are *not* reconciled to a description, however spirited, of a basilisk. A viper might do; but not, if you please, a dragoness or a harpy. The describer knows, as well as any of us the spectators know, that he is romancing; the *incredulus odi* overmasters us all; and we cannot submit to be detained by a picture which, according to the shifting humor of the poet, angry or laughing, is a lie where it is not a jest, is an affront to the truth of nature, where it is not confessedly an extravagance of drollery. In a playful fiction, we can submit with pleasure to the most enormous exaggerations; but then they must be offered as such. These of Pope's are not *so* offered, but as serious portraits; and in that character they affect us as odious and malignant libels. The malignity was not real, — as indeed nothing was real, but a condiment for hiding insipidity. Let us examine two or three of them, equally with a view to the possibility of the object described, and to the delicacy of the description.

'How soft is Silia! fearful to offend;
The frail one's advocate, the weak one's friend.
To *her* Calista proved her conduct nice;
And good Simplicius asks of *her* advice.'

Here we have the general outline of Silia's character; not particularly striking, but intelligible. She has a suavity of disposition that accommodates itself to all infirmities. And the worst thing one apprehends in her is — falseness: people with such honeyed breath for *present* frailties, are apt to exhale their rancor upon them when a little out of hearing. But really now this is no foible of Silia's. One likes her very well, and would be glad of her company to tea. For the dramatic reader knows who Calista is; and if Silia has indulgence for *her*, she must be a thoroughly tolerant creature. Where is her fault, then? You shall hear —

> 'Sudden she storms! she raves! — You tip the wink;
> But spare your censure; Silia does *not* drink.
> All eyes may see from what the change arose:
> All eyes may see — (see what?) — a pimple on her nose.'

Silia, the dulcet, is suddenly transformed into Silia the fury. But why? The guest replies to that question by *winking* at his fellow-guest; which most atrocious of vulgarities is expressed by the most odiously vulgar of phrases — he *tips* the wink — meaning to tip an insinuation that Silia is intoxicated. Not so, says the poet — drinking is no fault of hers — everybody may see [why not the winker then?] that what upsets her temper is a pimple on the nose. Let us understand you, Mr. Pope. A pimple! — what, do you mean to say that pimples jump up on ladies' faces at the unfurling of a fan? If they really *did* so in the 12th of George II., and a lady, not having a pimple on leaving her dressing-room, might grow one whilst taking tea, then we think that a saint might be excused for storming a little. But how is it that the wretch who winks, does *not* see the pimple, the *causa teterrima* of the sudden wrath; and Silia, who has no looking-glass at her girdle, *does*? And then who is it that Silia 'storms' at — the company, or the pimple? If at the company, we cannot defend her; but if at the pimple — oh, by all means — storm and welcome — she can't say anything worse than it deserves. Wrong or right, however, what moral does Silia illustrate more profound than this — that a particular lady, otherwise very amiable, falls into a passion upon suddenly finding her face disfigured? But then one remembers the song — '*My face is my fortune, sir, she said, sir, she said*' — it is a part of *every* woman's fortune, so long as she is young. Now to find one's fortune dilapidating by changes so rapid as this — pimples rising as suddenly as April clouds — is far too trying a calamity, that a little fretfulness should merit either reproach or sneer. Dr. Johnson's opinion was, that the man who cared little for dinner, could not be reasonably supposed to care much for anything. More truly it may be said, that the woman who is reckless about her face must be an unsafe person to trust with a secret. But seriously, what moral, what philosophic thought can be exemplified by a case so insipid, and so imperfectly explained as this? But we must move on.

Next, then, let us come to the case of Narcissa: —

> 'Odious! in *woollen?*[7] 'Twould a saint provoke,'
> Were the last words that poor Narcissa spoke.
> 'No, let a charming chintz and Brussels lace
> Wrap my cold limbs and shade my lifeless face;
> One would not sure be frightful when one's dead:
> And, Betty, give this cheek a little red.'

Well, what's the matter now? What's amiss with Narcissa, that a satirist must be called in to hold an inquest upon her corpse, and take Betty's evidence against her mistress? Upon hearing any such question, Pope would have started up in the character (very unusual with *him*) of religious censor, and demanded whether one approved of a woman's fixing her last dying thought upon the attractions of a person so soon to dwell with darkness and worms? Was *that* right — to provide for coquetting in her coffin? Why no, not strictly right, its impropriety cannot be denied; but what strikes one even more is, the suspicion that it may be a lie. Be this as it may, there are two insurmountable objections to the case of Narcissa, even supposing it not fictitious — viz. first, that so far as it offends at all, it offends the religious sense, and not any sense of which satire takes charge; secondly, that without reference to the special functions of satire, *any* form of poetry whatever, or *any* mode of moral censure, concerns itself not at all with anomalies. If the anecdote of Narcissa were other than a fiction, then it was a case too peculiar and idiosyncratic to furnish a poetic illustration; neither moral philosophy nor poetry condescends to the monstrous or the abnormal; both one and the other deal with the catholic and the representative.

There is another *Narcissa* amongst Pope's tulip-beds of ladies, who is even more open to criticism — because offering not so much an anomaly in one single trait of her character, as an utter anarchy in all. *Flavia* and *Philomedé* again present the same multitude of features with the same absence of all central principle for locking them into unity. They must have been distracting to themselves; and they are distracting to us a century later. *Philomedé*, by the way, stands for the second Duchess of Marlborough,[7] daughter of the great Duke. And these names lead us naturally to Sarah, the original, and (one may call her) the *historical* Duchess, who is libelled under the name of *Atossa.* This character amongst all Pope's satiric sketches has been celebrated the most, with the single exception of his *Atticus.* But the *Atticus* rested upon a different basis — it was true; and it was noble. Addison really *had* the infirmities of envious jealousy, of stimulated friendship, and of treacherous collusion with his friend's enemies — which Pope imputed to him under the happy parisyllabic name of Atticus; and the mode of imputation, the tone of expostulation — indignant as regarded Pope's own injuries, but yet full of respect for Addison, and even of sorrowful tenderness; all this in combination with the interest attached to a feud between two men so eminent, has sustained the *Atticus* as a classic remembrance in satiric literature. But the *Atossa* is a mere chaos of incompatibilities, thrown together as into some witch's cauldron. The witch, however, had sometimes an unaffected malignity, a sincerity of venom in her wrath, which acted chemically as a solvent for combining the hetorogeneous ingredients in her kettle; whereas the want of truth and earnestness in Pope leave the incongruities in his kettle of description to their natural incoherent operation on the reader. We have a great love for the great Duchess of Marlborough, though too young by a hundred years[8] or so to have been that true and faithful friend which, as contemporaries, we *might* have been.

What we love Sarah for, is partly that she has been

ill used by all subsequent authors, one copying from another a fury against her which even in the first of these authors was not real. And a second thing which we love is her very violence, qualified as it was. Sulphureous vapors of wrath rose up in columns from the crater of her tempestuous nature against him that *deeply* offended her, but she neglected petty wrongs. Wait, however, let the volcanic lava have time to cool, and all returned to absolute repose. It has been said that she did not write her own book. We are of a different opinion. The mutilations of the book were from other and inferior hands: but the main texture of the narrative and of the comments were, and must have been, from herself, since there could have been no adequate motive for altering them, and nobody else could have had the same motive for uttering them. It is singular that, in the case of the Duchess, as well as that of the Lady M. W. Montagu, the same two men, without concert, were the original aggressors amongst the *gens de plume*, viz. Pope, and subsequently Horace Walpole. Pope suffered more from his own libellous assault upon *Atossa*, through a calumny against himself rebounding from it, than *Atossa* could have done from the point-blank shot of fifty such batteries. The calumny circulated was, that he had been bribed by the Duchess with a thousand pounds to suppress the character — which of itself was bad enough; but as the consummation of baseness it was added, that after all, in spite of the bribe, he caused it to be published. This calumny we believe to have been utterly without foundation. It is repelled by Pope's character, incapable of any act so vile, and by his position, needing no bribes. But what we wish to add is, that the calumny is equally repelled by Sarah's character, incapable of any propitiation so abject. Pope wanted no thousand pounds; but neither did Sarah want his clemency. *He* would have rejected the £1000 cheque with scorn; but *she* would have scorned to offer it. Pope cared little for Sarah; but Sarah cared less for Pope.

What *is* offensive, and truly so, to every generous reader, may be expressed in two items: first, not pretending to have been himself injured by the Duchess, Pope was in this instance meanly adopting some third person's malice, which sort of intrusion into other people's quarrels is a sycophantic act, even where it may not have rested upon a sycophantic motive; secondly, that even as a second-hand malice it is not sincere. More shocking than the malice is the self-imposture of the malice: in the very act of puffing out his cheeks like Æolus, with ebullient fury, and conceiting himself to be in a passion perfectly diabolic, Pope is really unmoved, or angry only by favor of dyspepsy; and at a word of kind flattery from Sarah, (whom he was quite the man to love,) though not at the clink of her thousand guineas, he would have fallen at her feet, and kissed her beautiful hand with rapture. To enter a house of hatred as a junior partner, and to take the stock of malice at a valuation — (we copy from advertisements) — *that* is an ignoble act. But then how much worse in the midst of all this unprovoked wrath, real as regards the persecution which it meditates, but false as the flatteries of a slave in relation to its pretended grounds, for the spectator to find its malice counterfeit, and the fury only a plagiarism from some personated fury in an opera.

There is no truth in Pope's satiric sketches of women — not even colorable truth; but if there were, how frivolous, how hollow, to erect into solemn monumental protestations against the whole female sex what, if examined, turn out to be pure casual eccentricities, or else personal idiosyncrasies, or else foibles shockingly caricatured, but, above all, to be such foibles as could not have connected themselves with *sincere* feelings of indignation in any rational mind.

The length and breadth [almost we might say — the *depth*] of the shallowness, which characterizes Pope's Philosophy, cannot be better reflected than from the four well known lines —

> 'For modes of faith let graceless zealots fight,
> *His* can't be wrong, whose life is in the right:
> For forms of government let fools contest,
> Whate'er is best administered is best.'

In the first couplet, what Pope says is, that a life, which is irreproachable on a *human* scale of appreciation, neutralizes and practically cancels all possible errors of creed, opinion, or theory. But this schism between the moral life of man and his moral faith, which takes for granted that either may possibly be true, whilst the other is entirely false, can wear a moment's plausibility only by understanding *life* in so limited a sense as the sum of a man's external actions, appreciable by man. He whose life is in the right, cannot, says Pope, in any sense calling for blame, have a wrong faith; that is, if his life *were* right, his creed might be disregarded. But the answer is — that his life, according to any adequate idea of life in a moral creature, *cannot* be in the right unless in so far as it bends to the influences of a true faith. How feeble a conception must that man have of the infinity which lurks in a human spirit, who can persuade himself that its total capacities of life are exhaustible by the few gross *acts* incident to social relations or open to human valuation! An act, which may be necessarily limited and without opening for variety, may involve a large variety of motives — motives again, meaning grounds of action that are distinctly recognised for such, may (numerically speaking) amount to nothing at all when compared with the absolutely infinite influxes of feeling or combinations of feeling that vary the thoughts of man; and the true internal *acts* of moral man are his thoughts — his yearnings — his aspirations — his sympathies — his repulsions of heart. This is the life of man as it is appreciable by heavenly eyes. The scale of an alphabet — how narrow is that! Four or six and twenty letters, and all is finished. Syllables range through a wider compass. Words are yet more than syllables. But what are words to thoughts? Every word has a thought corresponding to it, so that not by so much as one solitary counter can the words outrun the thoughts. But every thought has *not* a word corresponding to it: so that the thoughts may outrun the words by many a thousand counters. In a developed nature they *do* so. But what are the thoughts when set against the modifications of thoughts by feelings, hidden even from him that feels them — or against the inter-combinations of such modifications with others — complex with complex, decomplex with decomplex — these can be unravelled by no human eye! This is the infinite music that God only can read upon the vast harp of the human heart. Some have fancied that musical combinations might be exhausted. A new Mozart might be impossible. All that he could do, might already have been done. Music laughs at *that,* as the sea laughs at palsy for its billows, as the morning laughs at old age and wrinkles for itself. But a harp, though a world in itself, is but a narrow world by comparison with the world of a human heart.

Now these thoughts, tinctured subtly with the perfume and coloring of human affections, make up the sum of what merits κατ' ἐξοχην the name of *life:* and these in a vast proportion depend for their possibilities of truth upon the degree of approach which the thinker makes to the appropriation of a pure faith. A man is thinking all day long, and putting thoughts into words: he is acting comparatively seldom. But are any man's thoughts brought into conformity with the openings to truth that a faith like the Christian's faith suggests? Far from it. Probably there never was one thought, from the foundation of the earth, that has passed through the mind of man, which did not offer some blemish, some sorrowful shadow of pollution, when it came up for review before a heavenly tribunal: that is, supposing it a thought entangled at all with human interests or human passions. But it is the *key* in which the thoughts move, that determines the stage of moral advancement. So long as we are human, many among the numerous and evanescent elements that enter (half-observed or not observed at all) into our thoughts, cannot *but* be tainted. But the governing, the predominant element it is which gives the character and the tendency to the thought: and this must become such, must become a governing element, through the quality of the ideals deposited in the heart by the quality of the religious faith. One pointed illustration of this suggests itself from another poem of Pope's, in which he reiterates his shallow doctrine. In his Universal Prayer he informs us, that it can matter little whether we pray to Jehovah or to Jove, so long as in either case we pray to the First Cause. To contemplate God under that purely ontological relation to the world, would have little more operative value for what is most important in man, than if he prayed to gravitation. And it would have been more honest in Pope to say, as virtually he has said in the couplet under examination, that it can matter little whether man prays at all to any being. It deepens the scandal of this sentiment, coming from a poet professing Christianity, that a clergyman (holding preferment in the English Church) viz., Dr. Joseph Warton, justifies Pope for this Pagan opinion, upon the ground that an ancient philosopher had uttered the same opinion long before. What sort of philosopher? A Christian? No: but a Pagan. What then is the value of the justification? To a Pagan it could be no blame that he should avow a reasonable Pagan doctrine. In Irish phrase, it was 'true for *him*.' Amongst gods that were all utterly alienated from any scheme of moral government, all equally remote from the executive powers for sustaining such a government, so long as there was a practical anarchy and rivalship amongst themselves, there could be no sufficient reason for addressing vows to one rather than to another. The whole pantheon collectively could do nothing for moral influences; *à fortiori*, no separate individual amongst them. Pope indirectly confesses this elsewhere by his own impassioned expression of Christian feelings, though implicitly denying it here by his mere understanding. For he reverberates elsewhere, by deep echoes, that power in Christianity, which even in a legendary tale he durst not on mere principles of good sense and taste have ascribed to Paganism. For instance, how could a God, having no rebellion to complain of in man, pretend to any occasion of large forgiveness of man, or of framing means for reconciling this forgiveness with his own attribute of perfect holiness? What room, therefore, for ideals of mercy, tenderness, long-suffering, under any Pagan religion — under any worship of Jove! How again from gods, disfigured by fleshly voluptuousness in every mode, could any countenance be derived to an awful ideal of purity? Accordingly we find, that even among the Romans (the most advanced, as regards moral principle, of all heathen nations) neither the deep fountain of benignity, nor that of purity, was unsealed in man's heart. So much of either was sanctioned as could fall within the purposes of the magistrate, but beyond that level neither fountain could have been permitted to throw up its column of water, nor could in fact have had any impulse to sustain it in ascending; and not merely because it would have been repressed by ridicule as a deliration of the human mind, but also because it would have been frowned upon gravely by the very principle of the Roman polity, as wandering away from *civic* objects. Even for so much of these great restorative ventilations as Rome enjoyed, she was indebted not to her religion, but to elder forces that act *in spite of* her religion, viz. the original law written upon the human heart. Now, on the other hand, Christianity has left a separate system of ideals amongst men, which (as regards their development) are continually growing in authority. Waters, after whatever course of wandering, rise to the level of their original springs. Christianity lying so far above all other fountains of religious influence, no wonder that its irrigations rise to altitudes otherwise unknown, and from which the distribution to every level of society becomes comparatively easy. Those men are reached oftentimes — choosing or not choosing — by the healing streams, who have not sought them nor even recognised them. Infidels of the most determined class talk in Christian lands the morals of Christianity, and exact that morality with their hearts, constantly mistaking it for a morality co-extensive with man; and why? Simply from having been moulded unawares by its universal pressure through infancy, childhood, manhood, in the nursery, in the school, in the market-place. Pope himself, not by system or by affectation an infidel, not in any coherent sense a doubter, but a careless and indolent assenter to such doctrines of Christianity as his own Church prominently put forward, or as social respectability seemed to enjoin, — Pope, therefore, so far a very lukewarm Christian, was yet unconsciously to himself searched profoundly by the Christian types of purity. This we may read in his

> 'Hark, the herald angels say,
> . —— Sister spirit, come away!'

Or, again, as some persons read the great lessons of spiritual ethics more pathetically in those that have transgressed them than in those that have been faithful to the end — read them in the Magdalen that fades away in penitential tears rather than in the virgin martyr triumphant on the scaffold — we may see in his own Eloisa, and in her fighting with the dread powers let loose upon her tempestuous soul, how profoundly Pope also had drunk from the streams of Christian sentiment through which a new fountain of truth had ripened a new vegetation upon earth. What was it that Eloisa fought with? What power afflicted her trembling nature, that any Pagan religions *could* have evoked? The human love, 'the nympholepsy of the fond despair,' might have existed in a Vestal Virgin of ancient Rome: but in the Vestal what counter-influence could have come into conflict with the passion of love through any operation whatever of religion? None of any ennobling character that could reach the Vestal's own heart. The way in which religion connected itself with the case was through a traditional superstition — not built upon any fine spiritual sense of female chastity as dear to heaven — but upon a gross fear of alienating a tutelary goddess by offering an imperfect sacrifice. This sacrifice, the sacrifice of the natural household[9] charities in a few injured women on the altar of the goddess, was selfish in all its stages — selfish in the dark deity that could be pleased by the sufferings of a human being simply *as* sufferings, and not at all under any fiction that they were voluntary ebullitions of religious devotion — selfish in the senate and people who demanded these sufferings as a ransom paid through sighs and tears for *their* ambition — selfish in the Vestal herself, as sustained altogether by fear of a punishment too terrific to face, sustained therefore by the meanest principle in her nature. But in Eloisa how grand is the collision between deep religious aspirations and the persecuting phantoms of her undying human passion! The Vestal feared to be walled up alive — abandoned to the pangs of hunger — to the trepidations of darkness — to the echoes of her own lingering groans — to the torments perhaps of frenzy rekindling at intervals the decaying agonies of flesh. Was *that* what Eloisa feared? Punishment she had none to apprehend: the crime was past, and remembered only by the criminals: there was none to accuse but herself: there was none to judge but God. Wherefore should Eloisa fear? Wherefore and with what should she fight? She fought by turns against herself and against God, against her human nature and against her spiritual yearnings. How grand were the mysteries of her faith, how gracious and forgiving its condescensions! How deep had been her human love, how imperishable its remembrance on earth! 'What is it,' the Roman Vestal would have said, 'that this Christian lady is afraid of? What is the phantom that she seems to see?' Vestal! it is not fear, but grief. She sees an immeasurable heaven that seems to touch her eyes: so near is she to its love. Suddenly, an Abelard — the glory of his race — appears, that seems to touch her lips. The heavens recede and diminish to a starry point twinkling in an unfathomable abyss; they are all but lost for *her*. Fire, it is in Eloisa that searches fire: the holy that fights with the earthly; fire that cleanses with fire that consumes: like cavalry the two fires wheel and counterwheel, advancing and retreating, charging and countercharging through and through each other. Eloïsa trembles, but she trembles as a guilty creature before a tribunal unveiled within the secrecy of her own nature: there was no such trembling in the heathen worlds, for there was no such secret tribunal. Eloisa fights with a shadowy enemy: there was no such fighting for Roman Vestals: because all the temples of our earth, (which is the crowned Vesta,) no, nor all the glory of her altars, nor all the pomp of her cruelties, could cite from the depths of a human spirit any such fearful shadow as Christian faith evokes from an afflicted conscience.

Pope, therefore, wheresoever his heart speaks loudly, shows how deep had been his early impressions from Christianity. That is shown in his intimacy with Crashaw, in his Eloisa, in his Messiah, in his adaptation to Christian purposes of the Dying Adrian, &c. It is remarkable also, that Pope betrays, in all places where he has occasion to *argue* about Christianity, how much grander and more faithful to that great theme were the subconscious perceptions of his heart than the explicit commentaries of his understanding. He, like so many others, was unable to read or interpret the testimonies of his own heart, which is a deep over which diviner agencies brood than are legible to the intellect. The cipher written on his heaven-visited heart was deeper than his understanding could interpret.

If the question were asked, What ought to have been the best among Pope's poems? most people would answer, the *Essay on Man.* If the question were asked, What *is* the worst? all people of judgment would say, the *Essay on Man.* Whilst yet in its rudiments, this poem claimed the first place by the promise of its subject; when finished, by the utter failure of its execution, it fell into the last. The case possesses a triple interest — first, as illustrating the character of Pope modified by his situation; secondly, as illustrating the true nature of that 'didactic' poetry to which this particular poem is usually referred; thirdly, as illustrating the anomalous condition to which a poem so grand in its ambition has been reduced by the double disturbance of its proper movement; one disturbance through the position of Pope, another through his total misconception of didactic poetry. First, as regards Pope's situation, it may seem odd — but it is not so — that a man's social position should overrule his intellect. The scriptural denunciation of riches, as a snare to any man that is striving to rise above worldly views, applies not at all less to the intellect, and to any man seeking to ascend by some aërial arch of flight above ordinary intellectual efforts. Riches are fatal to those continuities of energy without which there is no success of that magnitude. Pope had £800 a year. *That* seems not so much. No, certainly not, with a wife and six children: but by accident Pope had no wife and no children. He was luxuriously at his ease: and this accident of his position in life fell in with a constitutional infirmity that predisposed him to indolence. Even his religious faith, by shutting him out from those public employments which else his great friends would have been too happy to obtain for him, aided his idleness, or sometimes invested it with a false character of conscientious self-denial. He cherished his religion confessedly as a plea for idleness. The result of all this was, that in his habits of thinking and of study, (if *study* we can call a style of reading so desultory as *his*,) Pope became a pure *dilettante;* in his intellectual eclecticism he was a mere epicure, toying with the delicacies and varieties of literature; revelling in the first bloom of moral speculations, but sated immediately; fastidiously retreating from all that threatened labor, or that exacted continuous attention; fathoming, throughout all his vagrancies amongst books, no foundation; filling up no chasms; and with all his fertility of thought expanding no germs of new life.

This career of luxurious indolence was the result of early luck which made it possible, and of bodily constitution which made it tempting. And when we remember his youthful introduction to the highest circles in the metropolis, where he never lost his footing, we cannot wonder that, without any sufficient motive for resistance, he should have sunk passively under his constitutional propensities, and should have fluttered amongst the flower-beds of literature or philosophy far more in the character of a libertine butterfly for casual enjoyment, than of a hard-working bee pursuing a premeditated purpose.

Such a character, strengthened by such a situation, would at any rate have disqualified Pope for composing a work severely philosophic, or where philosophy did more than throw a colored light of pensiveness upon some sentimental subject. If it were necessary that the philosophy should enter substantially into the very texture of the poem, furnishing its interest and prescribing its movement, in that case Pope's combining and theorizing faculty would have shrunk as from the labor of building a pyramid. And wo to him where it did *not*, as really happened in the case of the Essay on Man. For his faculty of execution was under an absolute necessity of shrinking in horror from the enormous details of such an enterprise to which so rashly he had pledged himself. He was sure to find himself, as find himself he did, landed in the most dreadful embarrassment upon reviewing his own work. A work, which, when finished, was not even begun; whose arches wanted their key-stones; whose parts had no coherency; and whose pillars, in the very moment of being thrown open to public view, were already crumbling into ruins. This utter prostration of Pope in a work so ambitious as an Essay on Man — a prostration predetermined from the first by the personal circumstances which we have noticed — was rendered still more irresistible in the *second* place by the general misconception in which Pope shared as to the very meaning of 'didactic' poetry. Upon which point we pause to make an exposition of our own views.

What *is* didactic poetry? What does 'didactic' mean when applied as a distinguishing epithet to such an idea as a poem? The predicate destroys the subject: it is a case of what logicians call *contradictio in adjecto* — the unsaying by means of an attribute the very thing which is the subject of that attribute you have just affirmed. No poetry can have the function of teaching. It is impossible that a variety of species should contradict the very purpose which contradistinguishes its *genus*. The several species differ partially; but not by the whole idea which differentiates their class. Poetry, or any one of the fine arts, (all of which alike speak through the genial nature of man and his excited sensibilities,) can teach only as nature teaches, as forests teach, as the sea teaches, as infancy teaches, viz. by deep impulse, by hieroglyphic suggestion. Their teaching is not direct or explicit, but lurking, implicit, masked in deep incarnations. To teach formally and professedly, is to abandon the very differential character and principle of poetry. If poetry could condescend to teach anything, it would be truths moral or religious. But even these it can utter only through symbols and actions. The great moral, for instance, the last result of the Paradise Lost, is once formally announced: but it teaches itself only by diffusing its lesson through the entire poem in the total succession of events and purposes: and even this succession teaches it only when the whole is gathered into unity by a reflex act of meditation; just as the pulsation of the physical heart can exist only when all the parts in an animal system are locked into one organization.

To address the *insulated* understanding is to lay aside the Prospero's robe of poetry. The objection, therefore, to didactic poetry, as vulgarly understood, would be fatal even if there were none but this logical objection derived from its definition. To be in self-contradiction is, for any idea whatever, sufficiently to destroy itself. But it betrays a more obvious and practical contradiction when a little searched. If the true purpose of a man's writing a didactic poem were to teach, by what suggestion of idiocy should he choose to begin by putting on fetters? wherefore should the simple man volunteer to handcuff and manacle himself, were it only by the encumbrances of metre, and perhaps of rhyme? But these he will find the very least of his encumbrances. A far greater exists in the sheer necessity of omitting in any poem a vast variety of details, and even capital sections of the subject, unless they will bend to purposes of ornament. Now this collision between two purposes, the purpose of use in mere teaching, and the purpose of poetic delight, shows, by the uniformity of its solution, which is the true purpose, and which the merely ostensible purpose. Had the true purpose been instruction, the moment that this was found incompatible with a poetic treatment, as soon as it was seen that the sound education of the reader-pupil could not make way without loitering to gather poetic flowers, the stern cry of 'duty' would oblige the poet to remember that he had dedicated himself to a didactic mission, and that he differed from other poets, as a monk from other men, by his vows of self-surrender to harsh ascetic functions. But, on the contrary, in the very teeth of this rule, wherever such a collision does really take place, and one or other of the supposed objects must give way, it is always the vulgar object of *teaching* (the pedagogue's object) which goes to the rear, whilst the higher object of poetic emotion moves on triumphantly. In reality not one didactic poet has ever yet attempted to use any parts or processes of the particular art which he made his theme, unless in so far as they seemed susceptible of poetic treatment, and only *because* they seemed so. Look at the poem of *Cyder*, by Philips, of the *Fleece* of Dyer or (which is a still weightier example) at the *Georgics* of Virgil, — does any of these poets show the least anxiety for the correctness of your principles, or the delicacy of your manipulations in the worshipful arts they affect to teach? No; but they pursue these arts through every stage that offers any attractions of beauty. And in the very teeth of all anxiety for teaching, if there existed traditionally any very absurd way of doing a thing which happened to be eminently picturesque, and, if opposed to this, there were some improved mode that had recommended itself to poetic hatred by being dirty and ugly, the poet (if a good one) would pretend never to have heard of this disagreeable improvement. Or if obliged, by some rival poet, not absolutely to ignore it, he would allow that such a thing could be done, but hint that it was hateful to the Muses or Graces, and very likely to breed a pestilence.

This subordination of the properly didactic function to the poetic, which, leaving the old essential distinction of poetry [viz. its sympathy with the genial motions of man's heart] to override all accidents of special variation, and showing that the essence of poetry never *can* be set aside by its casual modifications, — will be compromised by some loose thinkers, under the idea that in didactic poetry the element of instruction is in fact one element, though subordinate and secondary. Not at all. What we are denying is, that the element of instruction enters *at all* into didactic poetry. The subject of the Georgics, for instance, is Rural Economy as practised by Italian farmers: but Virgil not only *omits* altogether innumerable points of instruction insisted on as articles of religious necessity by Varro, Cato, Columella, &c., but, even as to those instructions which he *does* communicate, he is careless whether they are made technically intelligible or not. He takes very little pains to keep you from capital mistakes in *practising* his instructions; but he takes good care that you shall not miss any strong impression for the eye or the heart to which the rural process, or rural scene, may naturally lead. He pretends to give you a lecture on farming, in order to have an excuse for carrying you all round the beautiful farm. He pretends to show you a good plan for a farm-house, as the readiest means of veiling his impertinence in showing you the farmer's wife and her rosy children. It is an excellent plea for getting a peep at the bonny milk-maids to propose an inspection of a model dairy. You pass through the poultry-yard, under whatever pretence, in reality to see the peacock and his harem. And so on to the very end, the pretended instruction is but in secret the connecting tie which holds together the laughing flowers going off from it to the right and to the left; whilst if ever at intervals this prosy thread of pure didactics is brought forward more obtrusively, it is so by way of foil, to make more effective upon the eye the prodigality of the floral magnificence.

We affirm, therefore, that the didactic poet is so far from seeking even a secondary or remote object in the particular points of information which he may happen to communicate, that much rather he would prefer the having communicated none at all. We will explain ourselves by means of a little illustration from Pope, which will at the same time furnish us with a miniature type of what we ourselves mean by a didactic poem, both in reference to what it *is* and to what it is *not.* In the Rape of the Lock there is a game at cards played, and played with a brilliancy of effect and felicity of selection, applied to the circumstances, which make it a sort of gem within a gem. This game was not in the first edition of the poem, but was an afterthought of Pope's, labored therefore with more than usual care. We regret that *ombre*, the game described, is no longer played, so that the entire skill with which the mimic battle is fought cannot be so fully appreciated as in Pope's days. The strategics have partly perished, which really Pope ought not to complain of, since he suffers only as Hannibal, Marius, Sertorius, suffered before him. Enough, however, survives of what will tell its own story. For what is it, let us ask, that a poet has to do in such a case, supposing that he were disposed to weave a didactic poem out of a pack of cards, as Vida has out of the chess-board? In describing any particular game he does not seek to *teach* you that game — he postulates it as *already* known to you — but he relies upon separate resources. 1st, he will revive in the reader's eye, for picturesque effect, the well-known personal distinctions of the several kings, knaves, &c., their appearances and their powers. 2dly, he will choose some game in which he may display a happy selection applied to the chances and turns of fortune, to the manœuvres, to the situations of doubt, of brightening expectation, of sudden danger, of critical deliverance, or of final defeat. The interest of a war will be rehearsed — *lis est de paupere regno* — that is true; but the depth of the agitation on such occasions, whether at chess, at draughts, or at cards, is not measured of necessity by the grandeur of the stake; he selects, in short, whatever fascinates the eye or agitates the heart by mimicry of life; but so far from *teaching*, he presupposes the reader already *taught*, in order that he may go along with the movement of the descriptions.

Now, in treating a subject so vast, indeed so inexhaustible, as man, this eclecticism ceases to be possible. Every part depends upon every other part: in such a *nexus* of truths to insulate is to annihilate. Severed from each other the parts lose their support, their coherence, their very meaning; you have no liberty to reject or to choose. Besides, in treating the ordinary themes proper for what is called didactic poetry — say, for instance, that it were the art of rearing silk-worms or bees — or suppose it to be horticulture, landscape-gardening, hunting, or hawking, rarely does there occur anything polemic; or if a slight controversy *does* arise, it is easily hushed asleep — it is stated in a line, it is answered in a couplet. But in the themes of Lucretius and Pope *everything* is polemic — you move only through dispute, you prosper only by argument and never-ending controversy. There is not positively one capital proposition or doctrine about man, about his origin, his nature, his relations to God, or his prospects, but must be fought for with energy, watched at every turn with vigilance, and followed into endless mazes, not under the choice of the writer, but under the inexorable dictation of the argument.

Such a poem, so unwieldy, whilst at the same time so austere in its philosophy, together with the innumerable polemic parts essential to its good faith and even to its evolution, would be absolutely unmanageable from excess and from disproportion, since often a secondary demur would occupy far more space than a principled section. Here lay the impracticable dilemma for Pope's Essay on Man. To satisfy the demands of the subject, was to defeat the objects of poetry. To evade the demands in the way that Pope has done, is to offer us a ruin for a palace. The very same dilemma existed for Lucretius, and with the very same result. The *De Rerum Naturâ* (which might, agreeably to its theme, have been entitled *De Omnibus Rebus*), and the Essay on Man (which might equally have borne the Lucretian title *De Rerum Naturâ*), are both, and from the same cause, fragments that could not have been completed. Both are accumulations of diamond-dust without principles of coherency. In a succession of pictures, such as usually form the materials of didactic poems, the slightest thread of interdependency is sufficient. But, in works essentially and everywhere argumentative and polemic, to omit the connecting links, as often as they are insusceptible of poetic effect, is to break up the unity of the parts, and to undermine the foundations, in what expressly offers itself as a systematic and architectural whole. Pope's poem has suffered even more than that of Lucretius from this want of cohesion. It is indeed the realization of anarchy; and one amusing test of this may be found in the fact, that different commentators have deduced from it the very opposite doctrines. In some instances this apparent antinomy is doubtful, and dependent on the ambiguities or obscurities of the expression. But in others it is fairly deducible: and the cause lies in the elliptical structure of the work: the ellipsis, or (as sometimes it may be called) the chasm, may be filled up in two different modes essentially hostile: and he that supplies the *hiatus*, in effect determines the bias of the poem this way or that — to a religious or to a sceptical result. In this edition the commentary of Warburton has been retained, which ought certainly to have been dismissed. The Essay is, in effect, a Hebrew word with the vowel-points omitted: and Warburton supplies one set of vowels, whilst Crousaz with equal right supplies a contradictory set.

As a whole, the edition before us is certainly the most agreeable of all that we possess. The fidelity of Mr. Roscoe to the interests of Pope's reputation, contrasts pleasingly with the harshness at times of Bowles, and the reckless neutrality of Warton. In the editor of a great classic, we view it as a virtue, wearing the grace of loyalty, that he should refuse to expose frailties or defects in a spirit of exultation. Mr. Roscoe's own notes are written with a peculiar good sense, temperance, and kind feeling. The only objection to them, which applies, however, still more to the notes of the former editors, is the want of compactness. They are not written under that austere instinct of compression and verbal parsimony, as the ideal merit in an annotator, which ought to govern all such ministerial labors in our days. Books are becoming too much the oppression of the intellect, and cannot endure any longer the accumulation of undigested commentaries, or that species of diffusion in editors which roots itself in laziness: the efforts of condensation and selection are painful; and they are luxuriously evaded by reprinting indiscriminately whole masses of notes — though often in substance reiterating each other. But the interests of readers clamorously call for the amendment of this system. The principle of selection must now be applied even to the *text* of great authors. It is no longer advisable to reprint the whole of either Dryden or Pope. Not that we would wish to see their works mutilated. Let such as are selected be printed in the fullest integrity of the text. But some have lost their interest;[10] others, by the elevation of public morals since the days of those great wits, are felt to be now utterly unfit for general reading. Equally for the reader's sake and the poet's, the time has arrived when they may be advantageously retrenched: for they are painfully at war with those feelings of entire and honorable esteem with which all lovers of exquisite intellectual brilliancy must wish to surround the name and memory of Pope.

NOTES.

Note 1. Page 148.

Charles I., for example, when Prince of Wales, and many others in his father's court, gained their known familiarity with Shakspeare — not through the original quartos, so slenderly diffused, nor through the first folio of 1623, but through the court representations of his chief dramas at Whitehall.

Note 2. Page 154.

The Canterbury Tales were not made public until 1380 or thereabouts: but the composition must have cost thirty or more years; not to mention that the work had probably been finished for some years before it was divulged.

Note 3. Page 156.

The reason why the broad distinctions between the two literatures of power and knowledge so little fix the attention, lies in the fact, that a vast proportion of books — history, biography, travels, miscellaneous essays, &c., lying in a middle zone, confound these distinctions by interblending them. All that we call 'amusement' or 'entertainment,' is a diluted form of the power belonging to passion, and also a mixed form; and where threads of direct *instruction* intermingle in the texture with these threads of *power*, this absorption of the duality into one representative *nuance* neutralizes the separate perception of either. Fused into a *tertium quid*, or neutral state, they disappear to the popular eye as the repelling forces, which in fact they are.

NOTE 4. Page 160.

And this purity of diction shows itself in many points arguing great vigilance of attention, and also great anxiety for using the language powerfully as the most venerable of traditions, when treating the most venerable of subjects. For instance, the Bible never condescends to the mean colloquial preterites of *chid* for *did chide*, or *writ* for *did write*, but always uses the full-dress word *chode*, and *wrote*. Pope might have been happier had he read his Bible more: but assuredly he would have improved his English. A question naturally arises — how it was that the elder writers — Shakspeare in particular, (who had seen so little of higher society when he wrote his youthful poems of Lucrece and Adonis,) should have maintained so much purer a grammar? Dr. Johnson indeed, but most falsely, says that Shakspeare's grammar is licentious. 'The style of Shakspeare' (these are the exact words of the Doctor in his preface) 'was in itself ungrammatical, perplexed, and obscure.' An audacious misrepresentation! In the doctor himself, a legislator for the language, we undertake to show more numerically of trespasses against grammar, but (which is worse still) more unscholarlike trespasses. Shakspeare is singularly correct in grammar. One reason, we believe, was this: from the restoration of Charles II. decayed the *ceremonious* exteriors of society. Stiffness and reserve melted away before the familiarity and impudence of French manners. Social meetings grew far more numerous as towns expanded; social pleasure far more began now to depend upon conversation; and conversation, growing less formal, quickened its pace. Hence came the call for rapid abbreviations: the *'tis* and *'twas*, the *can't* and *don't* of the two post-Miltonic generations arose under this impulse; and the general impression has ever since subsisted amongst English writers — that language, instead of being an exquisitely beautiful vehicle for the thoughts — a robe that never can be adorned with too much care or piety — is in fact a dirty high-road which all people detest whilst all are forced to use it, and to the keeping of which in repair no rational man ever contributes a trifle that is not forced from him by some severity of Quarter Sessions. The great corrupter of English was the conversational instinct for rapidity. A more honorable source of corruption lay in the growth of new ideas, and the continual influx of foreign words to meet them. Spanish words arose, like *reformado*, *prixado*, *desperado*, and French ones past counting. But as these retained their foreign forms of structure, they reacted to vitiate the language still more by introducing a piebald aspect of books which it seemed a matter of necessity to tolerate for the interests of wider thinking. The perfection of this horror was never attained except amongst the Germans.

Note 5. Page 168.

It was *after* his connection with Warburton that Pope introduced several of his *living* portraits into the Satires.

Note 6. Page 172.

By what might seem a strange oversight, but which in fact is a very natural oversight to one who was not uttering one word in which he seriously believed, Pope, in a prose note on verse 207, roundly asserts 'that the particular characters of women are *more various* than those of men.' It is no evasion of this insufferable contradiction, that he couples with the greater variety of *characters* in women a greater uniformity in what he presumes to be their *ruling passion*. Even as to this ruling passion he cannot agree with himself for ten minutes; generally he says, that it is the love of pleasure; but sometimes (as at verse 208) forgetting this monotony, he ascribes to women a dualism of passions — love of pleasure and love of power — which dualism of itself must be a source of self-conflict, and therefore of inexhaustible variety in character:

> 'Those only fix'd, they first or last obey —
> The love of pleasure and the love of sway.'

Note 7. Page 175.

This refers to the Act of Parliament for burying corpses in woollen, which greatly disturbed the fashionable costume in coffins *comme il faut*.

Note 7. Page 177.

The sons of the Duke having died, the title and estates were so settled as to descend through this daughter, who married the Earl of Sunderland. In consequence of this arrangement, *Spenser* (until lately) displaced the great name of *Churchill;* and the Earl became that second Duke of Marlborough, about whom Smollett tells us in his History of England (Reign of George II.) so remarkable and to this hour so mysterious a story.

Note 8. Page 177.

The Duchess died in the same year as Pope, viz. just in time by a few months to miss the Rebellion of 1745, and the second Pretender; spectacles which for little reasons (vindictive or otherwise) both of them would have enjoyed until the spring of 1746.

Note 9. Page 186.

The Vestals not only renounced marriage, at least for those years in which marriage could be a natural blessing, but also left their fathers' houses at an age the most trying to the human heart as regards the pangs of separation.

Note 10. Page 200.

We do not include the Dunciad in this list. On the contrary, the arguments by which it has been generally undervalued, as though antiquated by lapse of time and by the fading of names, are all unsound. We ourselves hold it to be the greatest of Pope's efforts. But for that very reason we retire from the examination of it, which we had designed, as being wholly disproportioned to the narrow limits remaining to us.

WILLIAM GODWIN.*

It is no duty of a notice so cursory, to discuss Mr. Godwin as a philosopher. Mr. Gilfillan admits, that in this character he did not earn much popularity by any absolute originality ; and of such popularity as he may have snatched surreptitiously without it, clearly all must have long since exhaled before it could be possible for 'a respectable person' to demand of Mr. Gilfillan '*Who's Godwin?*' A question which Mr. Gilfillan justly thinks it possible that 'some readers,' of the present day, November, 1845, may repeat. That is, we must presume, *not* who is Godwin the novelist? but who is Godwin the political philosopher? In that character he is now forgotten. And yet in *that* he carried one single shock into the bosom of English society, fearful but momentary, like that from the electric blow of the gymnotus; or, perhaps, the intensity of the brief panic which, fifty years ago, he impressed on the public mind, may be more adequately expressed by the case of a ship in the middle ocean suddenly scraping, with her keel, a rag-

* 'A Gallery of Literary Portraits.' By George Gilfillan.

ged rock, hanging for one moment, as if impaled upon the teeth of the dreadful *sierra*, then, by the mere *impetus* of her mighty sails, grinding audibly, to powder, the fangs of this accursed submarine harrow, leaping into deep water again, and causing the panic of ruin to be simultaneous with the deep sense of deliverance. In the *quarto* (that is, the original) edition of his 'Political Justice,' Mr. Godwin advanced against thrones and dominations, powers and principalities, with the air of some Titan slinger or monarchist from Thebes and Troy, saying, — 'Come hither, ye wretches, that I may give your flesh to the fowls of the air.' But, in the second, or *octavo* edition, — and under what motive has never been explained, — he recoiled, absolutely, from the sound himself had made: everybody else was appalled by the fury of the challenge; and, through the strangest of accidents, Mr. Godwin also was appalled. The second edition, as regards principles, is not a recast, but absolutely a travesty of the first: nay, it is all but a palinode. In this collapse of a tense excitement, I myself find the true reason for the utter extinction of the 'Political Justice,' and of its author considered as a philosopher. Subsequently, he came forward as a philosophical speculator, in 'The Enquirer,' and elsewhere; but here it was always some minor question which he raised, or some mixed question, rather allied to philosophy than philosophical. As regarded the main creative *nisus* of his philosophy, it remained undeniable that, in relation to the hostility of the world, he was like one who, in some piratical ship, should drop his anchor before Portsmouth, — should defy the navies of

England to come out and fight, and then, whilst a thousand vessels were contending for the preference in blowing him out of the seas, should suddenly slip his cables and run.

But it is as a novelist, not as a political theorist, that Mr. Gilfillan values Godwin ; and specially for his novel of 'Caleb Williams.' Now, if this were the eccentric judgment of one unsupported man, however able, and had received no countenance at all from others, it might be injudicious to detain the reader upon it. It happens, however, that other men of talent have raised 'Caleb Williams' to a station in the first rank of novels: whilst many more, amongst whom I am compelled to class myself, can see in it no merit of any kind. A schism, which is really perplexing, exists in this particular case ; and, that the reader may judge for himself, I will state the outline of the plot, out of which it is that the whole interest must be supposed to grow ; for the characters are nothing, being mere generalities, and very slightly developed. Thirty-five years it is since I read the book; but the nakedness of the incidents makes them easily rememberable. — Falkland, who passes for a man of high-minded and delicate honor, but is, in fact, distinguished only by acute sensibility to the opinion of the world, receives a dreadful insult in a most public situation. It is, indeed, more than an insult, being the most brutal of outrages. In a ball-room, where the local gentry and his neighbors are assembled, he is knocked down, kicked, dragged along the floor, by a ruffian squire, named Tyrrel. It is vain to resist; he himself is slightly built, and his antagonist is a powerful man. In these circumstances, and under the eyes of all the ladies in the county witnessing every step of his humiliation, no man could severely have blamed him, nor would our English law have severely punished him, if, in the frenzy of his agitation, he had seized a poker and laid his assailant dead upon the spot. Such allowance does the natural feeling of men, such allowance does the sternness of the judgment-seat make for human infirmity when tried to extremity by devilish provocation. But Falkland does not avenge himself thus: he goes out, makes his little arrangements, and, at a later hour of the night, he comes, by surprise, upon Tyrrel, and murders him in the darkness. Here is the first vice in the story. With any gleam of generosity in his nature, no man in pursuit of vengeance would have found it in such a catastrophe. That an enemy should die by apoplexy, or by lightning, would be no gratification of wrath to an impassioned pursuer: to make it a retribution for *him*, he himself must be associated to the catastrophe in the consciousness of his victim. Falkland for some time evades or tramples on detection. But his evil genius at last appears in the shape of Caleb Williams; and the agency through which Mr. Caleb accomplishes his mission is not that of any grand passion, but of vile eavesdropping inquisitiveness. Mr. Falkland had hired him as an amanuensis; and in that character Caleb had occasion to observe that some painful remembrance weighed upon his master's mind; and that something or other — documents or personal memorials connected with this remembrance — were deposited in a trunk visited at intervals by Falkland. But of what nature could these memorials be? Surely Mr. Falkland would not keep in brandy the gory head of Tyrrel; and anything short of *that* could not proclaim any murder at all, much less the particular murder. Strictly speaking, nothing *could* be in the trunk, of a nature to connect Falkland with the murder more closely than the circumstances had already connected him; and those circumstances, as we know, had been insufficient. It puzzles one, therefore, to imagine any evidence which the trunk could yield, unless there were secreted within it some known personal property of Tyrrel's; in which case the aspiring Falkland had committed a larceny as well as a murder. Caleb, meantime, wastes no labor in hypothetic reasonings, but resolves to have ocular satisfaction in the matter. An opportunity offers: an alarm of fire is given in the day-time; and whilst Mr. Falkland, with his people, is employed on the lawn manning the buckets, Caleb skulks off to the trunk; feeling, probably, that his first duty was to himself, by extinguishing the burning fire of curiosity in his own heart, after which there might be time enough for his second duty, of assisting to extinguish the fire in his master's mansion. Falkland, however, misses the absentee. To pursue him, to collar him, and, we may hope, to kick him, are the work of a moment. Had Caleb found time for accomplishing his inquest? I really forget; but no matter: either now, or at some luckier hour, he does so: he becomes master of Falkland's secret; consequently, as both fancy, of Falkland's life. At this point commences a flight of Caleb, and a chasing of Falkland, in order to watch his motions, which forms the most spirited part of the story. Mr. Godwin tells us that he derived this situation, the continual flight and continual pursuit, from a South American tradition of some Spanish vengeance. Always the Spaniard was riding *in* to any given town on the road, when his destined victim was riding *out* at the other end; so that the relations of 'whereabouts' were never for a moment lost: the trail was perfect. Now, this might be possible in certain countries; but in England! — heavens! could not Caleb double upon his master, or dodge round a gate (like Falkland when he murdered Mr. Tyrrel), or take a headlong plunge into London, where the scent might have lain cold for forty years? * Other accidents by thousands would interrupt the chase. On the hundredth day, for instance, after the flying parties had become well known on the road, Mr. Falkland would drive furiously up to some King's Head or White Lion, putting his one question to the waiter, 'Where's Caleb?' And the waiter would reply, 'Where's Mr. Caleb, did you say, Sir? Why, he went off at five by the Highflyer, booked inside the whole way to Doncaster; and Mr. Caleb is now, Sir, precisely forty-five miles a-head.' Then would Falkland furiously demand 'four horses on;' and then would the waiter plead a contested election in excuse for having no horses at all. Really, for dramatic

* 'Forty years:' so long, according to my recollection of Boswell, did Dr. Johnson walk about London before he met an old Derbyshire friend, who also had been walking about London with the same punctual regularity for every day of the same forty years. The *nodes* of intersection did not come round sooner.

effect, it is a pity that the tale were not translated forward to the days of railroads. Sublime would look the fiery pursuit, and the panic-stricken flight, when racing from Fleetwood to Liverpool, to Birmingham, to London; then smoking along the Great Western, where Mr. Caleb's forty-five miles a-head would avail him little, to Bristol, to Exeter; thence doubling back upon London, like the steam leg in Mr. H. G. Bell's admirable story.

But, after all, what was the object, and what the result of all this racing? Once I saw two young men facing each other upon a high road, but at a furlong's distance, and playing upon the foolish terrors of a young woman, by continually heading her back from one to the other, as alternately she approached towards either. Signals of some dreadful danger in the north being made by the northern man, back the poor girl flew towards the southern, who, in *his* turn, threw out pantomimic warnings of an equal danger to the south. And thus, like a tennis-ball, the simple creature kept rebounding from one to the other, until she could move no farther through sheer fatigue; and then first the question occurred to her, What was it that she had been running from? The same question seems to have struck at last upon the obtuse mind of Mr. Caleb; it was quite as easy to play the part of hunter, as that of hunted game, and likely to be cheaper. He turns therefore sharp round upon his master, who in *his* turn is disposed to fly, when suddenly the sport is brought to a dead lock by a constable, who tells the murdering squire that he is 'wanted.' Caleb has lodged informations; all parties meet for a final 'reunion' before the magistrate ; Mr. Falkland, oddly enough, regards himself in the light of an ill-used man ; which theory of the case, even more oddly, seems to be adopted by Mr. Gilfillan ; but, for all that he can say, Mr. Falkland is fully committed : and as laws were made for every degree, it is plain that Mr. Falkland (however much of a pattern-man) is in some danger of swinging. But this catastrophe is intercepted : a novelist may raise his hero to the peerage ; he may even confer the garter upon him ; but it shocks against usage and courtesy that he should hang him. The circulating libraries would rise in mutiny, if he did. And therefore it is satisfactory to believe, (for all along I speak from memory,) that Mr. Falkland reprieves himself from the gallows by dying of exhaustion from his travels.

Such is the fable of 'Caleb Williams,' upon which by the way is built, I think, Colman's drama of 'The Iron Chest.' I have thought it worth the trouble (whether for the reader, or for myself,) of a flying abstract ; and chiefly with a view to the strange collision of opinions as to the merit of the work ; some, as I have said, exalting it to the highest class of novels, others depressing it below the lowest of those which achieve any notoriety. They who vote against it are in a large majority. The Germans, whose literature offers a free port to all the eccentricities of the earth, have never welcomed 'Caleb Williams.' Chenier, the ruling *litterateur* of Paris, in the days of Napoleon, when reviewing the literature of his own day, dismisses Caleb contemptuously as coarse and vulgar. It is not therefore to the German taste, it is not to the

French. And as to our own country, Mr. Gilfillan is undoubtedly wrong in supposing that it 'is in every circulating library, and needs more frequently, than almost any novel, to be replaced.' If this were so, in presence of the immortal novels which for one hundred and fifty years have been gathering into the garners of our English literature, I should look next to see the race of men returning from venison and wheat to their primitive diet of acorns. But I believe that the number of editions yet published, would at once discredit this account of the book's popularity. Neither is it likely, *à priori*, that such a popularity could arise even for a moment. The interest from secret and vindictive murder, though coarse, is undoubtedly deep. What would make us thrill in real life, the case for instance of a neighbor lying under the suspicion of such a murder, would make us thrill in a novel. But then it must be managed with art, and covered with mystery. For a long time it must continue doubtful, both as to the fact, and the circumstances, and the motive. Whereas, in the case of Mr. Falkland, there is little mystery of any kind; not much, and only for a short time, to Caleb; and none at all to the reader, who could have relieved the curiosity of Mr. Caleb from the first, if he were placed in communication with him.

Differing so much from Mr. Gilfillan, as to the effectiveness of the novel, I am only the more impressed with the eloquent images and expressions by which he has conveyed his own sense of its power. Power there must be, though many of us cannot discern it, to react upon us, through impressions so powerful in other minds. Some of Mr. Gilfillan's impressions, as they are clothed in striking images by himself, I will here quote : — 'His,' Godwin's, 'heat is never that of the sun with all his beams around him ; but of the round rayless orb seen shining from the summit of Mont Blanc, still and stripped in the black ether. He has more passion than imagination. And even his passion he has learned more by sympathy than by personal feeling. And amid his most tempestuous scenes, you see the calm and stern eye of philosophic analysis looking on. His imagery is not copious, nor always original ; but its sparseness is its strength, the flash comes sudden as the lightning. No preparatory flourish, or preliminary sound : no sheets of useless splendor : each figure is a fork of fire, which strikes and needs no second blow. Nay, often his images are singularly common-place, and you wonder how they move you so, till you resolve this into the power of the hand which jaculates its own energy in *them.*' And again, 'His novels resemble the paintings of John Martin, being a gallery, nay a world, in themselves. In both, monotony and mannerism are incessant : but the monotony is that of the sounding deep, the mannerism that of the thunderbolts of heaven. Martin might append to his one continual flash of lightning, which is present in all his pictures — now to reveal a deluge, now to garland the brow of a fiend — now to rend the veil of a temple, and now to guide the invaders through the breach of a city — the words, *John Martin, his mark.* Godwin's novels are not less terribly distinguished to those who understand their cipher — the deep scar of misery branded upon the brow of the 'victim of society.'

And as to the earliest of these novels, the 'Caleb Williams,' he says, 'There is about it a stronger suction and swell of interest than in any novel we know, with the exception of one or two of Sir Walter's. You are in it ere you are aware. You put your hand playfully into a child's, and are surprised to find it held in the grasp of a giant. It becomes a fascination. Struggle you may, and kick, but he holds you by his glittering eye.' In reference, again, to 'St. Leon,' the next most popular of Godwin's novels, there is a splendid passage upon the glory and pretensions of the ancient alchemist, in the infancy of scientific chemistry. It rescues the character from vulgarity, and displays it idealized as sometimes, perhaps, it must have been. I am sorry that it is too long for extracting; but, in compensation to the reader, I quote two very picturesque sentences, describing what, to Mr. Gilfillan, appears the quality of Godwin's style: — 'It is a smooth succession of short and simple sentences, each clear as crystal, and none ever distracting the attention from the subject to its own construction. It is a style in which you cannot explain how the total effect rises out of the individual parts, and which is forgotten as entirely during perusal as is the pane of glass through which you gaze at a comet or a star.' Elsewhere, and limiting his remark to the style of the 'Caleb Williams,' he says finely: — 'The writing, though far from elegant or finished, has in parts the rude power of those sentences which criminals, martyrs, and maniacs, scrawl upon their walls or windows in the eloquence of desperation.' *

These things perplex me. The possibility that any individual in the minority can have regarded Godwin with such an eye, seems to argue that we of the majority must be wrong. Deep impressions seem to justify themselves. *We* may have failed to perceive things which *are* in the object; but it is not so easy for others to perceive things which are *not;* or, at least, hardly in a case like this, where (though a minority) these 'others' still exist in number sufficient to check and to confirm each other. On the other hand, Godwin's name seems sinking out of remembrance; and he is remembered less by the novels that succeeded, or by the philosophy that he abjured, than as the man that had Mary Wolstonecraft for his wife, Mrs. Shelley for his daughter, and the immortal Shelley as his son-in-law.

---

* 'Desperation.' Yet, as *martyrs* are concerned in the picture, it ought to have been said, 'of desperation and of farewell to earth,' or something equivalent.

JOHN FOSTER.

Mr. Gilfillan * possibly overrates the power of this essayist, and the hold which he has upon the public mind. It is singular, meantime, that whatever might be its degree, much or little, originally his influence was due to an accident of position which in some countries would have tended to destroy it. He was a Dissenter. Now, in England, *that* sometimes operates as an advantage. To dissent from the established form of religion, which could not affect the value of a writer's speculations, may easily become the means of diffusing their reputation, as well as of facilitating their introduction. And in the following way: The great mass of the reading population are absolutely indifferent to such deflexions from the national standard. The man, suppose, is a Baptist: but to be a Baptist is still to be a Protestant, and a Protestant agreeing with his countrymen in every thing essential to purity of life and faith. So far there is the most entire neutrality in the public mind, and readiness to receive any impression which the man's powers enable him to make.

* 'Gallery of Literary Portraits.'

There is, indeed, so absolute a carelessness for all inoperative shades of religious difference lurking in the background, that even the ostentatiously liberal hardly feel it a case for parading their liberality. But, on the other hand, his own sectarian party are as energetic to push him forward as all others are passive. They favor him as a brother, and also as one whose credit will react upon their common sect. And this favor, pressing like a wedge upon the unresisting neutrality of the public, soon succeeds in gaining for any able writer among sectarians an exaggerated reputation. Nobody is against him ; and a small section acts *for* him in a spirit of resolute partisanship.

To this accident of social position, and to his connection with the *Eclectic Review*, Mr. Foster owed his first advantageous presentation before the public. The misfortune of many an able writer is, not that he is rejected by the world, but that virtually he is never brought conspicuously before them : he is not dismissed unfavorably, but he is never effectually introduced. From this calamity at the outset, Foster was saved by his party. I happened myself to be in Bristol at the moment when his four essays were first issuing from the press; and everywhere I heard so pointed an account of the expectations connected with Foster by his religious party, that I made it a duty to read his book without delay. It is a distant incident to look back upon ; gone by for more than thirty years; but I remember my first impressions, which were these : — first, That the novelty or weight of the thinking was hardly sufficient to account for the sudden popularity, without some *extra* influence at work ; and, secondly, That the contrast was remarkable between the uncolored style of his general diction, and the brilliant felicity of occasional images embroidered upon the sober ground of his text. The splendor did not seem spontaneous, or growing up as part of the texture within the loom; it was intermitting, and seemed as extraneous to the substance as the flowers which are chalked for an evening upon the floors of ball-rooms.

Subsequently, I remarked two other features of difference in his manner, neither of which has been overlooked by Mr. Gilfillan, viz. first, The unsocial gloom of his eye, travelling over all things with dissatisfaction; second, (Which in our days seemed unaccountable,) the remarkable limitation of his knowledge. You might suppose the man, equally by his ignorance of passing things and by his ungenial moroseness, to be a specimen newly turned out from the silent cloisters of La Trappe. A monk he seemed by the repulsion of his cloistral feelings, and a monk by the superannuation of his knowledge. Both peculiarities he drew in part from that same sectarian position, operating for evil, to which, in another direction as a conspicuous advantage, he had been indebted for his favorable public introduction. It is not that Foster was generally misanthropic; neither was he, as a sectarian, 'a good hater' at any special angle; that is, he was not a zealous hater; but, by temperament, and in some measure by situation, as one pledged to a polemic attitude by his sect, he was a general disliker and a general suspecter. His confidence in human nature was small; for he saw the clay of the composite statue, but not its gold; and apparently his satisfaction with himself was not much greater. Inexhaustible was his jealousy; and for that reason his philanthropy was everywhere checked by frost and wintry chills. This blight of asceticism in his nature is not of a kind to be briefly illustrated, for it lies diffused through the texture of his writings. But of his other monkish characteristic, his abstraction from the movement and life of his own age, I may give this instance, which I observed by accident about a year since in some *late* edition of his Essays. He was speaking of the term *radical* as used to designate a large political party; but so slightly was he acquainted with the history of that party, so little had he watched the growth of this important interest in our political system, that he supposes the term 'Radical' to express a mere scoff or movement of irony from the antagonists of that party. It stands, as he fancies, upon the same footing as 'Puritan,' 'Roundhead,' &c. amongst our fathers, or 'Swaddler,' applied to the Evangelicals amongst ourselves. This may seem a trifle; nor do I mention the mistake for any evil which it can lead to, but for the dreamy inattention which it argues to what was most important in the agitations around him. It may cause nothing; but how much does it presume? Could a man, interested in the motion of human principles, or the revolutions of his own country, have failed to notice the rise of a new party which loudly proclaimed its own mission and purposes in the very name which it assumed? The term 'Radical' was used elliptically: Mr. Hunt, and all about him, constantly gave out that they were reformers who went to the *root* — *radical* reformers; whilst all previous political parties they held to be merely masquerading as reformers, or, at least, wanting in the determination to go deep enough. The party-name 'Radical' was no insult of enemies; it was a cognizance self-adopted by the party which it designates, and worn with pride; and whatever might be the degree of *personal* weight belonging to Mr. Hunt, no man, who saw into the composition of society amongst ourselves, could doubt that his principles were destined to a most extensive diffusion — were sure of a permanent settlement amongst the great party interests — and, therefore, sure of disturbing thenceforwards for ever the previous equilibrium of forces in our English social system. To mistake the origin or history of a word — is nothing; but to mistake it when that history of a word ran along with the history of a *thing* destined to change all the aspects of our English present and future — implies a sleep of Epimenides amongst the shocks which are unsettling the realities of earth.

The four original essays, by which Foster was first known to the public, are those by which he is still best known. It cannot be said of them that they have any *practical* character calculated to serve the uses of life. They terminate in speculations that apply themselves little enough to any business of the world. Whether a man should write memoirs of himself cannot have any personal interest for one reader in a myriad. And two of the essays have even a misleading tendency. That upon 'Decision of Character' places a very exaggerated valuation upon one quality of human temperament, which is neither rare, nor at all necessarily allied with the most elevated features of moral grandeur. Coleridge, because he had no business talents himself, admired them preposterously in others; or fancied them vast when they existed only in a slight degree. And, upon the same principle, I suspect that Mr. Foster rated so highly the quality of decision in matters of action, chiefly because he wanted it himself. Obstinacy is a gift more extensively sown than Foster was willing to admit. And *his* scale of appreciation, if it were practically applied to the men of history, would lead to judgments immoderately perverse. Milton would rank far below Luther. In reality, as Mr. Gilfillan justly remarks, 'Decision of character is not, strictly, a moral power; and it is extremely dangerous to pay that homage to any intellectual quality, which is sacred to virtue alone.' But even this estimate must often tend to exaggeration; for the most inexorable decision is much more closely connected with bodily differences of temperament than with any superiority of mind. It rests too much upon a physical basis; and of all qualities whatever, it is the most liable to vicious varieties of degeneration. The worst result from this essay is not merely speculative; it trains the feelings to false admirations; and upon a path which is the more dangerous, as the besetting temptation of our English life lies already towards an estimate much too high of all qualities bearing upon the active and the practical. We need no spur in that direction.

The essay upon the use of technically religious language seems even worse by its tendency, although the necessities of the subject will for ever neutralize

Foster's advice. Mr. Gilfillan is, in this instance, disposed to defend him: 'Foster does not ridicule the use, but the abuse, of technical language, as applied to divine things; and proposes, merely as an experiment, to translate it, in accommodation to fastidious tastes.' Safely, however, it may be assumed, that, in all such cases, the fastidious taste is but another aspect of hatred to religious themes,—a hatred which there is neither justice nor use in attempting to propitiate. Cant words ought certainly to be proscribed, as degrading to the majesty of religion; the word 'prayerful,' for instance, so commonly used of late years, seems objectionable; and such words as 'savory,' which is one of those cited by Foster himself, are absolutely abominable, when applied to spiritual or intellectual objects. It is not fastidiousness, but manliness and good feeling, which are outraged by such vulgarities. On the other hand, the word 'grace' expresses an idea so exclusively belonging to Christianity, and so indispensable to the wholeness of its philosophy, that any attempt to seek for equivalent terms of mere human growth, or amongst the vocabularies of mere worldly usage, must terminate in conscious failure, or else in utter self-delusion. Christianity, having introduced many ideas that are absolutely new, such as *faith*, *charity*, *holiness*, the nature of *God*, of human *frailty*, &c. is as much entitled (nay as much obliged and pledged) to a peculiar language and terminology as chemistry. Let a man try if he can find a word in the market-place fitted to be the substitute for the word *gas* or *alkali*. The danger, in fact, lies exactly in the opposite direction to that indicated by Foster. No fear that men of elegant taste should be revolted by the use of what, after all, is scriptural language; for it is plain that he who *could* be so revolted, wants nothing seriously with religion. But there is great fear that any general disposition to angle for readers of *extra* refinement, or to court the effeminately fastidious by sacrificing the majestic simplicities of scriptural diction, would and must end in a ruinous dilution of religious truths; along with the characteristic language of Christian philosophy, would exhale its characteristic doctrines.

WILLIAM HAZLITT.*

This man, who would have drawn in the scales against a select vestry of Fosters, is for the present deeper in the world's oblivion than the man with whom I here connect his name. *That* seems puzzling. For, if Hazlitt were misanthropic, so was Foster: both as writers were splenetic and more than peevish; but Hazlitt requited his reader for the pain of travelling through so gloomy an atmosphere, by the rich vegetation which his teeming intellect threw up as it moved along. The soil in *his* brain was of a volcanic fertility; whereas, in Foster, as in some tenacious clay, if the life were deep, it was slow and sullen in its throes. The reason for at all speaking of them in connection is, that both were essayists; neither in fact writing anything of note *except* essays, moral or critical; and both were bred at the feet of Dissenters. But how different were the results from that connection! Foster turned it to a blessing, winning the jewel that is most of all to be coveted, peace and the *fallentis semita vitæ.* Hazlitt, on the other hand, sailed wilfully away

* 'Gallery of Literary Portraits.' By George Gilfillan.

from this sheltering harbor of his father's profession, — for sheltering it might have proved to *him*, and *did* prove to his youth, — only to toss ever afterwards as a drifting wreck at the mercy of storms. Hazlitt was not one of those who *could* have illustrated the benefits of a connection with a sect, *i. e.* with a small confederation hostile by position to a larger; for the hostility from without, in order to react, presumes a concord from within. Nor does *his* case impeach the correctness of what I have said on that subject in speaking of Foster. He owed no introduction to the Dissenters; but it was because he *would* owe none. The Ishmaelite, whose hand is against every man, yet smiles at the approach of a brother, and gives the salutation of 'Peace be with you!' to the tribe of his father. But Hazlitt smiled upon no man, nor exchanged tokens of peace with the nearest of fraternities. Wieland in his 'Oberon,' says of a benign patriarch —

'*His* eye a smile on all creation beam'd.'

Travestied as to one word, the line would have described Hazlitt —

'*His* eye a scowl on all creation beam'd.'

This inveterate misanthropy was constitutional; exasperated it certainly had been by accidents of life, by disappointments, by mortifications, by insults, and still more by having wilfully placed himself in collision from the first with all the interests that were in the sunshine of this world, and with all the persons that were then powerful in England. But my impression was, if I had a right to *have* any impression with regard to one whom I knew so slightly, that no change of position or of fortunes could have brought Hazlitt into reconciliation with the fashion of this world, or of this England, or 'this now.' It seemed to me that he hated those whom hollow custom obliged him to call his 'friends,' considerably more than those whom notorious differences of opinion entitled him to rank as his enemies. At least within the ring of politics this was so. Between those particular Whigs whom literature had connected him with, and the whole gang of *us* Conservatives, he showed the same difference in his mode of fencing and parrying, and even in his style of civilities, as between the domestic traitor, hiding a stiletto among his robes of peace, and the bold enemy who sends a trumpet before him, and rides up sword-in-hand against your gates. *Whatever is* — so much I conceive to have been a fundamental lemma for Hazlitt — *is wrong*. So much he thought it safe to postulate. *How* it was wrong, might require an impracticable investigation; you might fail for a century to discover: but *that* it was wrong, he nailed down as a point of faith, that could stand out against all counter-presumptions from argument, or counter-evidences from experience. A friend of his it was, a friend wishing to love him, and admiring him almost to extravagance, who told me, in illustration of the dark sinister gloom which sat for ever upon Hazlitt's countenance and gestures, that involuntarily when Hazlitt put his hand within his waistcoat, (as a mere unconscious trick of habit,) he himself felt a sudden recoil of fear, as from one who was searching for a hidden dagger. Like 'a Moor of Malabar,' as described in the Faery Queen, at intervals Hazlitt threw up his angry eyes, and dark locks, as if wishing to affront the sun, or to search the air for hostility. And the same friend, on another occasion, described the sort of feudal fidelity to his belligerent duties, which in company seemed to animate Hazlitt, as though he were mounting guard on all the citadels of malignity, under some *sacramentum militaire*, by the following trait,—that, if it had happened to Hazlitt to be called out of the room, or to be withdrawn for a moment from the current of the general conversation, by a fit of abstraction, or by a private whisper to himself from some person sitting at his elbow, always on resuming his place as a party to what might be called the public business of the company, he looked round him with a mixed air of suspicion and defiance, such as seemed to challenge everybody by some stern adjuration into revealing whether, during his own absence or inattention, anything had been said demanding condign punishment at his hands. 'Has any man uttered or presumed to insinuate,' he seemed to insist upon knowing, 'during this *interregnum*, things that I ought to proceed against as treasonable to the interests which I defend?' He had the unresting irritability of Rousseau, but in a nobler shape; for Rousseau transfigured every possible act or design of his acquaintances into some personal relation to himself. The vile act was obviously meant, as a child could understand, to injure the person of Rousseau, or his interests, or his reputation. It was meant to wound his feelings, or to misrepresent his acts calumniously, or secretly to supplant his footing. But, on the contrary, Hazlitt viewed all personal affronts or casual slights towards himself, as tending to something more general, and masquing under a pretended horror of Hazlitt, the author, a real hatred, deeper than it was always safe to avow, for those social interests which he was reputed to defend. 'It was not Hazlitt whom the wretches struck at; no, no — it was democracy, or it was freedom, or it was Napoleon, whose shadow they saw in the rear of Hazlitt; and Napoleon, not for anything in him that might be really bad, but in revenge of that consuming wrath against the thrones of Christendom, for which (said Hazlitt) let us glorify his name eternally.'

Yet Hazlitt, like other men, and perhaps with more bitterness than other men, sought for love and for intervals of rest, in which all anger might sleep, and enmity might be laid aside like a travelling dress, after tumultuous journeys: . . .

'Though the sea-horse on the ocean
  Own no dear domestic cave,
Yet he slumbers without motion
  On the still and halcyon wave.

If, on windy days, the raven
  Gambol like a dancing skiff,
Not the less he loves his haven
  On the bosom of a cliff.

If almost with eagle pinion
  O'er the Alps the chamois roam,
Yet he has some small dominion,
  Which, no doubt, he calls his home.'

But Hazlitt, restless as the sea-horse, as the raven, as the chamois, found not their respites from storm; he sought, but sought in vain. And for *him* the closing stanza of that little poem remained true to his dying hour: in the person of the 'Wandering Jew,' *he* might complain,—

> 'Day and night my toils redouble:
> Never nearer to the goal,
> Night and day I feel the trouble
> Of the wanderer in my soul.'

Domicile he had not, round whose hearth his affections might gather: rest he had not, for the sole of his burning foot... One chance of regaining some peace, or a chance as he trusted for a time, was torn from him at the moment of gathering its blossoms. He had been divorced from his wife, not by the law of England, which would have argued criminality in *her*, but by Scottish law, satisfied with some proof of frailty in himself. Subsequently he became deeply fascinated by a young woman, in no very elevated rank, for she held some domestic office of superintendence in a boarding-house kept by her father, but of interesting person, and endowed with strong intellectual sensibilities. She had encouraged Hazlitt; had gratified him by reading his works with intelligent sympathy; and, under what form of duplicity it is hard to say, had partly engaged her faith to Hazlitt as his future wife, whilst secretly she was holding a correspondence, too tender to be misinterpreted, with a gentleman resident in the same establishment. Suspicions were put aside for a time; but they returned, and gathered too thickly for Hazlitt's penetration to cheat itself any longer. Once and for ever he resolved to satisfy himself. On a Sunday, fatal to him and his farewell hopes of domestic happiness, he had reason to believe that she, whom he now loved to excess, had made some appointment out-of-doors with his rival. It was in London; and through the crowds of London, Hazlitt followed her steps to the rendezvous. Fancying herself lost in the multitude that streamed through Lincolns-inn-fields, the treacherous young woman met her more favored lover without alarm, and betrayed, too clearly for any further deception, the state of her affections by the tenderness of her manner. *There* went out the last light that threw a guiding ray over the storm-vexed course of Hazlitt. He was too much in earnest, and he had witnessed too much, to be deceived or appeased. 'I whistled her down the wind,' was his own account of the catastrophe: but, in doing so, he had torn his own heart-strings, entangled with her 'jesses.' Neither did he, as others would have done, seek to disguise his misfortune. On the contrary, he cared not for the ridicule attached to such a situation amongst the unfeeling: the wrench within had been too profound to leave room for sensibility to the sneers outside. A fast friend of his at that time, and one who never ceased to be his apologist, described him to me as having become absolutely maniacal during the first pressure of this affliction. He went about proclaiming the case, and insisting on its details, to every stranger that would listen. He even published the whole story to the world, in his 'Modern Pygmalion.' And people generally, who could not be aware of his feelings, or the way in which this treachery acted upon his mind as a ratification of all other treacheries and wrongs that he had suffered through life, laughed at him, or expressed disgust for him as too coarsely indelicate in making such disclosures. But there was no indelicacy in such an act of confidence, growing, as it did, out of his lacerated heart. It was an explosion of frenzy. He threw out his clamorous anguish to the clouds, and to the winds, and to the air; caring not *who* might listen, *who* might sympathize, or *who* might sneer. Pity was no demand of his; laughter was no wrong: the sole necessity for *him* was — to empty his over-burdened spirit.

After this desolating experience, the exasperation of Hazlitt's political temper grew fiercer, darker, steadier. His 'Life of Napoleon' was prosecuted subsequently to this, and perhaps under this remembrance, as a reservoir that might receive all the vast overflows of his wrath, much of which was not merely political, or in a spirit of bacchanalian partisanship, but was even morbidly anti-social. He hated, with all his heart, every institution of man, and all his pretensions. He loathed his own relation to the human race.

It was but on a few occasions that I ever met Mr. Hazlitt myself; and those occasions, or all but one, were some time subsequent to the case of female treachery which I have here described. Twice, I think, or it might be three times, we walked for a few miles together: it was in London, late at night, and after leaving a party. Though depressed by the spectacle of a mind always in agitation from the gloomier passions, I was yet amused by the pertinacity with which he clung, through bad reasons or no reasons, to any public slander floating against men in power, or in the highest rank. No feather, or dowl of a feather, but was heavy enough for *him.* Amongst other instances of this willingness to be deluded by rumors, if they took a direction favorable to his own bias, Hazlitt had adopted the whole strength of popular hatred which for many years ran violently against the King of Hanover, at that time Duke of Cumberland. A dark calumny had arisen against this prince, amongst the populace of London, as though he had been accessary to the death of his valet. This valet [Sellis] had, in fact, attempted to murder the prince; and all that can be said in palliation of his act, is, that he *believed* himself to have sustained, in the person of his beautiful wife, the heaviest dishonor incident to man. How that matter stood, I pretend not to know: the attempt at murder was baffled; and the valet then destroyed himself with a razor. All this had been regularly sifted by a coroner's inquest; and I remarked to Hazlitt, that the witnesses seemed to have been called, indifferently, from all quarters likely to have known the facts; so that, if this inquest had failed to elicit the truth, we might, with equal reason, presume as much of all other inquests. From the verdict of a jury, except in very peculiar cases, no candid and temperate man will allow himself to believe any appeal sustainable: for, having the witnesses before them face to face, and hearing the *whole* of the evidence, a jury have always some means of forming a judgment which cannot be open to him who depends upon an abridged report. But, on this subject, Hazlitt would hear no reason. He said — 'No:

all the princely houses of Europe have the instinct of murder running in their blood; — they cherish it through their privilege of making war, which being wholesale murder, once having reconciled themselves to *that*, they think of retail murder, committed on you or me, as of no crime at all.' Under this obstinate prejudice against the duke, Hazlitt read everything that he did, or did *not* do, in a perverse spirit. And, in one of these nightly walks, he mentioned to me, as something quite worthy of a murderer, the following little trait of casuistry in the royal duke's distribution of courtesies. 'I saw it myself,' said Hazlitt, 'so no coroner's jury can put me down.' His royal highness had rooms in St. James's; and, one day, as he was issuing from the palace into Pall-Mall, Hazlitt happened to be immediately behind him; he could therefore watch his motions along the whole line of his progress. It is the custom in England, wheresoever the persons of the royal family are familiar to the public eye, as at Windsor, &c., that all passengers in the streets, on seeing them, walk bareheaded, or make some signal of dutiful respect. On this occasion, all the men, who met the prince, took off their hats; the prince acknowledging every such obeisance by a separate bow. Pall-Mall being finished, and its whole harvest of royal salutations gathered in, next the duke came to Cockspur street. But here, and taking a station close to the crossing, which daily he beautified and polished with his broom, stood a Negro sweep. If human at all, which some people doubted, he was pretty nearly as abject a representative of our human family divine as can ever have existed. Still he was held to be a man by the law of the land, which would have hanged any person, gentle or simple, for cutting his throat. Law, (it is certain,) conceived him to be a man, however poor a one; though Medicine, in an under-tone, muttered, sometimes, a demur to that opinion. But here the sweep *was*, whether man or beast, standing humbly in the path of royalty: vanish he would not; he was, (as *The Times* says of the Corn-League,) 'a great fact,' if rather a muddy one; and though, by his own confession, (repeated one thousand times a day,) both 'a nigger' and a sweep, ['Remember poor nigger, your honor!' 'remember poor sweep!'] yet the creature could take off his rag of a hat, and earn the bow of a prince, as well as any white native of St. James's. What was to be done? A great case of cônscience was on the point of being raised in the person of a paralytic nigger; nay, possibly a state question — Ought a son of England,* could a son of England,

* 'Son of England;' *i. e.*, prince of the blood in the *direct*, and not in the collateral, line. I mention this for the sake of some readers, who may not be aware that this beautiful formula, so well known in France, is often transferred by the French writers of memoirs to our English princes, though little used amongst ourselves. Gaston, Duke of Orleans, brother of Louis XIV., was 'a *son* of France,' as being a child of Louis XIII. But the son of Gaston, viz., the Regent Duke of Orleans, was a *grandson* of France. The first wife of Gaston, our Princess Henrietta, was called '*Fille* d'Angleterre,' as being a daughter of Charles I. The Princess Charlotte, again, was a *daughter* of England; her present majesty, a *grand-daughter* of England. But all these ladies collectively would be called, on the French principle, the children of England.

descend from his majestic pedestal to gild with the rays of his condescension such a grub, such a very doubtful grub, as this? Total Pall-Mall was sagacious of the coming crisis; judgment was going to be delivered; a precedent to be raised; and Pall-Mall stood still, with Hazlitt at its head, to learn the issue. How if the black should be a Jacobin, and (in the event of the duke's bowing) should have a bas-relief sculptured on his tomb, exhibiting an English prince, and a German king, as two separate personages, in the act of worshipping his broom? Luckily, it was not the black's province to settle the case. The Duke of Cumberland, seeing no counsel at hand to argue either the *pro* or the *contra*, found himself obliged to settle the question *de plano;* so, drawing out his purse, he kept his hat as rigidly settled on his head, as William Penn and Mead did before the Recorder of London. All Pall-Mall applauded: *contradicente* Gulielmo Hazlitt, and Hazlitt only. The black swore that the prince gave him half-a-crown; but whether he regarded this in the light of a god-send to his avarice, or a shipwreck to his ambition — whether he was more thankful for the money gained, or angry for the honor lost — did not transpire. 'No matter,' said Hazlitt, 'the black might be a fool; but I insist upon it, that he was entitled to the bow, since all Pall-Mall had it before him; and that it was unprincely to refuse it.' Either as a black or as a scavenger, Hazlitt held him 'qualified' for sustaining a royal bow: as a black, was he not a specimen (if rather a damaged one) of the *homo sapiens* described by Linnæus? As a sweep, in possession (by whatever title) of a lucrative crossing, had he not a kind of estate in London? Was he not, said Hazlitt, a fellow-subject, capable of committing treason, and paying taxes into the treasury? Not perhaps in any direct shape, but indirect taxes most certainly on his tobacco — and even on his broom?

These things could not be denied. But still, when my turn came for speaking, I confessed frankly that (politics apart) my feeling in the case went along with the duke's. The bow would not be so useful to the black as the half-crown: he could not possibly have both; for how could any man make a bow to a beggar when in the act of giving him half-a-crown? Then, on the other hand, this bow, so useless to the sweep, and (to speak by a vulgar adage) as superfluous as a side-pocket to a cow, would react upon the other bows distributed along the line of Pall-Mall, so as to neutralize them one and all. No honor could continue such in which a paralytic negro sweep was associated. This distinction, however, occurred to me; that if, instead of a prince and a subject, the royal dispenser of bows had been a king, he ought *not* to have excluded the black from participation; because, as the common father of his people, he ought not to know of any difference amongst those who are equally his children. And in illustration of that opinion, I sketched a little scene which I had myself witnessed, and with great pleasure, upon occasion of a visit made to Drury Lane by George IV. when regent. At another time I may tell it to the reader. Hazlitt, however, listened fretfully to me when praising the deportment and beautiful gestures of one conservative leader; though he had compelled *me* to hear the most disadvantageous comments on another.

As a lecturer, I do not know what Hazlitt was, having never had an opportunity of hearing him. Some qualities in his style of composition were calculated to assist the purposes of a lecturer, who must produce an effect oftentimes by independent sentences and paragraphs, who must glitter and surprise, who must turn round within the narrowest compass, and cannot rely upon any sort of attention that would cost an effort. Mr. Gilfillan says, that 'He proved more popular than was expected by those who knew his uncompromising scorn of all those tricks and petty artifices which are frequently employed to pump up applause. His manner was somewhat abrupt and monotonous, but earnest and energetic.' At the same time, Mr. Gilfillan takes an occasion to express some opinions, which appear very just, upon the unfitness (generally speaking) of men whom he describes as 'fiercely inspired,' for this mode of display. The truth is, that all genius implies originality, and sometimes uncontrollable singularity, in the habits of thinking, and in the modes of viewing, as well as of estimating objects. Whereas a miscellaneous audience is best conciliated by that sort of talent which reflects the average mind, which is not overweighted in any one direction, is not tempted into any extreme, and is able to preserve a steady, rope-dancer's equilibrium of posture upon themes where a man of genius is most apt to lose it.

It would be interesting to have a full and accurate list of Hazlitt's works, including, of course, his contributions to journals and encyclopædias. These last, as shorter, and oftener springing from an *impromptu* effort, are more likely, than his regular books, to have been written with a pleasurable enthusiasm: and the writer's proportion of pleasure, in such cases, very often becomes the regulating law for his reader's. Amongst the philosophical works of Hazlitt, I do not observe that Mr. Gilfillan is aware of two that are likely to be specially interesting. One is an examination of David Hartley, at least as to his law of association. Thirty years ago, I looked into it slightly; but my reverence for Hartley offended me with its tone; and afterwards, hearing that Coleridge challenged for his own most of what was important in the thoughts, I lost all interest in the essay. Hazlitt, having heard Coleridge talk on this theme, must have approached it with a mind largely preoccupied as regarded the weak points in Hartley, and the particular tactics for assailing them. But still the great talents for speculative research which Hazlitt had from nature, without having given to them the benefit of much culture or much exercise, would justify our attentive examination of the work. It forms part of the volume which contains the 'Essay on Human Action;' which volume, by the way, Mr. Gilfillan supposes to have won the special applause of Sir James Mackintosh, then in Bengal. This, if accurately stated, is creditable to Sir James's generosity: for, in this particular volume it is, that Hazlitt makes a pointed assault, in sneering terms, and very unnecessarily, upon Sir James.

The other little work unnoticed by Mr. Gilfillan, is an examination (but under what title I cannot say) of Lindley Murray's English Grammar. This may seem, by its subject, a trifle; yet Hazlitt could hardly have had a motive for such an effort but in some philosophic perception of the ignorance betrayed by many grammars of our language, and sometimes by that of Lindley Murray; which Lindley, by the way, though resident in England, was an American. There is great room for a useful display of philosophic subtlety in an English grammar, even though meant for schools. Hazlitt could not *but* have furnished something of value towards such a display. And if (as I was once told) his book was suppressed, I imagine that this suppression must have been purchased by some powerful publisher interested in keeping up the current reputation of Murray.

'Strange stories,' says Mr. Gilfillan, 'are told about his [Hazlitt's] latter days, and his death-bed.' I know not whether I properly understand Mr. Gilfillan. The stories which I myself have happened to hear, were not so much 'strange,' since they arose, naturally enough, out of pecuniary embarrassments, as they were afflicting in the turn they took. Dramatically viewed, if a man were speaking of things so far removed from our own times and interests as to excuse that sort of language, the circumstances of Hazlitt's last hours might rivet the gaze of a critic as fitted, harmoniously, with almost scenic art, to the whole tenor of his life; fitted equally to rouse his wrath, to deepen his dejection, and in the hour of death to justify his misanthropy. But I have no wish to utter a word on things which I know only at second-hand, and cannot speak upon without risk of misstating facts or doing injustice to persons. I prefer closing this section with the words of Mr. Gilfillan:

'Well says Bulwer, that of all the mental wrecks which have occurred in our era, this was the most melancholy. Others may have been as unhappy in their domestic circumstances, and gone down steeper places of dissipation than he; but they had meanwhile the breath of popularity, if not of wealth and station, to give them a certain solace.' What had Hazlitt of this nature? Mr. Gilfillan answers, — 'Absolutely nothing to support and cheer him. With no hope, no fortune, no *status* in society; no certain popularity as a writer, no domestic peace, little sympathy from kindred spirits, little support from his political party, no moral management, no definite belief; with great powers, and great passions within, and with a host of powerful enemies without, it was his to enact one of the saddest tragedies on which the sun ever shone. Such is a faithful portraiture of an extraordinary man, whose restless intellect and stormy passions have now, for fifteen years, found that repose in the grave which was denied them above it.' Mr. Gilfillan concludes with expressing his conviction, in which I desire to concur, that both enemies and friends will *now* join in admiration for the man; 'both will readily concede *now*, that a subtle thinker, an eloquent writer, a lover of beauty and poetry, and man and truth, one of the best of critics, and not the worst of men, expired in William Hazlitt.' *Requiescat in pace!*

NOTES ON WALTER SAVAGE LANDOR.*

NOBODY in this generation reads *The Spectator.* There are, however, several people still surviving who have read No. 1; in which No. 1 a strange mistake is made. It is there asserted, as a general affection of human nature, that it is impossible to read a book with satisfaction, until one has ascertained whether the author of it be tall or short, corpulent or thin, and as to complexion, whether he be a 'black' man, (which, in the *Spectator's* time, was the absurd expression for a swarthy man,) or a fair man, or a sallow man, or perhaps a green man, which Southey affirmed[1] to be the proper description of many stout artificers in Birmingham, too much given to work in metallic fumes; on which account the name of Southey is an abomination to this day in certain furnaces of Warwickshire. But can anything be more untrue than this Spectatorial doctrine? Did ever the youngest of female novel readers, on a sultry day, decline to eat a bunch of grapes until she knew whether the fruiterer were a good-looking man? Which of us ever heard a stranger inquiring for a 'Guide to the Trosachs,'

---

* The Works of Walter Savage Landor. 2 vols.

but saying, 'I scruple, however, to pay for this book, until I know whether the author is heather-legged.' On this principle, if any such principle prevailed, we authors should be liable to as strict a revision of our physics before having any right to be read, as we all are before having our lives insured from the medical advisers of insurance offices; fellows that examine one with stethescopes; that pinch one, that actually punch one in the ribs, until a man becomes savage, and — in case the insurance should miss fire in consequence of the medical report — speculates on the propriety of prosecuting the medical ruffian for an assault, for a most unprovoked assault and battery, and, if possible, including in the indictment the now odious insurance office as an accomplice before the fact. Meantime the odd thing is, not that Addison should have made a mistake, but that he and his readers should, in this mistake, have recognised a hidden truth, — the sudden illumination of a propensity latent in all people, but now first exposed; for it happens that there really *is* a propensity in all of us, very like what Addison describes very different, and yet, after one correction, the very same. No reader cares about an author's person *before* reading his book: it is *after* reading it, and supposing the book to reveal something of the writer's *moral* nature, as modifying his intellect; it is for his fun, his fancy, his sadness, possibly his craziness, that any reader cares about seeing the author in person. Afflicted with the very satyriasis of curiosity, no man ever wished to see the author of a *Ready Reckoner*, or of a treatise on the *Agistment Tithe*, or on the *Present deplorable Dry-rot in Potatoes.*

'Bundle off, Sir, as fast as you can,' the most diligent reader would say to such an author, in case he insisted on submitting his charms to inspection. 'I have had quite enough distress of mind from reading your works, without needing the additional dry-rot of your bodily presence.' Neither does any man, on descending from a railway train, turn to look whether the carriage in which he has ridden happens to be a good-looking carriage, or wish for an introduction to the coach-maker. Satisfied that the one has not broken his bones, and that the other has no writ against his person, he dismisses with the same frigid scowl both the carriage and the author of its existence.

But, with respect to Mr. Landor, as at all connected with this reformed doctrine of the *Spectator*, a difficulty arises. He is a man of great genius, and, as such, he *ought* to interest the public. More than enough appears of his strong, eccentric nature, through every page of his now extensive writings, to win, amongst those who have read him, a corresponding interest in all that concerns him personally; in his social relations, in his biography, in his manners, in his appearance. Out of two conditions for attracting a *personal* interest, he has powerfully realized one. His moral nature, shining with colored light through the crystal shrine of his thoughts, will not allow of your forgetting it. A sunset of Claude, or a dying dolphin *can* be forgotten, and generally *is* forgotten; but not the fiery radiations of a human spirit, built by nature to animate a leader in storms, a martyr, a national reformer, an arch-rebel, as circumstances might dictate, but whom too much wealth,[2] and the accidents of education, have turned aside into a contemplative recluse. Had Mr. Landor, therefore, been read in any extent answering to his merits, he must have become, for the English public, an object of prodigious personal interest. We should have had novels upon him, lampoons upon him, libels upon him ; he would have been shown up dramatically on the stage ; he would, according to the old joke, have been 'traduced' in French, and also 'overset' in Dutch. Meantime he has *not* been read. It would be an affectation to think it. Many a writer is, by the sycophancy of literature, reputed to be read, whom in all Europe not six eyes settle upon through the revolving year. Literature, with its cowardly falsehoods, exhibits the largest field of conscious Phrygian adulation that human life has ever exposed to the derision of the heavens. Demosthenes, for instance, or Plato, is not read to the extent of twenty pages annually by ten people in Europe. The *sale* of their works would not account for three readers; the other six or seven are generally conceded as possibilities furnished by the great public libraries. But, then, Walter Savage Landor, though writing a little in Latin, and a *very* little in Italian, does not write at all in Greek. So far he has some advantage over Plato ; and, if he writes chiefly in dialogue, which few people love to read any more than novels in the shape of letters, *that* is a crime common to both. So that he has the d——l's luck and his own, all Plato's chances, and one of his own beside — viz. his English. Still, it is no use counting chances; facts are the thing. And printing-presses, whether of Europe or of England, bear witness that neither Plato nor Landor is a marketable commodity.

In fact, these two men resemble each other in more particulars than it is at present necessary to say. Especially they were both inclined to be luxurious: both had a hankering after purple and fine linen; both hated 'filthy dowlas' with the hatred of Falstaff, whether in appareling themselves or their diction; and both bestowed pains as elaborate upon the secret *art* of a dialogue, as a lapidary would upon the cutting of a sultan's rubies.

But might not a man build a reputation on the basis of *not* being read? To be read is undoubtedly something: to be read by an odd million or so, is a sort of feather in a man's cap; but it is also a distinction that he has been read absolutely by nobody at all. There have been cases, and one or two in modern times, where an author could point to a vast array of his own works, concerning which no evidence existed that so much as one had been opened by human hand, or glanced at by human eye. That was awful: such a sleep of pages by thousands in one eternal darkness, never to be visited by light; such a rare immunity from the villanies of misconstruction; such a Sabbath from the impertinencies of critics! You shuddered to reflect that, for anything known to the contrary, *there* might lurk jewels of truth explored in vain, or treasure for ever intercepted to the interests of man. But such a sublimity supposes *total* defect of readers; whereas it can be proved against Mr. Landor, that he has been read by at least a score of people, all wide awake; and if any treason is buried in a page of *his*, thank Heaven, by this time it must have been found out and reported to the authorities. So that neither can Landor plead the unlimited popularity of a novelist, aided by the interest of a tale, and by an artist, nor the total obscuration of a German metaphysician. Neither do mobs read him, as they do M. Sue ; nor do all men turn away their eyes from him, as they do from Hegel.[3]

This, however, is true only of Mr. Landor's prose works. His first work was a poem, viz. *Gebir;* and it had the sublime distinction, for some time, of having enjoyed only two readers; which two were Southey and myself. It was on first entering at Oxford that I found 'Gebir' printed and (nominally) published; whereas, in fact, all its advertisements of birth and continued existence, were but so many notifications of its intense privacy. Not knowing Southey at that time, I vainly conceited myself to be the one sole purchaser and reader of this poem. I even fancied myself to have been pointed out in the streets of Oxford, where the Landors had been well known in times preceding my own, as the one inexplicable man authentically known to possess 'Gebir,' or even (it might be whispered mysteriously) to have read 'Gebir.' It was not clear but this reputation might stand in lieu of any independent fame, and might raise me to literary distinction. The preceding generation had greatly esteemed the man called '*Single-Speech Hamilton ;*' not at all for the speech (which, though good, very few people had read,) but entirely for the supposed fact that he had exhausted himself in that one speech, and had become physically incapable of making a second: so that afterwards, when he really *did* make a second, everybody was incredulous ; until, the thing being past denial, naturally the world was disgusted, and most people dropped his acquaintance. To be a Mono-Gebirist was quite as good a title to notoriety; and five years after, when I found that I had 'a brother near the throne,' viz. Southey, mortification would have led me willingly to resign altogether in *his* favor. Shall I make the reader acquainted with the story of Gebir?

Gebir is the king of Gibraltar; which, however, it would be an anachronism to *call* Gibraltar, since it drew that name from this very Gebir; and doubtless, by way of honor to his memory. Mussulmans tell a different story: but who cares for what is said by infidel dogs? King, then, let us call him of Calpe; and a very good king he is; young, brave, of upright intentions; but being also warlike, and inflamed by popular remembrances of ancient wrongs, he resolves to seek reparation from the children's children of the wrong-doers; and he weighs anchor in search of Mr. Pitt's 'indemnity for the past,' though not much regarding that right honorable gentleman's 'security for the future.' Egypt was the land that sheltered the wretches that represented the ancestors that had done the wrong. To Egypt, therefore, does king Gebir steer his expedition, which counted ten thousand picked men:

——————— 'Incenst
By meditating on primeval wrongs,
He blew his battle-horn; at which uprose
Whole nations: here ten thousand of most might
He called aloud; and soon Charoba saw
His dark helm hover o'er the land of Nile.'

Who is Charoba? As respects the reader, she is the heroine of the poem: as respects Egypt, she is queen by the grace of God, defender of the faith, and so forth. Young and accustomed to unlimited obedience, how could she be otherwise than alarmed by the descent of a host far more martial than her own effeminate people, and assuming a religious character — avengers of wrong in some forgotten age? In her trepidation, she turns for aid and counsel to her nurse Dalica. Dalica, by the way, considered as a word, is a dactyle; that is, you must not lay the accent on the *i*, but on the first syllable. Dalica, considered as a woman, is about as bad a one as even Egypt could furnish. She is a thorough gipsy; a fortune-teller, and something worse, in fact. She is a sorceress, 'stiff in opinion:' and it needs not Pope's authority to infer that —— of course she 'is always in the wrong.' By her advice, but for a purpose known best to herself, an interview is arranged between Charoba and the invading monarch. At this interview, the two youthful sovereigns, Charoba the queen of hearts and Gebir the king of clubs, fall irrevocably in love with each other. There's an end of club law: and Gebir is ever afterwards disarmed. But Dalica, that wicked Dalica, that sad old dactyle, who sees everything clearly that happens to be twenty years distant, cannot see a pikestaff if it is close before her nose; and of course she mistakes Charoba's agitations of love for paroxysms of anger. Charoba is herself partly to blame for this; but you must excuse her. The poor child readily confided her *terrors* to Dalica; but how can she be expected to make a *love* confidante of a tawny old witch like her? Upon this mistake, however, proceeds the whole remaining plot. *Dr.* Dalica (which means *doctor* D., and by no means *dear* D.,) having totally mistaken the symptoms, the diagnosis, the prognosis, and everything that ends in *osis*, necessarily mistakes also the treatment of the case, and, like some other doctors, failing to make a cure, covers up her blunders by a general slaughter. She visits her sister, a sorceress more potent than herself, living

'Deep in the wilderness of woe, Masar.'

Between them they concert hellish incantations. From these issues a venomous robe, like that of the centaur Nessus. This, at a festal meeting between the two nations and their princes, is given by Charoba to her lover — her lover, but as yet not recognised as such by *her*, nor until the moment of his death, avowed as such by himself. Gebir dies — the accursed robe, dipped in the 'viscous poison' exuding from the gums of the grey cerastes, and tempered by other venomous juices of plant and animal, proves too much for his rocky constitution — Gibraltar is found not impregnable — the blunders of Dalica, the wicked nurse, and the arts of her sister Myrthyr, the wicked witch, are found too potent; and in one moment the union of two nations, with the happiness of two sovereigns, is wrecked for ever. The closing situation of the parties — monarch and monarch, nation and nation, youthful king and youthful queen, dying or despairing — nation and nation that had been reconciled, starting asunder once again amidst festival and flowers — these objects are scenically effective. The conception of the grouping is good ; the *mise en scene* is good; but, from want of pains-taking, not sufficiently brought out into strong relief; and the dying words of Gebir, which wind up the whole, are too bookish; they seem to be part of some article which he had been writing for the Gibraltar Quarterly.

There are two episodes, composing jointly about two-sevenths of the poem, and by no means its weakest parts. One describes the descent of Gebir to Hades. His guide is a man — who *is* this man?

'Living — they called him Aroar.'

Is he *not* living, then? No. Is he dead, then? No, nor dead either. Poor Aroar cannot live, and cannot die — so that he is in an almighty fix. In this disagreeable dilemma, he contrives to amuse himself with politics — and, rather of a jacobinical cast: like the Virgilian Æneas, Gebir is introduced not to the shades of the past only, but of the future. He sees the pre-existing ghosts of gentlemen who are yet to come, silent as ghosts ought to be, but destined at some far distant time to make a considerable noise in our upper world. Amongst these is our worthy old George III., who (strange to say !) is not foreseen as galloping from Windsor to Kew, surrounded by an escort of dragoons, nor in a scarlet coat riding after a fox, nor taking his morning rounds amongst his sheep and his turnips; but in the likeness of some savage creature, whom really, were it not for his eyebrows and his '*slanting*' forehead, the reader would never recognise:

'Aroar! what wretch that nearest us? what wretch
Is that, with eyebrows white and slanting brow?
———————————— O king!
Iberia bore him; but the breed accurst
Inclement winds blew blighting from north-east.'

Iberia is spiritual England; and *north-east* is mystical Hanover. But what, then, were the 'wretch's' crimes? The white eyebrows I confess to; those were certainly crimes of considerable magnitude: but what else? Gebir has the same curiosity as myself, and propounds something like the same fishing question:

'He was a warrior then, nor feared the gods?'

To which Aroar answers —

'Gebir! he feared the demons, not the gods;
Though them, indeed, his daily face ador'd,
And was no warrior; yet the thousand lives
Squander'd as if to exercise a sling, &c. &c.'

Really Aroar is too *Tom-Painish*, and seems up to a little treason. He makes the poor king answerable for more than his own share of national offences, if such they were. All of us in the last generation were rather fond of fighting and assisting at fights in the character of mere spectators. I am sure *I* was. But if *that* is any fault, so was Plato, who (though probably inferior as a philosopher to you and me, reader,) was much superior to either of us as a cock-fighter. So was Socrates in the preceding age; for, as he notoriously haunted the company of Alcibiades at all hours, he must often have found his pupil diverting himself with these fighting quails which he kept in such numbers. Be assured that the oracle's 'wisest of men' lent a hand very cheerfully to putting on the spurs when a main was to be fought; and, as to betting, probably *that* was the reason that Xantippe was so often down upon him when he went home at night. To come home reeling from a fight, without a drachma left in his pocket, would naturally provoke any woman. Posterity has been very much misinformed about these things; and, no doubt, about Xantippe, poor woman, in particular. If *she* had had a disciple to write books, as her cock-fighting husband had, perhaps we should have read a very different story. By the way, the propensity to *scandalum magnatum* in Aroar was one of the things that fixed my youthful attention, and perhaps my admiration, upon Gebir. For myself, as perhaps the reader may have heard, I was and am a Tory; and in some remote geological æra, my bones may be dug up by some future Buckland as a specimen of the fossil Tory. Yet, for all that, I loved audacity; and I gazed with some indefinite shade of approbation upon a poet whom the attorney-general might have occasion to speak with.

This, however, was a mere condiment to the main attraction of the poem. *That* lay in the picturesqueness of the images, attitudes, groups, dispersed everywhere. The eye seemed to rest everywhere upon festal processions, upon the panels of Theban gates, or upon sculptured vases. The very first lines that by accident met my eye, were those which follow. I cite them in mere obedience to the fact as it really was; else there are more striking illustrations of this sculpturesque faculty in Mr. Landor; and for this faculty it was that both Southey and myself separately and independently had named him the English Valerius Flaccus.

GEBIR ON REPAIRING TO HIS FIRST INTERVIEW WITH CHAROBA.

'But Gebir, when he heard of her approach,
Laid by his orbed shield: his vizor helm,
His buckler and his corslet he laid by,
And bade that none attend him: at his side
Two faithful dogs that urge the silent course,
Shaggy, deep-chested, croucht; the crocodile,
Crying, oft made them raise their flaccid ears,
And push their heads within their master's hand.
There was a lightning paleness in his face,
Such as Diana rising o'er the rocks
Shower'd on the lonely Latmian; on his brow
Sorrow there was, but there was nought severe.'

'And the long moonbeam on the hard wet sand
Lay like a jasper column half up-rear'd.'

'The king, who sate before his tent, descried
The dust rise redden'd from the setting sun.'

Now let us pass to the imaginary dialogues: —

Marshal Bugeaud and Arab Chieftain. — This dialogue, which is amongst the shortest, would not challenge a separate notice, were it not for the freshness in the public mind, and the yet uncicatrized rawness of that atrocity which it commemorates. Here is an official account from the commander-in-chief: — 'Of seven hundred refractory and rebellious who took refuge in the caravans, thirty,' [says the glory-hunting Marshal], 'and thirty only, are alive; and of these thirty there are four only who are capable of labor, or indeed of motion.' How precious to the Marshal's heart must be that harvest of misery from which he so reluctantly allows the discount of about one-half per cent. Four only out of seven hundred, he is happy to assure Christendom, remain capable of hopping about; as to working, or getting honest bread, or doing any service in this world to themselves or others, it is truly delightful to announce, for public information, that all such practices are put a stop to for ever.

Amongst the fortunate four, who retain the power of hopping, we must reckon the *Arab Chieftain*, who is introduced into the colloquy in the character of respondent. He can hop, of course, *ex hypothesi*, being one of the ever lucky quaternion; he can hop a little also as a rhetorician; indeed, as to *that* he is too much for the Marshal; but on the other hand he cannot see; the cave has cured him of any such impertinence as staring into other people's faces; he is also lame, the cave has shown him the absurdity of rambling about; — and, finally, he is a beggar; or, if he will not allow himself to be called by that name, upon the argument [which seems plausible] that he cannot be a beggar if he never begs, it is not the less certain that, in case of betting a sixpence, the chieftain would find it inconvenient to stake the cash.

The Marshal, who apparently does not pique himsef upon politeness, addresses the Arab by the following assortment of names — 'Thief, assassin, traitor! blind greybeard! lame beggar!' The three first titles being probably mistaken for compliments, the Arab pockets in silence; but to the double-barrelled discharges of the two last he replies thus: — 'Cease *there*. Thou canst never make me beg for bread, for water, or for life; my grey beard is from God; my blindness and lameness are from thee.' This is a pleasant way of doing business; rarely does one find little accounts so expeditiously settled and receipted. Beggar? But how if I do not beg? Greybeard? Put that down to the account of God. Cripple? Put that down to your own. Getting sulky under this mode of fencing from the desert-born, the Marshal invites him to enter one of his new-made law courts, where he will hear of something probably *not* to his advantage. Our Arab friend, however, is no connoisseur in courts of law: small wale[4] of courts in the desert; he does not so much 'do himself the honor to decline' as he turns a deaf ear to this proposal, and on *his* part presents a little counter invitation to the Marshal for a *pic-nic* party to the caves of Dahra. 'Enter' (says the unsparing Sheik) 'and sing and whistle in the cavern where the bones of brave men are never to bleach, are never to decay. Go, where the mother and infant are inseparable for ever — one mass of charcoal; the breasts that gave life, the lips that received it — all, all, save only where two arms, in color and hardness like corroded iron, cling round a brittle stem, shrunken, warped, and where two heads are calcined. Even this massacre, no doubt, will find defenders in *your* country, for it is the custom of *your* country, to cover blood with lies, and lies with blood.' 'And (says the facetious French Marshal) here and there a sprinkling of ashes over both.' ARAB. 'Ending in merriment, as befits ye. But *is* it ended?' But *is* it ended? Aye; the wilderness beyond Algiers returns an echo to those ominous words of the blind and mutilated chieftain. No, brave Arab, although the Marshal scoffingly rejoins that at least it is ended for *you*, ended it is not; for the great quarrel by which human nature pleads with such a fiendish spirit of warfare, carried on under the countenance of him who stands first in authority under the nation that stands second in authority amongst the leaders of civilization; — quarrel of that sort, once arising, does not go to sleep again until it is righted for ever. As the English martyr at Oxford said to his fellow martyr — 'Brother, be of good cheer, for we shall this day light up a fire in England that, by the blessing of God, cannot be extinguished for ever,' — even so the atrocities of these hybrid campaigns between baffled civilization and barbarism, provoked into frenzy, will, like the horrors of the middle passage rising up from the Atlantic deep, suddenly, at the bar of the British senate, sooner or later reproduce themselves, in strong reactions of the social mind throughout Christendom, upon *all* the horrors of war that are wilful and superfluous. In that case there will be a consolation in reserve for the compatriots of those, the brave men, the women, and the innocent children, who died in that fiery furnace at Dahra.

'Their moans
The vales redoubled to the hills, and *they*
To heaven.' [5]

The caves of Dahra repeated the woe to the hills, and the hills to God. But such a furnace, though fierce, may be viewed as brief indeed if it shall terminate in permanently pointing the wrath of nations, (as in this dialogue it has pointed the wrath of genius,) to the particular outrage and class of outrages which it concerns. The wrath of nations is a consuming wrath, and the scorn of intellect is a withering scorn, for all abuses upon which either one or the other is led, by strength of circumstances, to settle itself *systematically*. The danger is for the most part that the very violence of public feeling should rock it asleep — the tempest exhausts itself by its own excesses — and the thunder of one or two immediate explosions, by satisfying the first clamors of human justice and indignation, is too apt to intercept that sustained roll of artillery which is requisite for the effectual assault of long established abuses. Luckily in the present case of the Dahra massacre there is the less danger of such a result, as the bloody scene has happened to fall in with a very awakened state of the public sensibility as to the evils of war generally, and with a state of expectation almost romantically excited as to the possibility of readily or soon exterminating these evils.

Hope meantime, even if unreasonable, becomes wise and holy when it points along a path of purposes that are more than usually beneficent. According to a fine illustration of Sir Phillip Sidney's, drawn from the practice of archery, by attempting more than we can possibly accomplish, we shall yet reach farther than ever we *should* have reached with a less ambitious aim; we shall do much for the purification of war, if nothing at all for its abolition; and atrocities of this Algerine order are amongst the earliest that will give way. They will sink before the growing illumination, and (what is equally important) before the growing *combination* of minds acting simultaneously from various centres, in nations otherwise the most at variance. By a rate of motion continually accelerated, the gathering power of the press, falling in with the growing facilities of personal intercourse, is, day by day, bringing Europe more and more into a state of fusion, in which the sublime name of *Christendom* will continually become more and more significant, and will express a unity of the most awful order, viz., in the midst of strife, long surviving as to inferior interests and subordinate opinions, will express an agreement continually more close, and an agreement continually more operative, upon all capital questions affecting human rights, duties, and the interests of human *progress.* Before that tribunal, which every throb of every steam engine, in printing houses and on railroads, is hurrying to establish, all flagrant abuses of belligerent powers will fall prostrate; and, in particular, no form of pure undisguised murder will be any longer allowed to confound itself with the necessities of honorable warfare.

Much already *has* been accomplished on this path; more than people are aware of; so gradual and silent has been the advance. How noiseless is the growth of corn! Watch it night and day for a week, and you will never see it growing; but return after two months, and you will find it all whitening for the harvest. Such, and so imperceptible, in the stages of their motion, are the victories of the press. Here is one instance. Just forty-seven years ago, on the shores of Syria, was celebrated by Napoleon Bonaparte, the most damnable carnival of murder that romance has fabled, or that history has recorded. Rather more than four thousand men — not, (like Tyrolese or Spanish guerillas,) even in pretence, 'insurgent rustics,' but regular troops, serving the Pacha and the Ottoman Sultan, not old men that might by odd fractions have been thankful for dismissal from a life of care or sorrow, but all young Albanians, in the early morning of manhood, the oldest not twenty-four — were exterminated by successive rolls of musketry, when helpless as infants, having their arms pinioned behind their backs like felons on the scaffold, and having surrendered their muskets, (which else would have made so desperate a resistance,) on the faith that they were dealing with soldiers and men of honor. I have elsewhere examined, as a question in casuistry, the frivolous pretences for this infamous carnage, but that examination I have here no wish to repeat; for it would draw off the attention from one feature of the case, which I desire to bring before the reader, as giving to this Jaffa tragedy a depth of atrocity wanting in that of Dahra. The four thousand and odd young Albanians had been seduced, trepanned, fraudulently decoyed, from a post of considerable strength, in which they could and would have sold their lives at a bloody rate, by a solemn promise of safety from authorized French officers. 'But,' said Napoleon, in part of excuse, 'these men, my aides-de-camp, were poltroons: to save their own lives, they made promises which they ought *not* to have made.' Suppose it so; and suppose the case one in which the supreme authority has a right to disavow his agents; what then? This entitles that authority to refuse his ratification to the terms agreed on; but this, at the same time, obliges him to replace the hostile parties in the advantages from which his agents had wiled them by these terms. A robber, who even owns himself such, will not pretend that he may refuse the price of the jewel as exorbitant, and yet keep possession of the jewel. And next comes a fraudulent advantage, not obtained by a knavery in the aid-de-camp, but in the leader himself. The surrender of the weapons, and the submission to the fettering of the arms, were not concessions from the Albanians, filched by the representatives of Napoleon, acting (as *he* says) without orders, but by express falsehoods, emanating from himself. The officer commanding at Dahra could not have reached his enemy without the shocking resource which he employed: Napoleon could. The officer at Dahra violated no covenant: Napoleon did. The officer at Dahra had not by lies seduced his victims from their natural advantages: Napoleon had. Such was the atrocity of Jaffa in the year 1799. Now, the relation of that great carnage to the press, the secret argument through which that vast massacre connects itself with the progress of the press, is this — That in 1799, and the two following years, when most it had become important to search the character and acts of Napoleon, excepting Sir Robert Wilson, no writer in Europe, no section of the press, cared much to insist upon this, by so many degrees, the worst deed of modern[6] military life. From that deed all the waters of the Atlantic would not have cleansed him; and yet, since 1804, we have heard much oftener of the sick men whom he poisoned in his Syrian hospital, (an act of merely erroneous humanity,) and more of the Duc d'Enghien's execution than of either; though this, savage as it was, admits of such palliations as belong to doubtful provocations in the sufferer, and to extreme personal terror in the inflicter. Here then, we have a case of wholesale military murder, emanating from Christendom, and not less treacherous than the worst which have been ascribed to the Mahometan Timur, or even to any Hindoo Rajah, which hardly moved a vibration of anger, or a solitary outcry of protestation from the European press, (then, perhaps, having the excuse of deadly fear for herself,) or even from the press of moral England, having no such excuse. Fifty years have passed; a less enormity is perpetrated, but again by a French leader: and, behold! Europe is *now* convulsed from side to side by unaffected indignation! So travels the press to victory: such is the light, and so broad, which it diffuses: such is the strength for action by which it combines the hearts of nations.

MELANCTHON AND CALVIN.

Of Mr. Landor's notions in religion it would be useless, and without polemic arguments it would be arrogant, to say that they are false. It is sufficient to say that they are degrading. In the dialogue between Melancthon and Calvin, it is clear that the former represents Mr. L. himself, and is not at all the Melancthon whom we may gather from his writings. Mr. Landor has heard that he was gentle and timid in action; and he exhibits him as a mere development of that keynote; as a compromiser of all that is severe in doctrine; and as an effeminate picker and chooser in morals. God, in *his* conception of him, is not a father so much as a benign, but somewhat weak, old grandfather; and we, his grandchildren, being now and then rather naughty, are to be tickled with a rod made of feathers, but, upon the whole, may rely upon an eternity of sugar-plums. For instance, take the puny idea ascribed to Melancthon upon *Idolatry;* and consider, for one moment, how little it corresponds to the vast machinery reared up by God himself against this secret poison and dreadful temptation of human nature. Melancthon cannot mean to question the truth or the importance of the Old Testament; and yet, if *his* view of idolatry (as reported by L.) be sound, the Bible must have been at the root of the worst mischief ever yet produced by idolatry. He begins by describing idolatry as '*Jewish;*' insinuating that it was an irregularity chiefly besetting the Jews. But how perverse a fancy! In the Jews, idolatry was a disease; in Pagan nations, it was the normal state. In a nation (if any such nation could exist) of *crétins* or of *lepers*, nobody would talk of cretinism or leprosy as of any morbid affection; *that* would be the regular and natural condition of man. But where either was spoken of with horror as a ruinous taint in human flesh, it would argue that naturally (and, perhaps, by a large majority) the people were uninfected. Amongst Pagans, nobody talked of idolatry — no such idea existed — because *that* was the regular form of religious worship. To be named at all, idolatry must be viewed as standing in opposition to some higher worship that is *not* idolatry. But, next, as we are all agreed that in idolatry there is something evil, and differ only as to the propriety of considering it a Jewish evil — in what does this evil lie? It lies, according to the profound Landorian Melancthon, in this — that different idolaters figure the Deity under different forms: if they could all agree upon one and the same mode of figuring the invisible Being, there need be no quarrelling; and in this case, consequently, there would be no harm in idolatry — none whatever. But, unhappily, it seems each nation, or sometimes section of a nation, has a different fancy: they get to disputing; and from that they get to boxing, in which, it is argued, lies the true evil of idolatry. It is an *extra* cause of broken heads. One tribe of men represent the Deity as a beautiful young man, with a lyre and a golden bow; another as a snake; and a third — Egyptians, for instance, of old — as a beetle or an onion; these last, according to Juvenal's remark, having the happy privilege of growing their own gods in their own kitchen-gardens. In all this there would be no harm, were it not for subsequent polemics and polemical assaults. Such, if we listen to Mr. L., is Melancthon's profound theory [7] of a false idolatrous religion. Were the police everywhere on an English footing, and the magistrates as unlike as possible to Turkish Cadis, nothing could be less objectionable; but, as things are, the beetle-worshipper despises the onion-worshipper; which breeds ill blood; whence grows a cudgel; and from the cudgel a constable; and from the constable an unjust magistrate. Not so, Mr. Landor; thus did not Melancthon speak: and if he *did*, and would defend it for a thousand times, then for a thousand times he would deserve to be trampled by posterity into that

German mire which he sought to evade by his Grecian disguise.[8] The true evil of idolatry is this: There is one sole idea of God, which corresponds adequately to his total nature. Of this idea, two things may be affirmed: the first being — that it is at the root of all absolute grandeur, of all truth, and of all moral perfection; the second being — that, natural and easy as it seems when once unfolded, it could only have been unfolded by revelation; and, to all eternity, he that started with a false conception of God, could not, through any effort of his own, have exchanged it for a true one. All idolaters alike, though not all in equal degrees, by intercepting the idea of God through the prism of some representative creature that *partially* resembles God, refract, splinter, and distort that idea. Even the idea of light, of the pure, solar light — the old Persian symbol of God — has that depraving necessity. Light itself, besides being an *imperfect* symbol, is an incarnation for us. However pure itself, or in its original divine manifestation, for us it is incarnated in forms and in matter that are *not* pure: it gravitates towards physical alliances, and therefore towards unspiritual pollutions. And all experience shows that the tendency for man, left to his own imagination, is downwards. The purest symbol, derived from created things, can and will condescend to the grossness of inferior human natures, by submitting to mirror itself in more and more carnal representative symbols, until finally the mixed element of resemblance to God is altogether buried and lost. God, by this succession of imperfect interceptions, falls more and more under the taint and limitation of the *alien* elements associated with all created things; and, for the ruin of all moral grandeur in man, every idolatrous nation left to itself will gradually bring round the idea of God into the idea of a powerful demon. Many things check and disturb this tendency for a time; but finally, and under that intense civilization to which man intellectually is always hurrying under the eternal evolution of physical knowledge, such a degradation of God's idea, ruinous to the *moral* capacities of man, would undoubtedly perfect itself, were it not for the kindling of a purer standard by revelation. Idolatry, therefore, is not merely *an* evil, and one utterly beyond the power of social institutions to redress, but, in fact, it is the fountain of all other evil that seriously menaces the destiny of the human race.

PORSON AND SOUTHEY.

The two dialogues between Southey and Porson relate to Wordsworth; and they connect Mr. Landor with a body of groundless criticism, for which vainly he will seek to evade his responsibility by pleading the caution posted up at the head of his Conversations, viz. — 'Avoid a mistake in attributing to the *writer* any opinions in this book but what are spoken under his own name.' If Porson, therefore, should happen to utter villanies that are indictable, *that* (you are to understand) is Porson's affair. Render unto Landor the eloquence of the dialogue, but render unto Porson any kicks which Porson may have merited by his atrocities against a man whom assuredly he never heard of, and probably never saw. Now, unless Wordsworth ran into Porson in the streets of Cambridge on some dark night about the era of the French Revolution, and capsized him into the kennel — a thing which is exceedingly improbable, considering that Wordsworth was never tipsy except once in his life, yet, on the other hand, is exceeding probable, considering that Porson was very seldom otherwise — barring this one opening for a collision, there is no human possibility or contingency known to insurance offices, through which Porson ever *could* have been brought to trouble his head about Wordsworth. It would have taken three witches, and three broom-sticks, clattering about his head, to have extorted from Porson any attention to a contemporary poet that did not give first-rate feeds. And a man that, besides his criminal conduct in respect of dinners, actually made it a principle to drink nothing but water, would have seemed so depraved a character in Porson's eyes that, out of regard to public decency, he would never have mentioned his name, had he even happened to know it. 'Oh no! he never mentioned *him*.' Be assured of *that*. As to Poetry, be it known that Porson read none whatever, unless it were either political or obscene. With no seasoning of either sort, 'wherefore,' he would ask indignantly, 'should I waste my time upon a poem?' Porson had read the Rolliad, because it concerned his political party; he had read the epistle of Obereea, Queen of Otaheite, to Sir Joseph Banks, because, if Joseph was rather too demure, the poem was *not*. Else, and with such exceptions, he condescended not to any metrical writer subsequent to the era of Pope, whose Eloisa to Abelard he could say by heart, and could even sing from beginning to end; which, indeed, he *would* do, whether you chose it or not, after a sufficient charge of brandy, and sometimes even though threatened with a cudgel, in case he persisted in his molestations. Waller he had also read, and occasionally quoted with effect. But as to a critique on Wordsworth, whose name had not begun to mount from the ground when Porson died,[9] as reasonably and characteristically might it have been put into the mouth of the Hetman Platoff. Instead of Porson's criticisms on writings which he never saw, let us hear Porson's account of a fashionable rout in an aristocratic London mansion: it was the only party of distinction that this hirsute but most learned Theban ever visited; and his history of what passed (comic alike and tragic) is better worth preserving than 'Brantome,' or even than Swift's 'Memoirs of a Parish Clerk.' It was by the hoax of a young Cantab that the Professor was ever decoyed into such a party: the thing was a swindle; but his report of its natural philosophy is not on that account the less picturesque: —

SOUTHEY. — Why do you repeat the word *rout* so often?

PORSON. — I was once *at* one by mistake; and really I saw there what you describe: and this made me repeat the word and smile. You seem curious.

SOUTHEY. — Rather, indeed.

PORSON. — I had been dining out; there were some who smoked after dinner: within a few hours, the fumes of their pipes produced such an effect on my head that I was willing to go into the air a little. Still I continued hot and thirsty; and an undergraduate, whose tutor was my old acquaintance, proposed that we should turn into an oyster-cellar, and refresh ourselves with oysters and porter. The rogue, instead of this, conducted me to a fashionable house in the neighborhood of St.

James's; and, although I expostulated with him, and insisted that we were going *up* stairs and not *down*, he appeared to me so ingenuous in his protestations to the contrary that I could well disbelieve him no longer. Nevertheless, receiving on the stairs many shoves and elbowings, I could not help telling him plainly — that, if indeed it *was* the oyster-cellar in Fleet Street, the company was much altered for the worse; and that, in future, I should frequent another. When the fumes of the pipes had left me, I discovered the deceit by the brilliancy and indecency of the dresses; and was resolved not to fall into temptation. Although, to my great satisfaction, no immodest proposal was directly made to me, I looked about anxious that no other man should know me beside *him* whose wantonness had conducted me thither; and I would have escaped, if I could have found the door, from which every effort I made appeared to remove me farther and farther. * * * A pretty woman said loudly, 'He has no gloves on!' 'What nails the creature has!' replied an older one — 'Piano-forte keys wanting the white.'

I pause to say that this, by all accounts which have reached posterity, was really no slander. The Professor's forks had become rather of the dingiest, probably through inveterate habits of scratching up Greek roots from diluvian mould, some of it older than Deucalion's flood, and very good, perhaps, for turnips, but less so for the digits which turn up turnips. What followed, however, if it were of a nature to be circumstantially repeated, must have been more trying to the sensibilities of the Greek oracle, and to the blushes of the policeman dispersed throughout the rooms, than even the harsh critique upon his nails; which, let the wits say what they would in their malice, were no doubt washed regularly enough once every three years. And, even if they were *not*, I should say that this is not so strong a fact as some that are reported about many a continental professor. Mrs. Cl——nt, with the two-fold neatness of an Englishwoman and a Quaker, told me that, on visiting Pestalozzi, the celebrated education professor, at Yverdun, about 1820, her first impression, from a distant view of his dilapidated premises, was profound horror at the grimness of his complexion, which struck her as no complexion formed by nature, but as a deposition from half a century of atmospheric rust—a most ancient *œrugo*. She insisted on a radical purification, as a *sine qua non* towards any interview with herself. The mock professor consented. Mrs. Cl. hired a stout Swiss charwoman, used to the scouring of staircases, kitchen floors, &c.; the professor, whom, on this occasion, one may call 'the prisoner,' was accommodated with a seat (as prisoners at the bar sometimes are with us) in the centre of a mighty washing-tub, and then scoured through a long summer forenoon, by the strength of a brawny Helvetian arm. 'And now, my dear friends,' said Mrs. Cl. to myself, 'is it thy opinion that this was cruel? Some people say it *was;* and I wish to disguise nothing;—it was not mere soap that I had him scoured with, but soap and sand; so, say honestly, dost thee call *that* cruel?' Laughing no more than the frailty of my human nature compelled me, I replied, 'Far from it; on the contrary, everybody must be charmed with her consideration for the professor, in not having him cleaned on the same principle as her carriage, viz., taken to the stable-yard, mopped severely,' ['*mobbed*, dost thee say?' she exclaimed; 'No, no,' I said, 'not mobbed, but *mopped*, until the gravel should be all gone,'] 'then pelted with buckets of water by firemen, and, finally, currycombed and rubbed down by two grooms, keeping a sharp *susurrus* between them, so as to soothe his wounded feelings; after all which, a feed of oats might not have been amiss.' The result, however, of this scouring extraordinary was probably as fatal as to Mambrino's helmet in Don Quixote. Pestalozzi issued, indeed, from the washing-tub like Aeson from Medea's kettle; he took his station amongst a younger and fairer generation; and the dispute was now settled whether he belonged to the Caucasian or Mongolian race. But his intellect was thought to have suffered seriously. The tarnish of fifty or sixty years seemed to have acquired powers of re-acting as a stimulant upon the professor's fancy, through the *rete mucosum*, or through — heaven knows what. He was too old to be converted to cleanliness; the Paganism of a neglected person at seventy becomes a sort of religion interwoven with the nervous system — just as the well known *Plica Polonica* from which the French armies suffered so much in Poland, during 1807–8, though produced by neglect of the hair, will not be cured by extirpation of the hair. The hair becomes matted into Medusa locks, or what look like snakes; and to cut these off is oftentimes to cause nervous frenzy, or other great constitutional disturbance. I never heard, indeed, that Pestalozzi suffered apoplexy from his scouring; but certainly his ideas on education grew bewildered, and will be found essentially damaged, after that great epoch — his baptism by water and sand.

Now, in comparison of an Orson like this man of Yverdun — this great Swiss reformer, who might, perhaps, have bred a pet variety of typhus fever for his own separate use — what signify nails, though worse than Caliban's or Nebuchadnezzar's?

This Greek professor Porson — whose knowledge of English was so limited that his total cargo might have been embarked on board a walnut-shell, on the bosom of a slop bason, and insured for three halfpence — astonishes me, that have been studying English for thirty years and upwards, by the strange discoveries that he announces in this field. One and all, I fear, are mares' nests. He discovered, for instance, on his first and last reception amongst aristocratic people, that in this region of society a female bosom is called her *neck*. But, if it really *had* been so called, I see no objection to the principle concerned in such disguises; and I see the greatest to that savage frankness which virtually is indicated with applause in the Porsonian remark. Let us consider. It is not that we *cannot* speak freely of the female bosom, and we do so daily. In discussing a statue, we do so without reserve; and in the act of suckling an infant, the bosom of every woman is an idea so sheltered by the tenderness and sanctity with which all but ruffians invest the organ of maternity, that no man scruples to name it, if the occasion warrants it. He suppresses it only as he suppresses the name of God; not as an idea that can itself contain any indecorum, but, on the contrary, as making other and more trivial ideas to become indecorous when associated with a conception rising so much above their own standard. Equally, the words, *affliction*, *guilt*, *penitence*, *remorse*, &c., are proscribed from the ordinary current of conversation amongst mere acquaintances; and for the same reason, viz., that they touch chords too impassioned and profound for harmonizing with the key in which the mere social civilities of life are exchanged. Meantime, it is not true that any custom ever prevailed in *any* class of calling a woman's bosom her neck. Porson goes on to say, that, for *his* part, he was born in an age when people had *thighs*. Well, a great many people have thighs still. But in all ages there must have been many of whom it is lawful to suspect such a fact zoologically; and yet, as men honoring our own race, and all its veils of mystery, not too openly to insist upon it, which, luckily, there is seldom any occasion to do.

Mr. Landor conceives that we are growing worse in the pedantries of false delicacy. I think not. His own residence in Italy has injured his sense of discrimination. It is not his countrymen that have grown conspicuously more demure and prudish, but he himself that has grown in Italy more tolerant of what is really a blameable coarseness. Various instances occur in these volumes of that faulty compliance with Southern grossness. The tendencies of the age, among ourselves, lie certainly in *one* channel towards excessive refinement. So far, however, they do but balance the opposite tendencies in some other channels. The craving for instant effect in style — as it brings forward many disgusting Germanisms and other barbarisms — as it transplants into literature much slang from the street — as it re-acts painfully upon the grandeurs of the antique scriptural diction, by recalling into *colloquial* use many consecrated words which thus lose their

Gothic beauty — also operates daily amongst journalists, by the temptations of apparent strength that lurk in plain speaking or even in brutality. What other temptation, for instance, can be supposed to govern those who, in speaking of hunger as it affects our paupers, so needlessly affect us by the very coarsest English word for the Latin word *venter*? Surely the word *stomach* would be intelligible to everybody, and yet disgust nobody. It would do for *him* that affects plain speaking; it would do for you and me that revolt from gross speaking. Signs from abroad speak the very same language, as to the *liberal* tendencies (in this point) of the nineteenth century. Formerly, it was treason for a Spaniard, even in a laudatory copy of verses, to suppose his own Queen lowered to the level of other females by the possession of legs! Constitutionally, the Queen was incapable of legs. How else her Majesty contrived to walk, or to dance, the Inquisition soon taught the poet was no concern of *his*. Royal legs for females were an inconceivable thing — except amongst Protestant nations; some of whom the Spanish Church affirmed to be even disfigured by tails! Having tails, of course they might have legs. But not *Catholic* Queens. Now-a-days, so changed is all this, that if you should even express your homage to her Most Catholic Majesty, by sending her a pair of embroidered garters — which certainly pre-suppose legs — there is no doubt that the Spanish Minister of Finance would gratefully carry them to account — on the principle that 'every little helps.' Mr. Porson is equally wrong, as I conceive, in another illustration of this matter, drawn from the human toes, and specifically from the great toe. It is true, that, in refined society, upon any rare necessity arising for alluding to so inconsiderable a member of the human statue, generally this is done at present by the French term *doigt-de-pied* — though not always — as may be seen in various honorary certificates granted to chiropodists within the last twenty months. And whereas Mr. Porson asks pathetically — What harm has the great toe done, that it is never to be named? I answer — The greatest harm; as may be seen in the first act of 'Coriolanus,' where *Menenius* justly complains, that this arrogant subaltern of the crural system,

> '——— Being basest, meanest, vilest,
> Still goeth foremost.'

Even in the villany of running away from battle, this unworthy servant still asserts precedency. I repeat, however, that the general tendencies of the age, as to the just limits of *parrhesia*, (using the Greek word in a sense wider than of old,) are moving at present upon two opposite tracks; which fact it is, as in some other cases, that makes the final judgment difficult.

ROMAN IMPERATOR.

Mr. Landor, though really learned, often puts his learning into his pocket.

Thus, with respect to the German Empire, Mr. L. asserts that it was a chimæra; that the *Imperium Germanicum* was a mere usage of speech, founded (if I understand him) not even in a legal fiction, but in a blunder; that a German *Imperator* never had a true historical existence; and, finally, that even the Roman title of *Imperator* — which, unquestionably, surmounted in grandeur all titles of honor that ever were or will be — ranged in dignity below the title of *Rex*.

I believe him wrong in every one of these doctrines; let us confine ourselves to the last. The title of Imperator was not *originally* either above or below the title of Rex, or even upon the same level; it was what logicians call *disparatē* — it radiated from a different centre, precisely as the modern title of *Decanus*, or *Dean*, which is originally astrological, [see the elder Scaliger on Manilius,] has no relation, whether of superiority or equality or inferiority, to the title of *Colonel*, nor the title of *Cardinal* any such relation to that of *Field-Marshal;* and quite as little had *Rex* to *Imperator*. Masters of Ceremonies, or Lord Chamberlains, may certainly *create* a precedency in favor of any title whatever in regard to any other title; but such a precedency for any of the cases before us would be arbitrary, and not growing out of any internal principle, though useful for purposes of convenience. As regards the Roman *Imperator*, originally like the Roman *Prætor* — this title and the official rank pointed exclusively to military distinctions. In process of time, the Prætor came to be a legal officer, and the Imperator to be the supreme political officer. But the motive for assuming the title of *Imperator*, as the badge or cognizance of the sovereign authority, when the great transfiguration of the Republic took place, seems to have been this. An essentially new distribution of political powers had become necessary, and this change masqued itself to Romans, published itself in menaces and muttering thunder to foreign states, through the martial title of *Imperator*. A new equilibrium was demanded by the changes which time and luxury and pauperism had silently worked in the composition of Roman society. If Rome was to be saved from herself — if she was to be saved from the eternal flux and reflux — action and re-action — amongst her oligarchy of immense estates [which condition of things it was that forced on the great *sine quâ non* reforms of Cæsar, against all the babble of the selfish Cicero, of the wicked Cato, and of the debt-ridden Senate] — then it was indispensable that a new order of powers should be combined for bridling her internal convulsions. To carry her off from her own self-generated vortex, which would, in a very few years, have engulphed her and drawn her down into fragments, some machinery as new as steam-power was required : her own native sails filled in the wrong direction. There were already powers in the constitution equal to the work, but distracted and falsely lodged. These must be gathered into one hand. And, yet, as names are all-powerful upon our frail race, this recast must be *verbally* disguised. The title must be such as, whilst flattering the Roman pride, might yet announce to Oriental powers a plenipotentiary of Rome who argued all disputed points, not so much strongly as (an Irish phrase) with 'a strong back' — not so much piquing himself on Aristotelian syllogisms that came within *Barbary* and *Celarent*, as upon thirty legions that stood within call. The Consulship was good for little ; *that*, with some reservations, could be safely resigned into subordinate hands. The Consular name, and the name of Senate, which was still suffered to retain an obscure vitality and power of resurrection, continued to throw a popular lustre over the government. Millions were duped. But the essential offices, the offices in which settled the organs of all the life in the administration, were these: — 1, of Military Commander-in-Chief (including such a partition of the provinces as might seal the authority in this officer's hands, and yet flatter the people through the Senate); 2, of Censor, so as to watch the action of morals and social usages upon politics; 3, of Pontifex Maximus; 4, and finally, of Tribune. The tribunitial power, next after the military power, occupied the earliest anxieties of the Cæsars. All these powers, and some others belonging to less dignified functions, were made to run through the same central rings (or what in mail-coach harness is called the *turrets*): the 'ribbons' were tossed up to one and the same imperial coachman, looking as amiable as he could, but, in fact, a very truculent personage, having powers more unlimited than was always safe for himself. And now, after all this change of things, what was to be the *name*? By what *title* should men know him? Much depended upon that. The tremendous symbols of S. P. Q. R. still remained; nor had they lost their power. On the contrary, the great idea of the Roman destiny, as of some vast phantom moving under God to some unknown end, was greater than ever: the idea was now *so* great, that it had outgrown all its representative realities. *Consul* and *Proconsul* would no longer answer, because they represented too exclusively the interior or domestic fountains of power, and not the external relations to the terraqueous globe which were beginning to expand with sudden accelerations of velocity. The *central* power could not be forgotten by any who were near enough to have tasted its wrath ; but now there was arising a necessity for expressing, by some great unity of denomination, so as no longer to lose the totality in the separate partitions — the enormity of the *circumference*. A necessity for this had repeatedly been found in negotiations, and in contests of ceremonial rank with oriental powers, as between ourselves and China. With Persia, the greatest of these powers, an instinct of inevitable collision [10] had, for some time, been ripening. It became requisite that there should be a representative officer for the whole Roman grandeur, and one capable of standing on the same level as the Persian king of kings ; and this necessity arose at the very same moment that a new organization was required of Roman power for *domestic* purposes. There is no doubt that both purposes were consulted in the choice of the title of *Imperator*. The chief alternative title was that of *Dictator*. But to this, as regarded Romans, there were two objections — first, that it was a mere *provisional* title, always commemorating a transitional emergency, and pointing to some happier condition, which the extraordinary powers of the officer ought soon to establish. It was in the nature of a problem, and continually asked for its own solution. The Dictator dictated. He was the greatest *ipse dixit* that ever was heard of. It reminded the people *verbally* of despotic powers and autocracy. Then again, as regarded foreign nations, unacquainted with the Roman constitution, and throughout the servile East incapable of understanding it, the title of *Dictator* had no meaning at all. *The*

Speaker is a magnificent title in England, and makes brave men sometimes shake in their shoes. But, yet, if from rustic ignorance it is not understood, even that title means nothing.

Of the proudest Speaker that England ever saw, viz., Sir Edward Seymour, it is recorded that his grandeur failed him, sank under him, like the Newgate drop, at the very moment when his boiling anger most relied upon and required it. He was riding near Barnet, when a rustic wagoner ahead of him, by keeping obstinately the middle of the road, prevented him from passing. Sir Edward motioned to him magnificently, that he must turn his horses to the left. The carter, on some fit of the sulks (perhaps from the Jacobinism innate in man), despised this pantomime, and sturdily persisted in his mutinous disrespect. On which Sir Edward shouted—'Fellow, do you know who I am?' '*Noo-ah*,' replied our rebellious friend, meaning, when faithfully translated, *no*. 'Are you aware, Sirrah,' said Sir Edward, now thoroughly incensed, 'that I am the right honorable the Speaker? At your peril, Sir, in the name of the Commons of England, in Parliament assembled, quarter instantly to the left.' This was said in that dreadful voice which sometimes reprimanded penitent offenders, kneeling at the bar of the House. The carter, more struck by the terrific tones than the words, spoke an aside to 'Dobbin,' (his 'thill' horse,) which procured an opening to the blazing Speaker, and then replied thus—'Speaker! Why, if so be as thou can'st speak, whoy-y-y-y-y,' (in the tremulous undulation with which he was used to utter his sovereign whoah-h-h-h to his horses,) 'Whoy-y-y-y didn't-a speak afore?' The wagoner, it seemed, had presumed Sir Edward, from his mute pantomime, to be a dumb man; and all which the proud Speaker gained, by the proclamation of his style and title, was, to be exonerated from that suspicion, but to the heavy discredit of his sanity. A Roman Dictator stood quite as poor a chance with foreigners, as our Speaker with a rustic. 'Dictator! let him dictate to his wife; but he sha'n't dictate to us.' Any title, to prosper with distant nations, must rest upon the basis of arms. And this fell in admirably with the political exigency for Rome herself. The title of *Imperator* was liable to no jealousy. Being entirely a military title, it clashed with no civil pretensions whatever. Being a military title, that recorded a triumph over external enemies in the field, it was dear to the patriotic heart; whilst it directed the eye to a quarter where all increase of power was concurrent with increase of benefit to the State. And again, as the honor had been hitherto purely titular, accompanied by some *auctoritas*, in the Roman sense, [not always honor, for Cicero was an Imperator for Cilician exploits, which he reports with laughter,] but no separate authority in our modern sense. Even in military circles it was open to little jealousy; nor apparently could ripen into a shape that ever *would* be so, since, according to all precedent, it would be continually balanced by the extension of the same title, under popular military suffrage, to other fortunate leaders. Who could foresee, at the inauguration of this reform, that this precedent would be abolished? who could guess that henceforwards no more triumphs, (but only a sparing distribution of triumphal decorations,) henceforwards no more imperatorial titles for anybody out of the one consecrated family? All this was hidden in the bosom of the earliest Imperator: he seemed, to the great mass of the people, perfectly innocent of civic ambition: he rested upon his truncheon, *i.e.*, upon S. P. Q. R.: like Napoleon, he said, 'I am but the first soldier of the republic,' that is, the most dutiful of her servants; and, like Napoleon, under cover of this martial *paludamentum*, he had soon filched every ensign of authority by which the organs of public power could speak. But, at the beginning, this title of *Imperator* was the one by far the best fitted to masque all this, to disarm suspicion, and to win the confidence of the people.

The title, therefore, began in something like imposture; and it was not certainly at first the gorgeous title into which it afterwards blossomed. The earth did not yet ring with it. The rays of its diadem were not then the first that said *All hail!* to the rising — the last that said *Farewell!* to the setting sun. But still it was already a splendid distinction; and, in a Roman ear, it must have sounded far above all competition from the trivial title (in *that* day) of 'Rex,' unless it were the Persian Rex, viz., 'Rex Regum.' Romans *gave* the title; they stooped not to accept it.[11] Even Mark Antony, in the all-magnificent description of him by Shakspeare's Cleopatra, could give it in showers — kings waited in his ante-room, 'and from his pocket fell crowns and sceptres.' The title of *Imperator* was indeed reaped in glory that transcended the glory of earth, but it was not, therefore, sown in dishonor.

We are all astonished at Mr. Landor — myself and three hundred select readers. What *can* he mean by tilting against the Imperator — Semper Augustus? Before *him* the sacred fire (that burned from century to century) went pompously in advance — before *him* the children of Europe and Asia — of Africa and the islands, rode as *dorypheroi; his somatophulakes* were princes; and *his* empire, when burning out in Byzantium, furnished from its very ruins the models for our western honors and ceremonial. Had it even begun in circumstances of ignominy, *that* would have been cured easily by its subsequent triumph. Many are the titles of earth that have found a glory in looking back to the humility of their origin as its most memorable feature. The fisherman who sits upon Mount Palatine, in some respects the grandest of all potentates, as one wielding both earthly and heavenly thunders, is the highest example of this. Some, like the Mamelukes of Egypt and the early Janizaries of the Porte, have glorified themselves in being slaves. Others, like the Caliphs, have founded their claims to men's homage in the fact of being *successors* to those who (between ourselves) were knaves. And once it happened to Professor Wilson and myself, that we travelled in the same post-chaise with a most agreeable madman, who, amongst a variety of other select facts which he communicated, was kind enough to give us the following etymological account of our much-respected ancestors the Saxons; which furnishes a further illustration [quite unknown to the learned] of the fact — that honor may glory in deducing itself from circumstances of humility. He assured us that these worthy Pagans were a league, comprehending every single brave man of German blood; so much so, that on sailing away they left that unhappy land in a state of universal cowardice, which accounts for the licking it subsequently received from Napoleon. The Saxons were very poor, as brave men too often are. In fact, they had no breeches, and, of course, no silk stockings. They had, however, *sacks*, which they mounted on their backs, whence naturally their name *Sax-on*. *Sacks-on!* was the one word of command, and *that* spoken, the army was ready. In reality, it was treason to take them off. But this indorsement of their persons was not assumed on any Jewish principle of humiliation; on the contrary, in the most flagrant spirit of defiance to the whole race of man. For they proclaimed that, having no breeches nor silk stockings of their own, they intended, wind and weather permitting, to fill these same sacks with those of other men. The Welshmen then occupying England were reputed to have a good stock of both, and in quest of this Welsh wardrobe the *Sacks-on* army sailed. With what success it is not requisite to say, since here in one post-chaise, four hundred and thirty years after, were three of their posterity, the Professor, the madman, and myself, indorsees (as you may say) of the original indorsers, who were all well equipped with the objects of this great *Sacks-on* exodus.

It is true that the word *emperor* is not in every situation so impressive as the word *king*. But *that* arises in part from the latter word having less of specialty about it; it is more catholic, and to that extent more poetic; and in part from accidents of position which disturb the relations of many other titles beside. The *Proconsul* had a grander sound, as regarded military expeditions, than the principal from whom he emanated. The *Surena* left a more awful remembrance of his title upon the comrades of Julian in his Persian expedition than the Surena's master. And there are many cases extant in which the word *angel* strikes a deeper key; cases where power is contemplated as well as beauty or mysterious existence, than the word archangel, though confessedly higher in the hierarchies of Heaven.

Let me now draw the reader's attention to *Count Julian*, a great conception of Mr. Landor's.

The fable of Count Julian (that is, when comprehending all the parties to that web, of which *he* is the centre) may be pronounced the grandest which modern history unfolds. It is, and it is *not*, scenical. In some portions (as the fate so mysterious of Roderick, and in a higher sense of Julian) it rises as much above what the stage could illustrate, as does Thermopylæ above the petty details of narration. The man was mad that, instead of breathing from a hurricane of harps some mighty ode over Thermopylæ, fancied the little conceit of weaving it into a metrical novel or succession of incidents. Yet, on the other hand, though rising higher, Count Julian sinks lower: though the passions rise far above Troy, above Marathon, above Thermopylæ, and are such passions as could not have existed under Paganism, in some respects they condescend and preconform to the stage. The characters are all different, all marked, all *in position;* by which, never assuming fixed attitudes as to purpose and interest, the passions are deliriously complex, and the situations are of corresponding grandeur. Metius Fuffetius, Alban traitor! that wert torn limb from limb by antagonist yet confederate chariots, thy tortures, seen by shuddering armies, were not comparable to the unseen tortures in Count Julian's mind; who — whether his treason prospered or not, whether his dear outraged daughter lived or died, whether his king were trampled in the dust by the horses of infidels, or escaped as a wreck from the fiery struggle, whether his dear native Spain fell for ages under misbelieving hounds, or, combining her strength, tossed off *them*, but then also *himself*, with one loathing from her shores — saw, as he looked out into the mighty darkness, and stretched out his penitential hands vainly for pity or for pardon, nothing but the blackness of ruin, and ruin that was too probably to career through centuries. 'To this pass,' as Cæsar said to his soldiers at Pharsalia, 'had his enemies reduced him;' and Count Julian might truly say, as he stretched himself a rueful suppliant before the Cross, listening to the havoc that was driving onwards before the dogs of the Crescent, '*My* enemies, because they would not remember that I was a man, forced *me* to forget that I was a Spaniard: — to forget thee, oh native Spain, — and, alas! thee, oh faith of Christ!'

The story is wrapt in gigantic mists, and looms upon one like the Grecian fable of Œdipus; and there will be great reason for disgust, if the deep Arabic researches now going on in the Escurial, or at Vienna, should succeed in stripping it of its grandeurs. For, as it stands at present, it is the most fearful lesson extant of the great moral, that crime propagates crime, and violence inherits violence; nay, a lesson on the awful *necessity* which exists at times, that one tremendous wrong should blindly reproduce itself in endless retaliatory wrongs. To have resisted the dread temptation, would have needed an angel's nature: to have yielded, is but human; should it, then, plead in vain for pardon? and yet, by some mystery of evil, to have perfected this human vengeance, is, finally, to land all parties alike, oppressor and oppressed, in the passions of hell.

Mr. Landor, who always rises with his subject, and dilates like Satan into Teneriffe or Atlas, when he sees before him an antagonist worthy of his powers, is probably the one man in Europe that has adequately conceived the situation, the stern self-dependency and the monumental misery of Count Julian. That sublimity of penitential grief, which cannot accept consolation from man, cannot hear external reproach, cannot condescend to notice insult, cannot so much as see the curiosity of by-standers; that awful carelessness of all but the troubled deeps within his own heart, and of God's spirit brooding upon their surface, and searching their abysses, never was so majestically described as in the following lines; it is the noble Spaniard, Hernando, comprehending and loving Count Julian in the midst of his treasons, who speaks: — Tarik, the gallant Moor, having said that at last the Count must be happy; for that

'Delicious calm
Follows the fierce enjoyment of revenge.'

Hernando replies thus: —

'That calm was never his; no other *will* be,
Not victory, that o'ershadows him, sees he:
No airy and light passion stirs abroad
To ruffle or to soothe him; all are quell'd
Beneath a mightier, sterner, stress of mind.
Wakeful he sits, and lonely, and unmov'd,
Beyond the arrows, shouts, and views of men.
As oftentimes an eagle, ere the sun
Throws o'er the varying earth his early ray,
Stands solitary — stands immovable
Upon some highest cliff, and rolls his eye,
Clear, constant, unobservant, unabas'd,
In the cold light above the dews of morn.'

One change suggests itself to me as possibly for the better, viz., if the magnificent line —

'Beyond the arrows, shouts, and views of men' —

were transferred to the secondary object, the eagle, placed after what is *now* the last line, it would give a fuller rhythmus to the close of the entire passage; it would be more *literally* applicable to the majestic and solitary bird, than to the majestic and solitary man; whilst the figurative expression even more impassioned might be found for the utter self-absorption of Count Julian's spirit — too grandly sorrowful to be capable of disdain.

It completes the picture of this ruined prince, that Hernando, the sole friend (except his daughter) still cleaving to him, dwells with yearning desire upon his death, knowing the necessity of this consummation to his own secret desires, knowing the forgiveness which would settle upon his memory after that last penalty should have been paid for his errors, comprehending the peace that would then swallow up the storm: —

'For his own sake I could endure his loss,
Pray for it, and thank God: yet mourn I must
Him above all, so great, so bountiful,
So blessed once!'

It is no satisfaction to Hernando that Julian should 'yearn for death with speechless love,' but Julian *does* so: and it is in vain now, amongst these irreparable ruins, to wish it otherwise.

''Tis not my solace that 'tis [12] *his* desire:
Of all who pass us in life's drear descent
We grieve the most for those who *wish'd* to die.'

How much, then, is in this brief drama of Count Julian, chiselled, as one might think, by the hands of that sculptor who fancied the great idea of chiselling Mount Athos into a demigod, which almost insists on being quoted; which seems to rebuke and frown on one for *not* quoting it: passages to which, for their solemn grandeur, one raises one's hat as at night in walking under the Coliseum; passages which, for their luxury of loveliness, should be inscribed on the phylacteries of brides, or upon the frescoes of Ionia, illustrated by the gorgeous allegories of Rubens.

'Sed fugit interea, fugit irreparibile tempus,
Singula dum capti circumvectamur amore.'

Yet, reader, in spite of time, one word more on the subject we are quitting. Father Time is certainly become very importunate and clamorously shrill since he has been fitted up with that horrid railway whistle; and even old Mother Space is growing rather impertinent, when she speaks out of monthly journals licensed to carry but small quantities of bulky goods; yet one thing I must say in spite of them both.

It is, that although we have had from men of memorable genius, Shelley in particular, both direct and indirect attempts (some of them powerful attempts) to realize the great idea of Prometheus, which idea is *so* great, that (like the primeval majesties of Human Innocence, of Avenging Deluges that are past, of Fiery Visitations yet to come) it has had strength to pass through many climates, and through many religions, without essential loss, but surviving, without tarnish, every furnace of chance and change; so it is that, after all has been done which intellectual power *could* do since Æschylus (and since, Milton in his Satan), no embodiment of the Promethean situation, none of the Promethean character, fixes the attentive eye upon itself with the same secret feeling of fidelity to the vast archetype, as Mr. Landor's 'Count Julian.' There is in this modern aerolith the same jewelly lustre, which cannot be mistaken; the same '*non imitabile fulgur*,' and the same character of 'fracture,' or *cleavage*, as mineralogists speak, for its beaming iridescent grandeur, redoubling under the crush of misery. The color and the coruscation are the same when splintered by violence; the tones of the rocky[13] harp are the same when swept by sorrow. There is the same spirit of heavenly persecution against his enemy, persecution that would have hung upon his rear, and 'burn'd after him to the bottomless pit,' though it had yawned for both; there is the same gulf fixed between the possibilities of their reconciliation, the same immortality of resistance, the same abysmal anguish. Did Mr. Landor *consciously* cherish this Æschylean ideal in composing 'Count Julian?' I know not: there it is.

NOTES.

Note 1. Page 242.

'*Southey affirmed:*'—viz. in the 'Letters of Espriella,' an imaginary Spaniard on a visit to England, about the year 1810.

Note 2. Page 244.

'*Too much wealth:*'—Mr. Landor, who *should* know best, speaks of himself (once, at least) as 'poor;' but *that* is all nonsense. I have known several people with annual incomes bordering on £20,000, who spoke of themselves, and seemed seriously to think themselves, unhappy 'paupers.' Lady Hester Stanhope, with £2700 a year, (of which about twelve arose from her government pension,) and without one solitary dependent in her train, thought herself rich enough to become a queen (an Arabic *maleky*) in the Syrian mountains, but an absolute pauper for London: 'for how, you know,' (as she would say, pathetically,) 'could the humblest of spinsters live decently upon that pittance?'

Note 3. Page 247.

'*From Hegel:*'—I am not prepared with an affidavit that no man ever read the late Mr. Hegel, that great master of the impenetrable. But sufficient evidence of that fact, as I conceive, may be drawn from those who have written commentaries upon him.

Note 4. Page 256.

Wale (Germanicè *wahl*) the old ballad word for *choice*. But the motive for using it in this place is in allusion to an excellent old Scottish story (not sufficiently known in the South), of a rustic laird, who profited by the hospitality of his neighbors, duly to get drunk once (and no more) every lawful night, returning in the happiest frame of mind under the escort of his servant Andrew. In spite of Andrew, however, it sometimes happened that the laird fell off his horse; and on one of these occasions, as he himself was dismounted from his saddle, his wig was dismounted from his cranium. Both fell into a peat-moss, and both were fished out by Andrew. But the laird, in his confusion, putting on the wig wrong side before, reasonably 'jaloused' that this could not be his own wig, but some other man's, which suspicion he communicated to Andrew, who argued *contra* by the memorable reply — 'Hout! laird, there's nae wale o' wigs i' a peat-moss.'

Note 5. Page 257.

Milton, in uttering his grief (but also his hopes growing out of this grief) upon a similar tragedy, viz., the massacre of the Protestant women and children by 'the bloody Piedmontese.'

Note 6. Page 261.

'*Modern military life:*' — By modern I mean since the opening of the thirty years' war. In this war, the sack, or partial sack, of Magdeburg, will occur to the reader as one of the worst amongst martial ruffianisms. But this happens to be a hoax. It is an old experience, that, when once the demure muse of history has allowed herself to tell a lie, she never retracts it. Many are the falsehoods in our own history, which our children read traditionally for truths, merely because our uncritical grandfathers believed them to be such. Magdeburg was *not* sacked. What fault there was in the case belonged to the King of Sweden, who certainly was remiss in this instance, though with excuses more than were hearkened to at that time. Tilly, the Bavarian General, had no reason for severity in this case, and showed none. According to the regular routine of war, Magdeburg had become forfeited to military execution; which, let the reader remember, was not, in those days, a right of the General as against the enemy, and by way of salutary warning to other cities, lest they also should abuse the right of a reasonable defence, but was a right of the soldiery as against their own leaders. A town stormed was then a little perquisite to the ill-fed and ill-paid soldiers. So of prisoners. If I made a prisoner of 'Signor Drew' [see Henry V.] it was *my* business to fix his ranson: the General had no business to interfere with that. Magdeburg, therefore, had incurred the common penalty (which she must have foreseen) of obstinacy; and the only difference between *her* case and that of many another brave little town, that quietly submitted to the usual martyrdom, without howling through all the speaking-trumpets of history, was this — that the penalty was, upon Magdeburg, but partially enforced. Harte, the tutor of Lord Chesterfield's son, first published, in his Life of Gustavus Adolphus, an anthentic diary of what passed at that time, kept by a Lutheran clergyman. This diary shows sufficiently that no real departures were made from the customary routine, except in the direction of mercy. But it is evident that the people of Magdeburg were a sort of German hogs, of whom, it is notorious, that if you attempt in the kindest way to shear them, all you get is horrible yelling, and (the proverb asserts) very little wool. The case being a classical one in the annals of military outrages, I have noticed its real features.

Note 7. Page 264.

'*Melanchthon's profound theory.*' — That the reader may not suppose me misrepresenting Mr. L., I subjoin his words, p. 224, vol. 1: — 'The evil of idolatry is this — rival nations have raised up rival deities; war hath been denounced in the name of heaven; men have been murdered for the love of God; and such impiety hath darkened all the regions of the world, that the Lord of all things hath been mocked by all simultaneously as the Lord of Hosts.' The evil or idolatry is, not that it disfigures the Deity, (in which, it seems, there might be no great harm,) but that one man's disfiguration differs from another man's; which leads to quarrelling, and *that* to fighting.'

NOTE 8. Page 265.

'*Grecian disguise:*' — The true German name of this learned reformer was *Schwarzerd* (black earth); but the homeliness and pun-provoking quality of such a designation induced Melanchthon to masque it in Greek. By the way, I do not understand how Mr. Landor, the arch-purist in orthography, reconciles *his* spelling of the name to Greek orthodoxy: there is no Greek word that *could* be expressed by the English syllable 'cthon.' Such a word as Melancthon * would be a hybrid monster — neither fish, flesh, nor good red herring.

NOTE 9. Page 268.

An equal mistake it is in Mr Landor to put into the mouth of Porson any vituperation of Mathias as one that had uttered opinions upon Wordsworth. In the *Pursuits of Literature*, down to the fifteenth edition, there is no mention of Wordsworth's name. Southey is mentioned slightingly, and chiefly with reference to his then democratic principles; but not Coleridge, and not Wordsworth. Mathias soon after went to Italy, where he passed the remainder of his life — died, I believe, and was buried — never, perhaps, having heard the name of Wordsworth. As to Porson, it is very true that Mathias took a few liberties with his private habits, such as his writing paragraphs in the little cabinet fitted up for the *gens de plume* at the *Morning Chronicle* Office, and other trifles. But these, though impertinences, were not of a nature seriously to offend. They rather flattered, by the interest which they argued in his movements. And with regard to Porson's main pretension, his exquisite skill in Greek, Mathias was not the

* The reader of this edition will notice that the American printer has altered the spelling in the text, without reference to Mr. De Quincey's remarks on Mr. Landor's method.

man to admire this too little: his weakness, *if in that point he had* a weakness, lay in the opposite direction. His own Greek was not a burthen that could have foundered a camel: he was neither accurate, nor extensive, nor profound. But yet Mr. Landor is wrong in thinking that he drew it from an Index. In his Italian, he had the advantage probably of Mr. Landor himself: at least, he wrote it with more apparent fluency and compass.

NOTE 10. Page 279.

Herod the Great, and his father Antipater, owed the favor of Rome, and, finally, the throne of Judæa, to the seasonable election which they made between Rome and Persia; but made not without some doubts, as between forces hardly yet brought to a satisfactory equation.

NOTE 11. Page 282.

'*Stooped not to accept it.*' — The notion that Julius Cæsar, who of all men must have held cheapest the title of *Rex*, had seriously intrigued to obtain it, arose (as I conceive) from two mistakes — first, From a misinterpretation of a figurative ceremony in the pageant of the Lupercalia. The Romans were ridiculously punctilious in this kind of jealousy. They charged Pompey at one time with a plot for making himself king, because he wore white bandages round his thighs; now *white*, in olden days, was as much the regal color as *purple*. Think, dear reader, of us — of you and me — being charged with making ourselves kings, because we may choose to wear white cotton drawers. Pompey was very angry, and swore bloody oaths that it was *not* ambition which had cased his thighs in white *fasciæ*. 'Why, what is it then?' said a grave citizen. 'What is it, man?' replied Pompey, 'it is rheumatism.' Dogberry must have had a hand in this charge: — 'Dost thou hear, thou varlet? Thou are charged with incivism; and it shall go hard with me but I will prove thee to thy face a false knave, and guilty of flat rheumatism.'. The other reason which has tended to confirm posterity in the belief that Cæsar really coveted the title of *Rex*, was the confusion of the truth arising with Greek writers. *Basileus*, the term by which indifferently they designated the mighty Artaxerxes and the pettiest *regulus*, was the original translation used for *Imperator*. Subsequently, and especially after Dioclesian had approximated the aulic pomps to Eastern models, the terms *Autocrator*, *Kaisar*, *Augustus*, *Sebastos*, &c., came more into use. But after Trajan's time, or even to that of Commodus, generally the same terms which expressed *Imperator* and *Imperitorial* [viz. *Basileus* and *Basilikos*] to a Grecian ear expressed *Rex* and *Regalis*.

NOTE 12. Page 289.

''Tis' : — Scotchmen and Irishmen (for a reason which it may be elsewhere worth while explaining) make the same mistake of supposing *'tis* and *'twas* admissible in prose : which is shocking to an English ear, for since 1740 they have become essentially poetic forms, and cannot, without a sense of painful affectation and sentimentality, be used in conversation or in *any* mode of prose. Mr. Landor does not make *that* mistake, but the reduplication of the *'tis* in this line, — will he permit me to say ? — is dreadful. He is wide awake to such blemishes in other men of all nations : so am I. He blazes away all day long against the trespasses of that class, like a man in spring protecting corn-fields against birds. So do I at times. And if ever I publish that work on *Style*, which for years has been in preparation, I fear that, from Mr. Landor, it will be necessary to cull some striking flaws in composition, were it only that in *his* works must be sought some of its most striking brilliancies.

NOTE 13. Page 290.

'*Rocky harp* :' — There are now known other cases, beside the ancient one of Memnon's statue, in which the 'deep-grooved' granites, or even the shifting sands of wildernesses, utter mysterious music to ears that watch and wait for the proper combination of circumstances.

DE QUINCEY'S WRITINGS.

I. CONFESSIONS OF AN ENGLISH OPIUM-EATER. 1 Vol. 16mo. 75 cents.

Contents. THE CONFESSIONS.
SUSPIRIA DE PROFUNDIS.

II. BIOGRAPHICAL ESSAYS. 1 Vol. 16mo. 75 cts.

Contents. SHAKSPEARE.
POPE.
LAMB.
GOETHE.
SCHILLER.

III. MISCELLANEOUS ESSAYS. 1 Vol. 16mo. 75 cts.

Contents. ON THE KNOCKING AT THE GATE IN MACBETH.
MURDER, CONSIDERED AS ONE OF THE FINE ARTS.
SECOND PAPER ON MURDER.
JOAN OF ARC.
THE ENGLISH MAIL-COACH.
THE VISION OF SUDDEN DEATH.
DINNER, REAL AND REPUTED.
ORTHOGRAPHIC MUTINEERS.

IV. THE CÆSARS. 1 Vol. 16mo. 75 cents.

V. LIFE AND MANNERS. 1 Vol. 16mo. 75 cents.

Contents. Early Days.
London.
Ireland.
The Irish Rebellion.
Premature Manhood.
Travelling.
My Brother.
Oxford.
German Literature.

VI. & VII. LITERARY REMINISCENCES. 2 Vols. 16mo. $1.50.

Contents. Literary Novitiate
Sir Humphry Davy.
William Godwin.
Mrs. Grant.
Recollections of Charles Lamb.
Walladmor.
Coleridge.
Wordsworth.
Southey.
Recollections of Grasmere.
The Saracen's Head.
Society of the Lakes.
Charles Lloyd.
Walking Stewart.
Edward Irving.
Talfourd.
The London Magazine.
Junius.
Clare.
Cunningham.
Attack by a London Journal.
Duelling.

VIII. & IX. NARRATIVE AND MISCELLANEOUS PAPERS. 2 Vols. 16mo. $1.50.

Contents. The Household Wreck.
The Spanish Nun.
Flight of a Tartar Tribe.
System of the Heavens as revealed by the Telescope.
Modern Superstition.
Coleridge and Opium-Eating.
Temperance Movement.
On War.
The Last Days of Immanuel Kant.

X. ESSAYS ON THE POETS AND OTHER ENGLISH WRITERS. 1 Vol. 16mo. 75 cents.

Contents. The Poetry of Wordsworth.
Percy Bysshe Shelley.
John Keats.
Oliver Goldsmith.
Alexander Pope.
William Godwin.
John Foster.
William Hazlitt.
Walter Savage Landor.

XI. & XII. HISTORICAL AND CRITICAL ESSAYS. 2 Vols. 16mo. $1.50.

Contents. Philosophy of Roman History.
The Essenes.
Philosophy of Herodotus.
Plato's Republic.
Homer and the Homeridæ.
Cicero.
Style.
Rhetoric.

www.ingramcontent.com/pod-product-compliance
Lightning Source LLC
LaVergne TN
LVHW020237110826
845151LV00003B/953
* 9 7 8 1 4 2 5 5 2 9 7 4 1 *